Help Me! Guide to iPhone 6

P9-DEI-411

By Charles Hughes

Table of Contents

Getting Started

Table of Contents

1. Button Layout

The iPhone 6 has five buttons and one switch. The rest of the functionality is controlled by the touchscreen. Each button has several functions, depending on the context in which it is used.

The buttons perform the following functions, as shown below:

Home Button

Figure 1: Front View

Home Button

- Shows the Home screen.
- Displays open applications when pressed twice quickly.
- Allows you to use TouchID to unlock the phone, and to make payments.

Figure 2: Left Side View

Volume Controls

- Controls the volume of the ringer. Refer to Adjusting Sound Settings to learn more about setting ringtones or the sound volume.
- Controls the volume of the earpiece or speakerphone during a conversation.
- Controls the media volume.

Vibration Switch

- Turns Vibration on or off.
- Turns the Sound on or off.

Figure 3: Bottom View

Headphone Jack - Allows headphones or speakers to be plugged in. Allows an AUX cable to be plugged in to listen to audio over the speakers in a car or stereo.

Lightning Connector - Connects the phone to a computer in order to transfer data. Connects the phone to a charger.

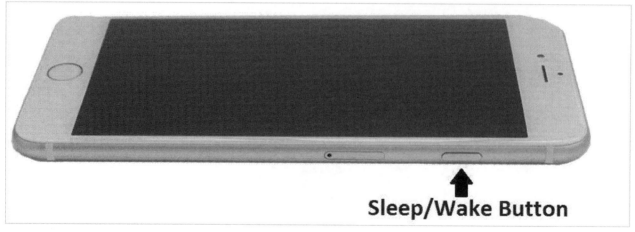

Figure 4: Right Side View

Sleep/Wake Button

- Turns the phone on and off.
- Locks and unlocks the phone.

2. Charging the Phone

To ensure that the phone works well, please follow these guidelines:
Discharge the phone completely at least once a month for optimal performance. When charging the battery, the meter in the upper right-hand corner of the screen (when unlocked) may show that it is fully charged; however, the charge is not complete until **100% Charged** appears on the lock screen. Insert the Lightning cable into the Lightning Connector on the bottom of the phone. The

lightning cable looks like this: . When the cable is inserted correctly, the indicator sound is played or the phone vibrates. Refer to "Tips and Tricks" on page 358 to learn about conserving battery life.

3. Turning the Phone On and Off

Use the Sleep/Wake button to turn the phone on or off. To turn the phone on, press and hold

the **Sleep/Wake** button for two seconds. The phone turns on and the logo is displayed. After the phone has finished starting up, the Lock screen is displayed.

Note: If the phone does not turn on after a few seconds, try charging the battery.

To turn the phone off, press and hold the **Sleep/Wake** button until the screen becomes dark. The

message "Slide to power off" appears. Touch the slider and move your finger to the right. The phone turns off.

Note: To keep the phone on, touch Cancel or do not take any action at all.

4. Installing a SIM Card

Insert the SIM card from an old phone to retain your personal information and phone number. The type of SIM card depends on your carrier. For instance, you cannot insert a Verizon SIM card into an AT&T phone, and vice-versa. To install a SIM card:

1. Insert the end of a paper clip or a SIM eject tool into the hole on the right side of the phone. The SIM card tray pops out, as shown in **Figure 5**.
2. Take out the old SIM card, if necessary, and insert the new SIM card with the short side facing upwards, as shown in **Figure 6**.
3. Re-insert the tray into the phone. The new SIM card is installed.

Figure 5: SIM Card Tray

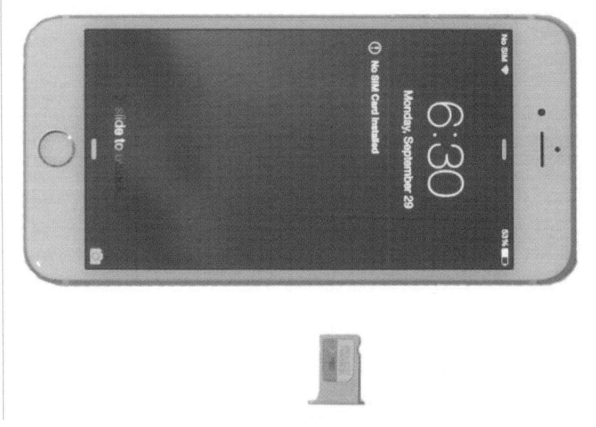

Figure 6: SIM Card in Tray

5. Setting Up the Phone for the First Time

You must set up the phone when you turn it on for the first time, unless an Apple associate or another specialist has already done so for you. To set up the phone:

1. Turn on the phone by pressing and holding the **Power** button until the icon appears. The phone starts up and the Welcome screen appears, as shown in **Figure 7**.
2. Touch the screen anywhere and move your finger to the right to begin setting up your phone. The Language screen appears, as shown in **Figure 8**.
3. Touch a language in the list. The language is selected, and the Country screen appears, as shown in **Figure 9**.
4. Touch the country where you reside. The country is selected, and the Wi-Fi Networks screen appears.
5. Touch a Wi-Fi network. The Password prompt appears.

6. Enter the network password, which is usually found on your wireless router. Touch **Join** in the upper right-hand corner of the screen. The phone connects to the selected Wi-Fi network and the Location Services screen appears, as shown in **Figure 10**. If you did not activate your iPhone in the store, you may need to confirm your phone number before the Location Services screen appears. Enter your billing zip code and the last four digits of your social security number to confirm.

7. Touch **Enable Location Services** if you want to turn the feature on. Touch **Disable Location Services** to leave the feature turned off. Some applications will not work with Location Services turned off. The Set Up iPhone screen appears, as shown in **Figure 11**.

8. Touch **Restore from iCloud Backup** or **Restore from iTunes Backup** if you have a data backup. You will need to connect the phone to your computer and run iTunes if you touch 'Restore from iTunes Backup'. Touch **Set Up as New iPhone** if you do not have an iCloud or iTunes backup. The Apple ID screen appears.

9. Touch **Sign In with your Apple ID** if you have an Apple ID or touch **Create a Free Apple ID**. The Terms and Conditions screen appears once you are signed in.

10. Touch **Agree** in the bottom right-hand corner of the screen. A confirmation dialog appears.

11. Touch **Agree** again. The iCloud screen appears.

12. Touch **Use iCloud** to use the feature or touch **Don't Use iCloud** to disable it. The Find My iPhone feature is turned on automatically when you use iCloud. The iMessage and FaceTime screen appears.

13. Touch a phone number or email address if you would like to enable it for iMessage or FaceTime. A blue check mark appears next to each selected address or number.

14. Touch **Next** in the upper right-hand corner of the screen when you are finished. The iCloud drive screen appears. iCloud Drive syncs all of your documents and images in iCloud, and updates them on all of your phone as you work.

15. Touch **Upgrade to iCloud Drive**. iCloud Drive is turned on, and the Passcode Creation screen appears, as shown in **Figure 12**.

16. Enter a passcode to set up a security lock for your phone, or touch **Don't Add Passcode** to do it later. The Display Zoom screen appears, as shown in **Figure 13**.

17. Touch the iPhone on the left to view the most amount of information on your screen. However, the fonts will be slightly harder to read. Touch the iPhone on the right to use your iPhone in zoomed view. Fonts will be easier to read, but the screen will not fit as much information. The Diagnostics screen appears.

18. Touch **Automatically Send** to have the phone send usage data to Apple or touch **Don't Send** to disable this feature. Usage Data contains anonymous statistics about the ways in which you use your phone.

19. Touch **Get Started**. The phone setup is complete.

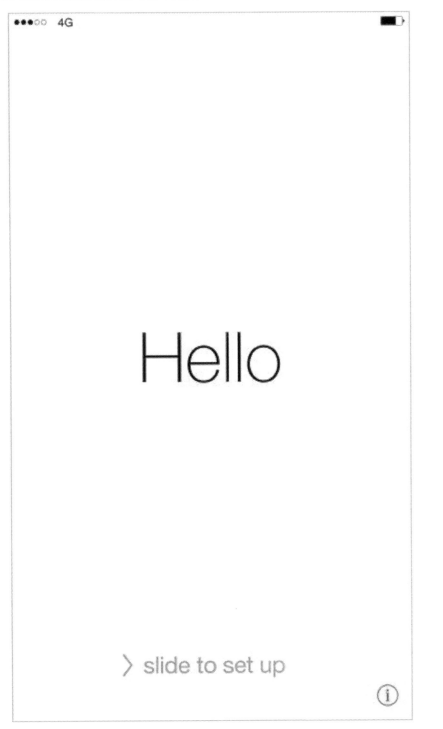

Figure 7: Welcome Screen

●●●○○ 4G   5:20 PM   ▰▯

English   >

Español   >

Français   >

Français (Canada)   >

Deutsch   >

简体中文   >

繁體中文   >

繁體中文（香港）   >

日本語   >

Nederlands   >

Italiano   >

Figure 8: Language Screen

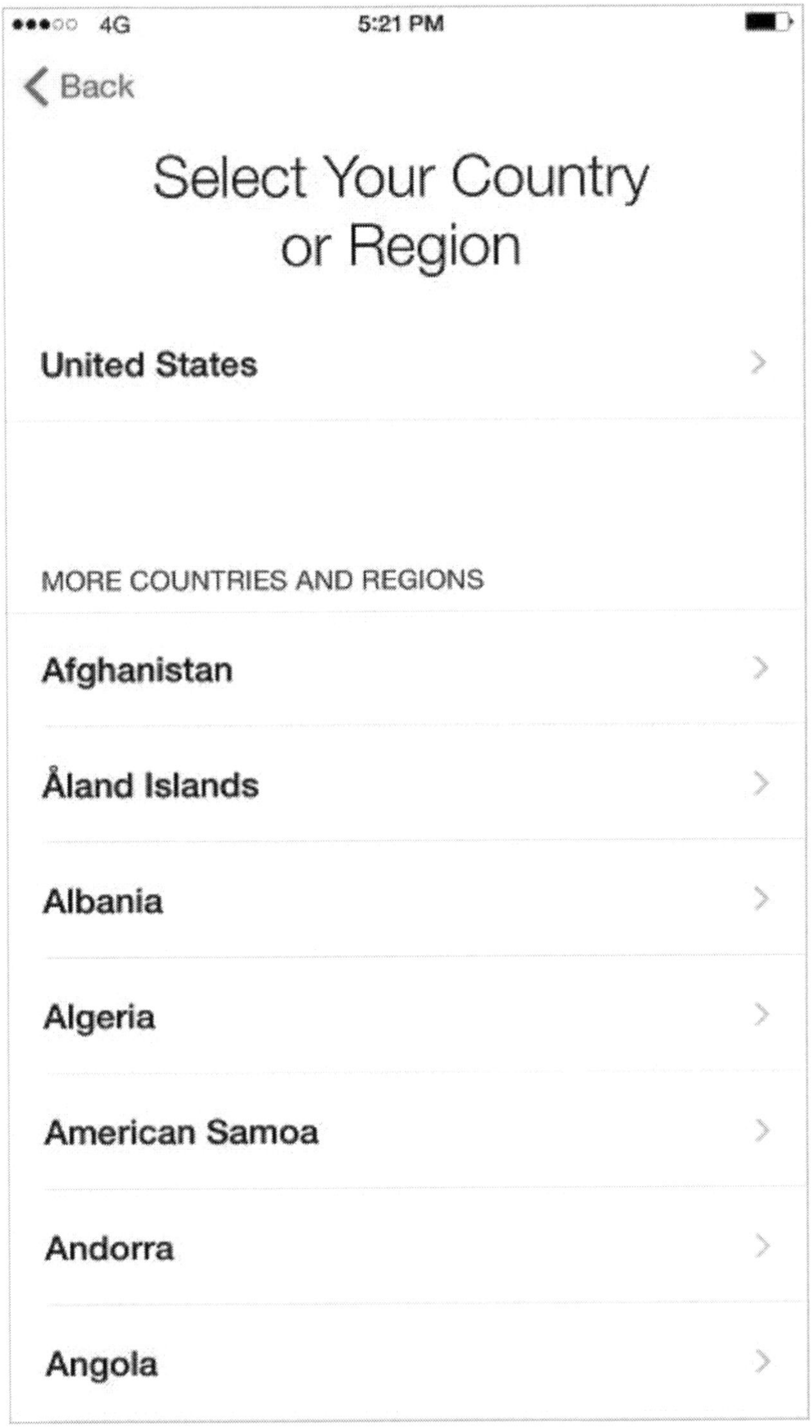

Figure 9: Country Screen

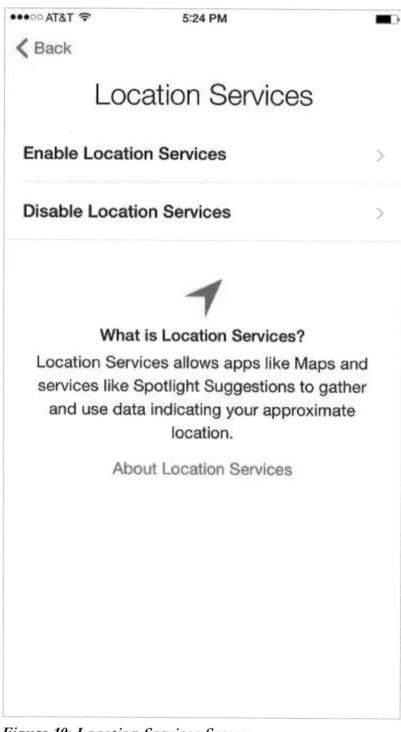

Figure 10: Location Services Screen

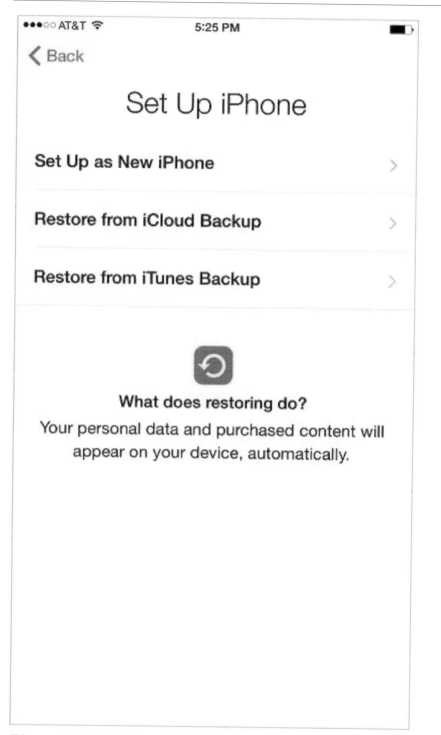

Figure 11: Wi-Fi Networks Screen

Figure 12: Passcode Creation Screen

Figure 13: Display Zoom Screen

6. Navigating the Screens

There are many ways to navigate the phone. Use the following tips to quickly navigate the screens of the phone:

- Use the **Home** button to return to the Home screen at any time. Any application or tool that you were using will be in the same state when you return to it.
- At the Home screen, slide your finger to the left to access additional pages. If nothing happens, the other pages are blank.
- Touch the center of the Home screen and slide your finger down to access the phone's search feature. You may search any data stored on your phone, including application data, as well as the web, iTunes, Application Store, movie show times, locations nearby, and much more.

7. Organizing Icons

You may wish to re-order the location of the application icons on the screens. To organize application icons:

1. Touch an icon and hold it until all of the icons begin to shake. The icons can now be moved around the screen.
2. Move the icon to the desired location and let go of the screen. The icon is relocated and the surrounding icons are re-ordered accordingly. If an icon that used to be on the screen is gone, then it has been moved to a different Home screen in the process.
3. To move an icon to another screen, move the icon to the edge of the current one and hold it there. The adjacent screen appears. Drop the icon in the desired location.
4. Press the **Home** button. The icons stop shaking.

8. Creating an Icon Folder

When there are many icons on the Home screens, you may wish to organize the icons into folders. Each folder can have a meaningful name to enable you to find the icons easily. To create a folder:

1. Touch an icon and hold it until all of the icons begin to shake. The icons can now be moved.
2. Move one icon on top of another and let go of the screen. A folder with the selected icons is created, as shown in **Figure 14**. Touch the ⊗ button to enter a name for the folder.
3. Enter a name for the folder, and touch **Done**. The new name is saved.
4. To exit the folder, touch anywhere outside of it. The folder closes.
5. Press the **Home** button. The icons stop shaking.

Note: To add more icons to a folder, just touch an icon while it is shaking and move it onto the folder.

Figure 14: A New Folder

9. Using Wi-Fi

Use a nearby Wi-Fi hotspot or a home router to avoid having to use data. Wi-Fi is required to download large applications. To turn on Wi-Fi:

1. Touch the ⚙ icon. The Settings screen appears, as shown in **Figure 15**.
2. Touch **Wi-Fi**. The Wi-Fi Networks screen appears, as shown in **Figure 16**.

3. Touch the ⬭ switch next to 'Wi-Fi'. Wi-Fi turns on and a list of available networks appears, as shown in **Figure 17**. If the network has an 🔒 icon next to it, a password is needed to connect to it.

4. Touch the network to which you would like to connect. The Wi-Fi Password prompt appears if the network is protected, as shown in **Figure 18**.

5. Enter the network password. Touch **Join**. Provided that you entered the correct password, a check mark appears next to the network name and the 📶 icon appears at the top of the screen. You are connected to the Wi-Fi network.

Note: If you enter an incorrect password, the message "Unable to join the network >Network Name<" appears, where '>Network Name<' is the name of your network. The network password is usually written on the modem given to you by your internet service provider. It is sometimes called a WEP Key.

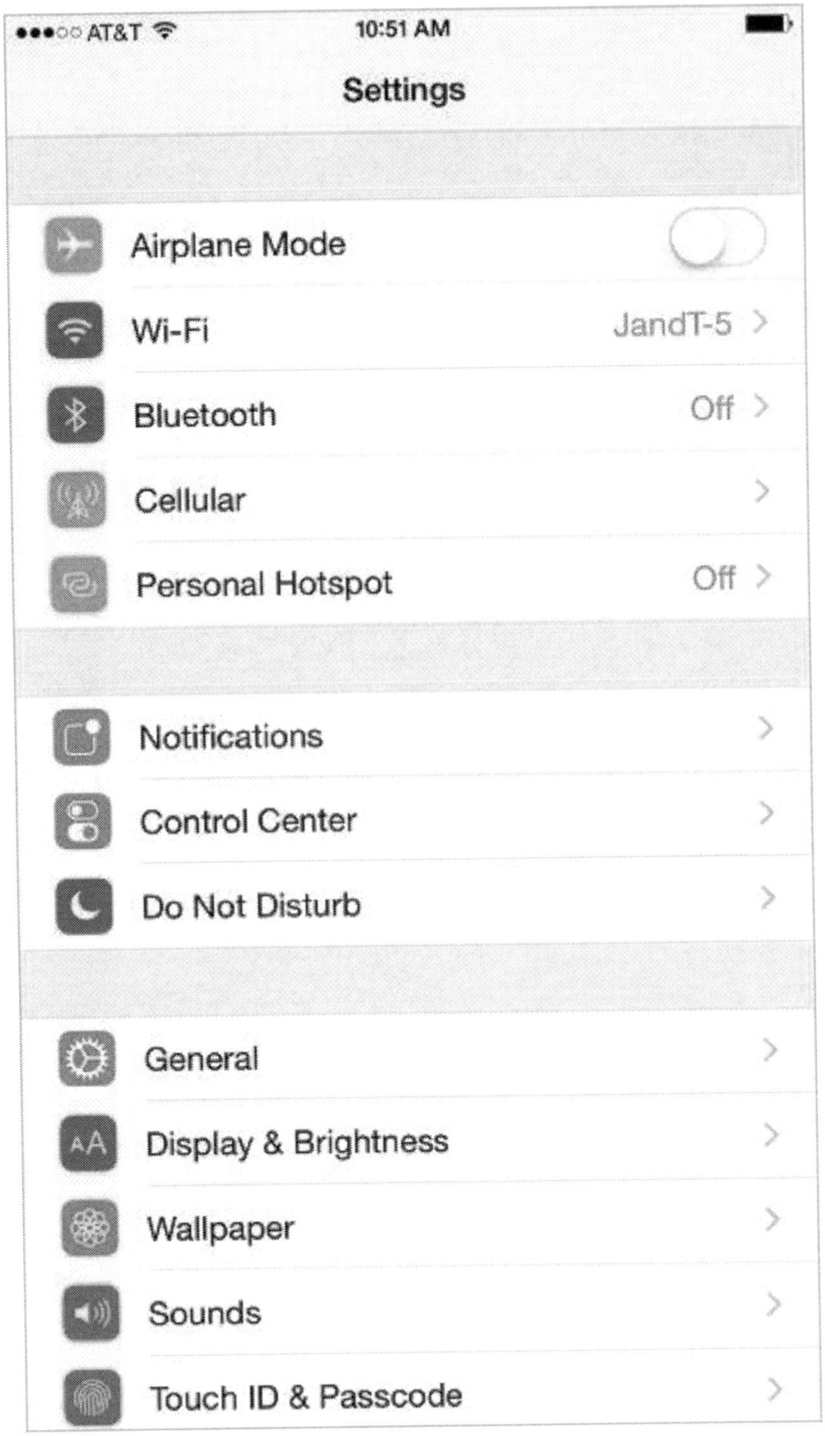

Figure 15: Settings Screen

Figure 16: Wi-Fi Networks Screen

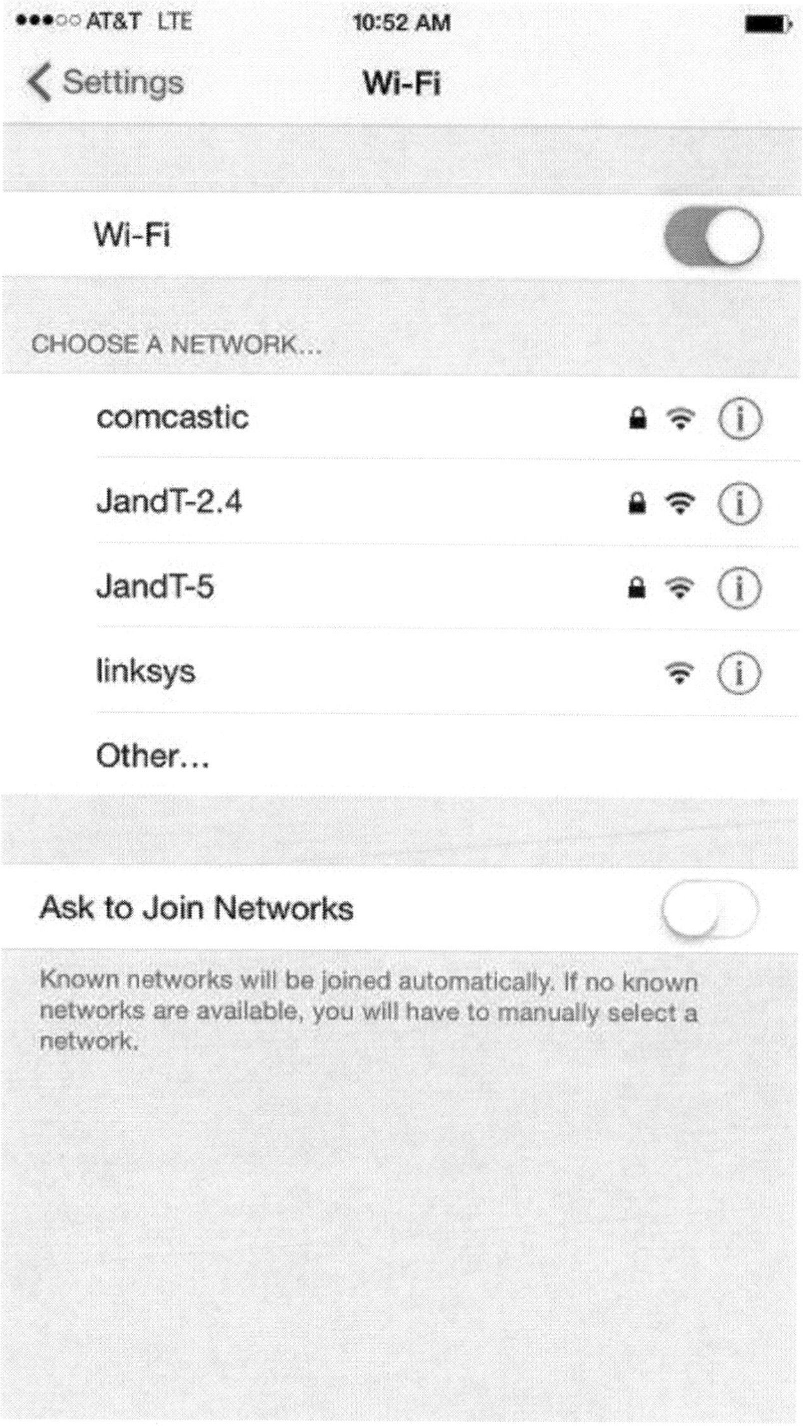

Figure 17: List of Available Wi-Fi Networks

Figure 18: Wi-Fi Password Prompt

10. Accessing Quick Settings through the Control Center

There are various settings that you can access without opening the Settings screen by using the Control Center. To use the Control Center:

1. Touch the bottom of the screen at any time and slide your finger up. The Control Center appears, as shown in **Figure 19**.
2. Touch one of the following icons at the top of the Control Center to turn on the corresponding function:

- Turns Airplane mode on or off.

- Turns Wi-Fi on or off.

- Turns Bluetooth on or off.

- Turns 'Do not disturb' on or off.

- Turns automatic screen rotation on or off.

A white icon, such as a   icon, indicates that the function is turned on.

3. Touch one of the following icons at the bottom of the Control Center to turn on the corresponding service:

- Turns the flashlight on or off .

- Opens the timer application.

- Opens the calculator application .

- Turns on the camera.

Figure 19: Control Center

11. Using the Notification Center

The Notification Center shows event reminders and all types of alerts, such as calendar events, received texts, and missed calls. To open the notification center, touch the top of the screen at any time and move your finger down. Touch a notification to open the corresponding application. For instance, touch a calendar event to open the calendar. You can also touch **All** or **Missed** at the top of the screen to view the corresponding call notifications. The Notifications Center is shown in **Figure 20**.

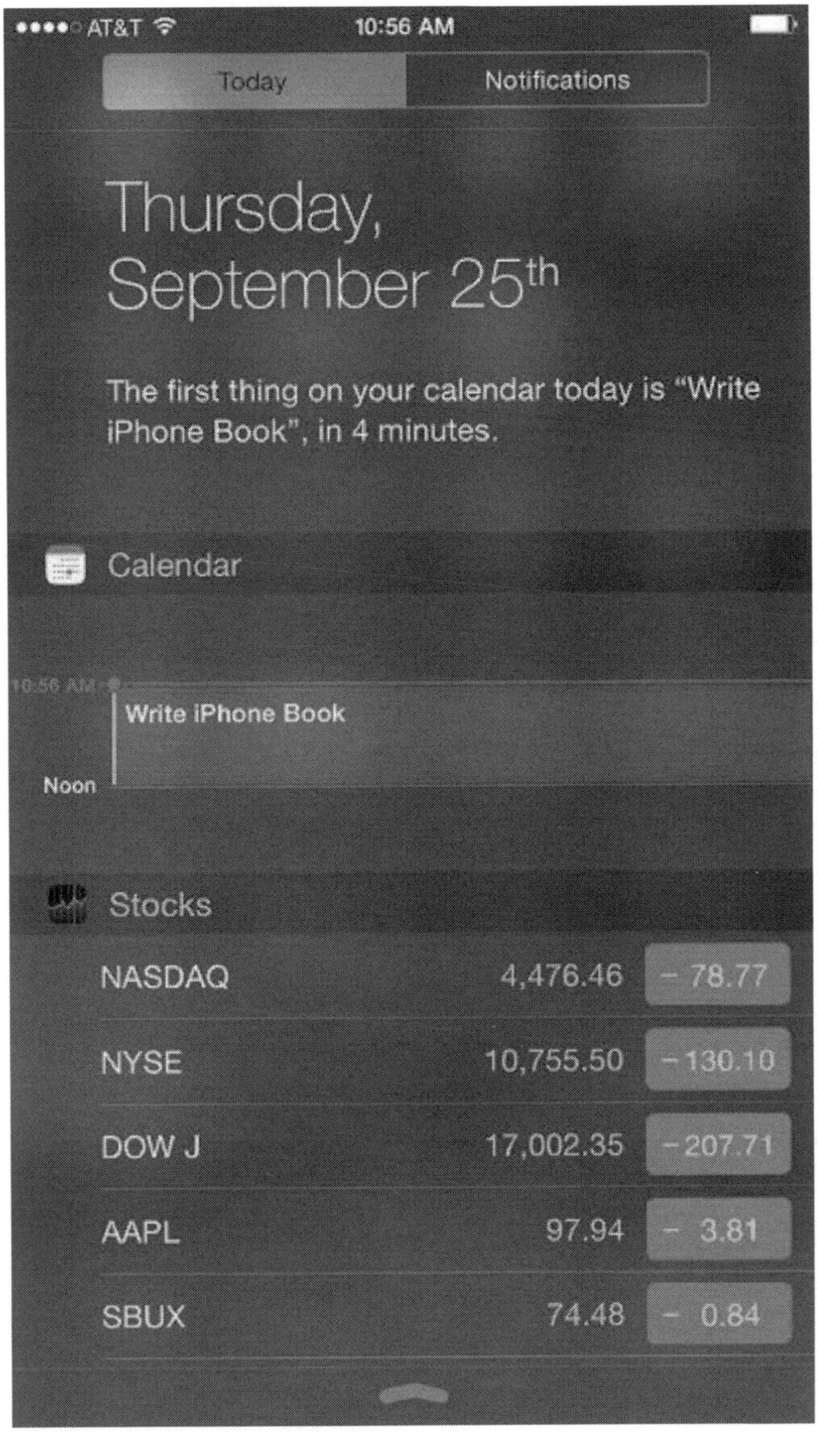

Figure 20: Notifications Center

Making Voice and Video Calls

Table of Contents

1. Dialing a Number

Numbers that are not in your Phonebook can be dialed on the keypad. To manually dial a phone number, touch the ⬛ icon on the Home screen. The keypad appears, as shown in **Figure 1**. Touch the ⬛ icon at the bottom of the screen, if you do not see the keypad. Enter the desired phone number and then touch the ⬛ at the bottom of the screen. The phone dials the number.

Figure 1: Keypad

2. Calling a Contact

If a number is stored in your Phonebook, you may touch the name of a contact to dial it. To call a contact already stored in your phone:

1. Touch the icon on the Home screen. The Phonebook appears, as shown in **Figure 2**.
2. Touch the name of the desired contact. The Contact Information screen appears, as shown in **Figure 3**.
3. Touch the desired phone number. The phone calls the contact's number. Refer to *"Managing Contacts"* on page 58 to learn more about adding or removing contacts.

Note: For some unexplained reason, Apple has decided to place the *icon in the Extras folder by default. If you cannot find it, look in that folder.*

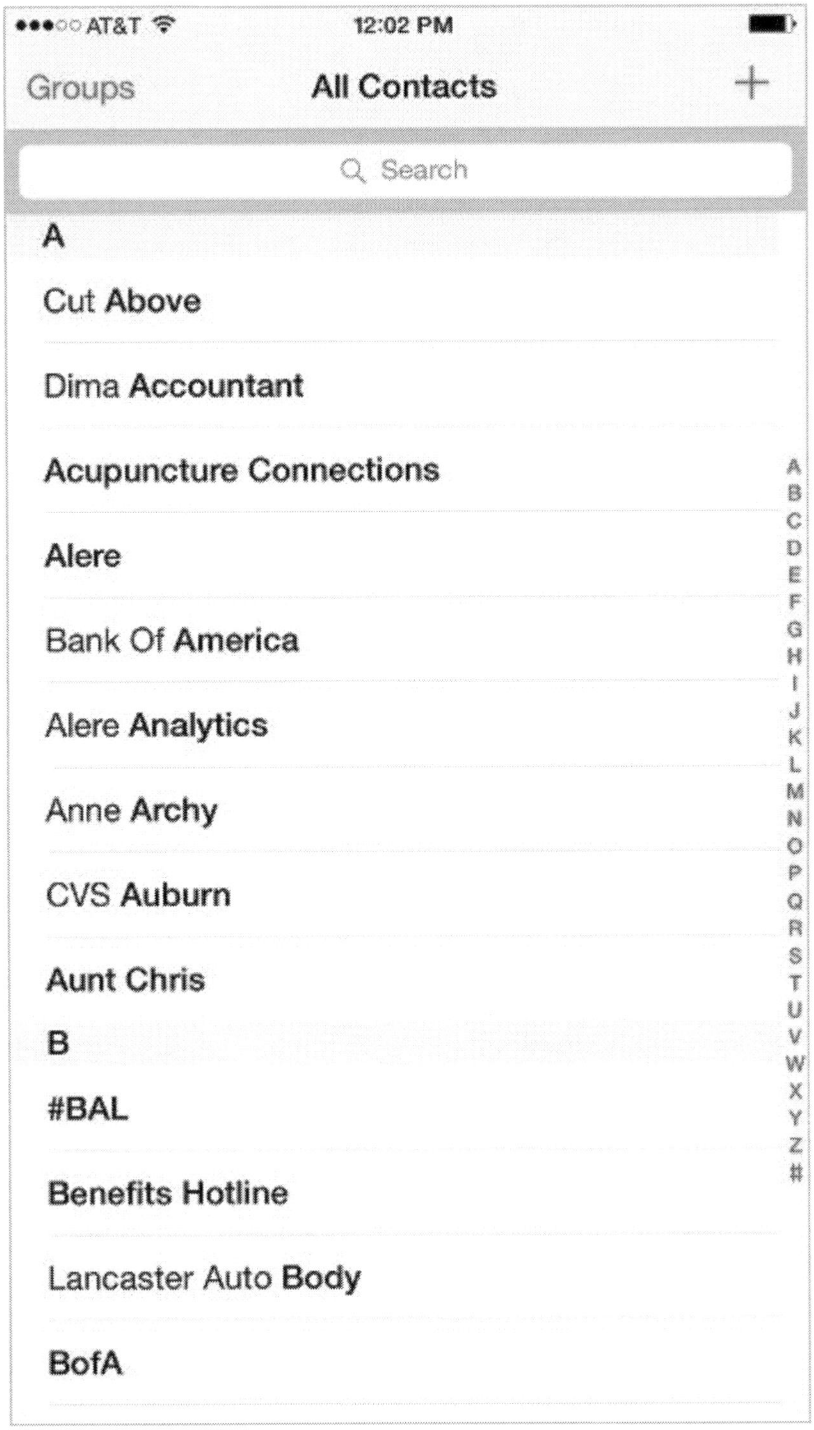

Figure 2: Phonebook

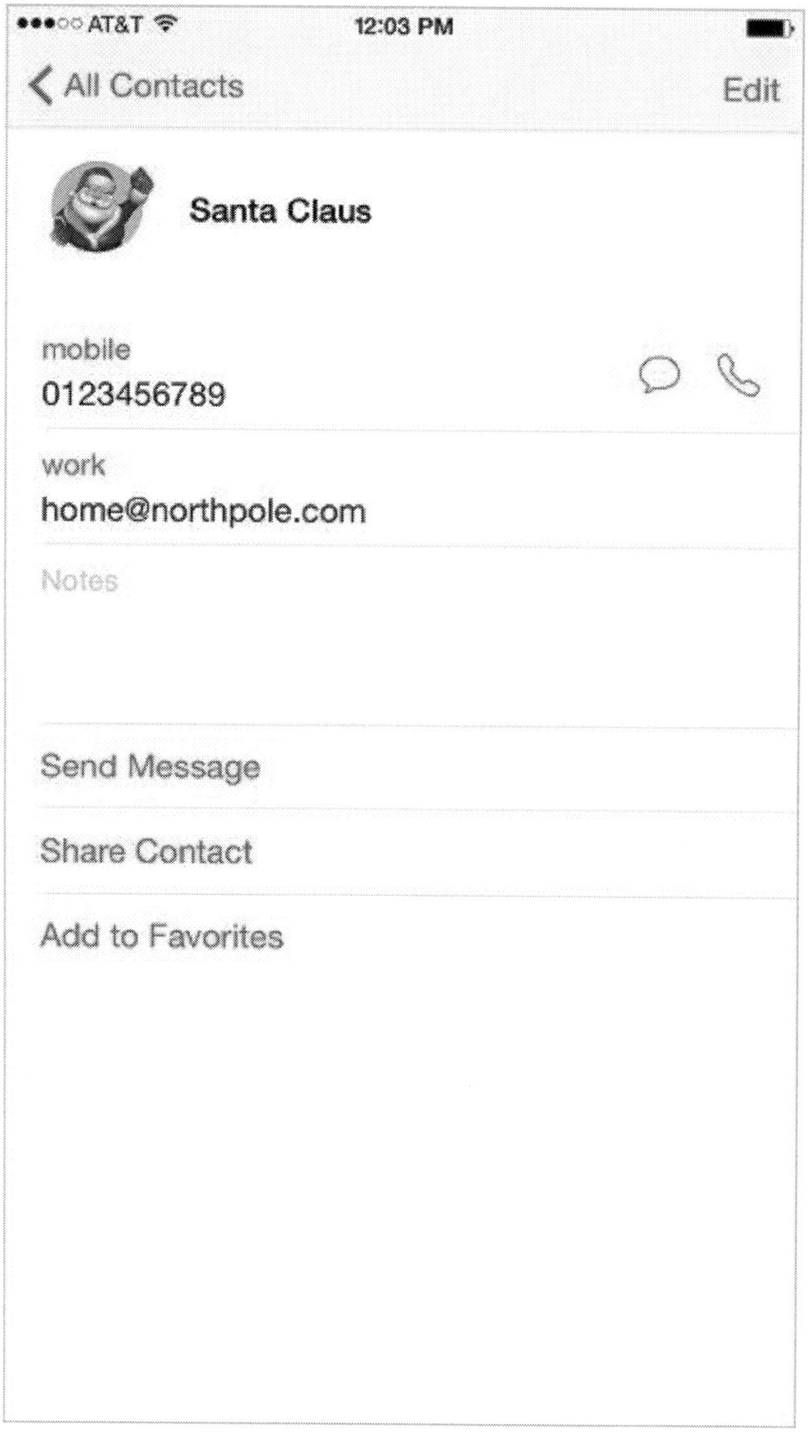

●●●○○ AT&T 📶   12:03 PM   ▬▮

‹ All Contacts   **Edit**

Santa Claus

mobile
0123456789   💬   📞

work
home@northpole.com

Notes

Send Message

Share Contact

Add to Favorites

Figure 3: Contact Information Screen

3. Calling a Favorite

There is no Speed Dial feature on phone. Instead, frequently dialed numbers can be saved as Favorites, which can be accessed more quickly than other contacts. To call a number stored in Favorites:

1. Touch the icon on the Home screen. The keypad screen appears.
2. Touch the icon at the bottom of the screen. The Favorites screen appears, as shown in **Figure 4**.
3. Touch the name of a Favorite. The device calls the selected number. Refer to *"Managing Contacts"* on page 58 to learn more about managing Favorites.

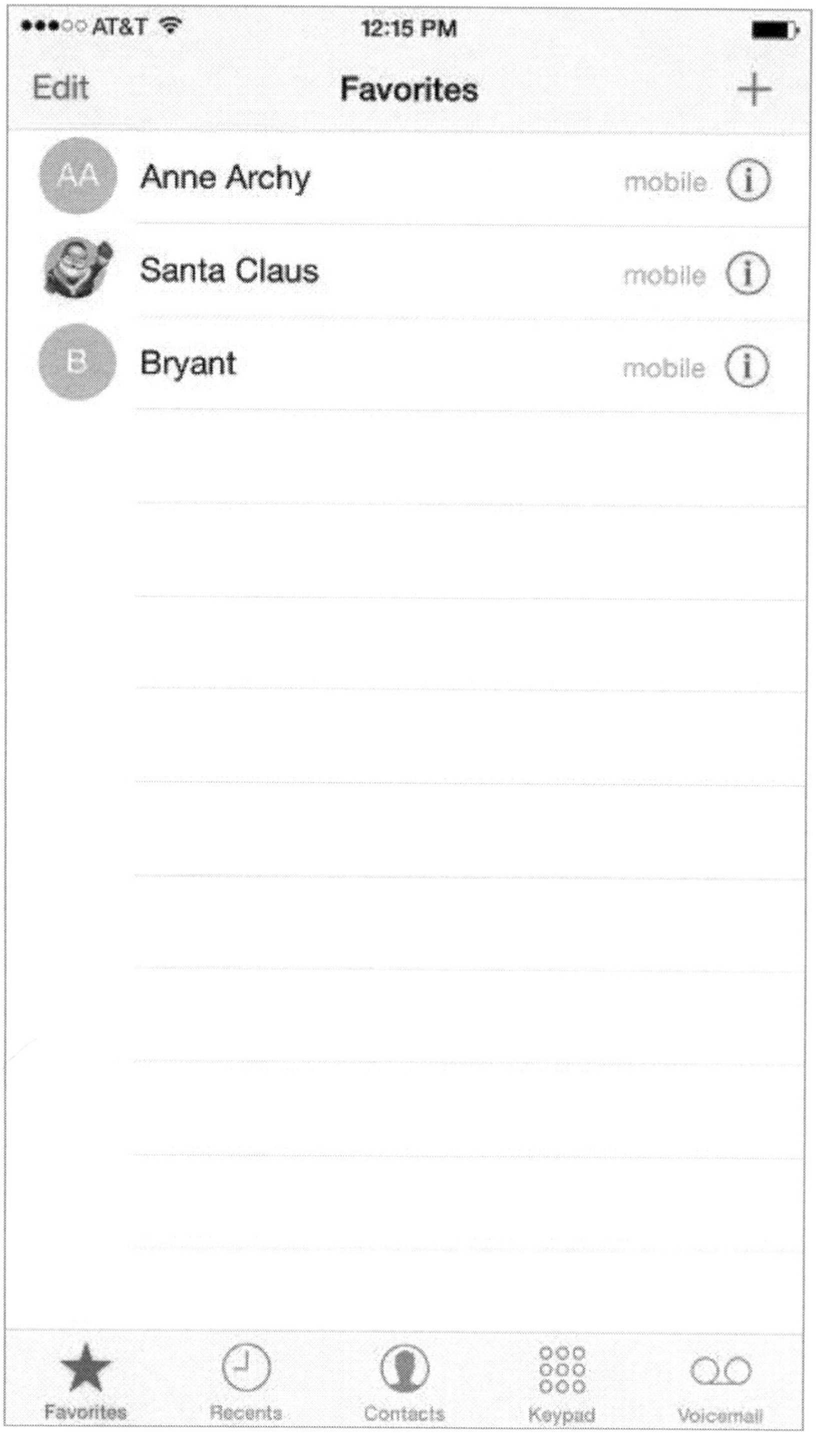

Figure 4: Favorites Screen

4. Returning a Recent Phone Call

After missing a call, your phone will notify you of who called and at what time. The phone also shows a history of all recently placed calls. To view and return a missed call or redial a recently entered number:

1. Touch the ![phone icon] icon on the Home screen. The Calling screen appears.
2. Touch the ![clock icon] icon at the bottom of the screen. The Recent Calls screen appears, with the most recent calls on top. Missed or declined calls are shown in red. The ![call icon] icon is shown next to a placed call, as shown in **Figure 5**.
3. Touch the name of a contact. The phone calls the contact.

*Note: To view only missed calls, touch **Missed** at the top of the Recent Calls screen.*

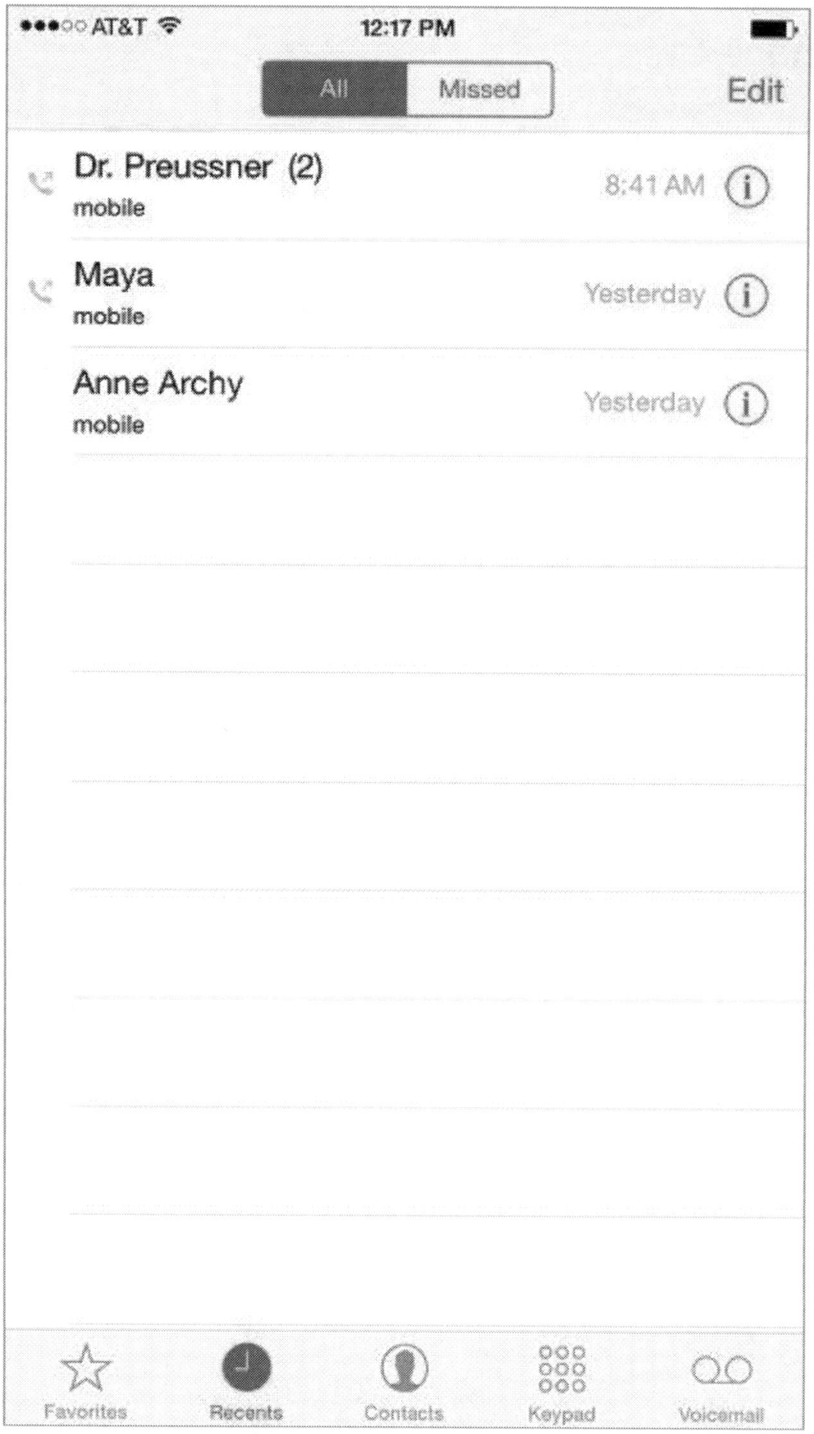

Figure 5: Recent Calls Screen

5. Receiving a Voice Call

There are several ways to accept or reject a voice call based on whether or not the screen is locked. Use the following tips when receiving a voice call:

- To receive an incoming voice call while the phone is locked, touch and move the on the slider, shown in **Figure 6**, to the right. The call is answered.
- To mute the ringer, press the Sleep/Wake button. To reject the incoming call, press the Sleep/Wake button again.
- To receive an incoming call while using an application (or viewing a Home screen), touch the button, as shown in **Figure 7**. To reject the incoming call, touch the button. The call is declined. The number then appears in red in the list of recent calls, signifying that it is a missed call, and a notification appears above the icon on the Home screen.
- Touch **Message** or **Remind Me** to decline a call if you are currently busy but wish to address it later. Refer to **Replying to an Incoming Call with a Text Message** or **Setting a Reminder to Return an Incoming Call** to learn more about these options.

Figure 6: Incoming Call, Phone Locked

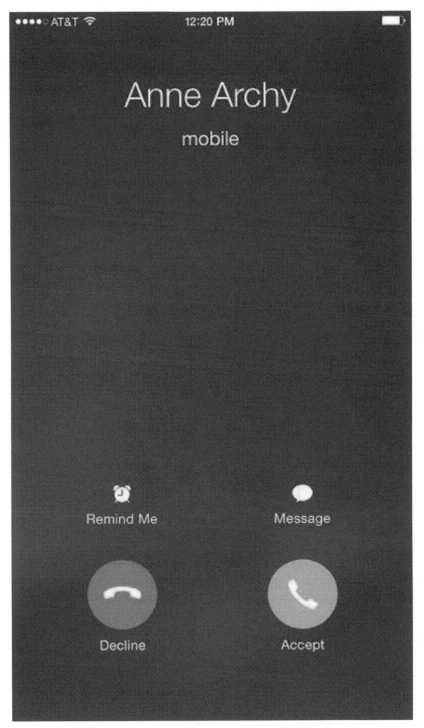

Figure 7: Incoming Call, Phone Unlocked

6. Replying to an Incoming Call with a Text Message

During an incoming call, you may reject it and automatically send a text message to the caller. To reply to an incoming call with a text message:

1. Touch **Message** during an incoming voice call. A list of pre-defined text messages appear.
2. Touch a message. The selected text message is sent to the caller. Alternatively, touch **Custom** to enter your own text message.
3. Touch the **Send** button. The phone sends the custom text message to the caller.

7. Setting a Reminder to Return an Incoming Call

During an incoming call, you may reject it and automatically set a reminder for yourself to return the call at a specified time or when you reach a specific location (such as work or home). To set a reminder to return an incoming call:

1. Touch **Remind Me** during an incoming voice call. The following reminder options appear: 'In 1 hour' and 'When I leave'.
2. Touch **In 1 hour**. The phone displays a pop-up after one hour has passed reminding you to call back. Alternatively, touch **When I leave** to have the phone remind you when you leave your current location.

8. Using the Speakerphone During a Voice Call

The phone has a built-in Speakerphone, which is useful when calling from a car or when several people need to hear the conversation. To use the Speakerphone during a phone call:

1. Place a voice call. The Calling Screen appears, as shown in **Figure 8**.
2. Touch the 🔊 icon. The Speakerphone is turned on. Adjust the volume of the Speakerphone by using the Volume Controls. Refer to *"Button Layout"* on page 10 to locate the Volume Controls.
3. Touch the 🔊 icon. The Speakerphone is turned off.

Figure 8: Calling Screen

---

9. Using the Keypad During a Voice Call

You may wish to use the keypad while on a call in order to input numbers in an automated menu or to enter an account number. To use the keypad during a phone call, place a voice call and touch the ▦ icon. The keypad appears. To hide the keypad again, touch **Hide Keypad**.

10. Using the Mute Function During a Voice Call

During a voice call, you may wish to mute your side of the conversation. When mute is turned on, the person on the other end of the line will not hear anything on your side. To use Mute during a call, place a voice call and touch the [icon] icon. The phone mutes your voice and the caller(s) can no longer hear you, but you are still able to hear them. Touch the [icon] icon. Mute is turned off.

11. Putting a Caller on Hold (hidden button)

Apple replaced the Hold button ([icon]) with the [icon] button on the iPhone 4 and later generations. However, the Hold function still exists. Press and hold the [icon] button while on a call until the [icon] button appears. Release the screen. The call is put on hold.

12. Starting a Conference Call (Adding a Call)

To talk to more than one person at a time, call another person while continuing the current call. To create a conference call, place a voice call and then touch the [icon] icon. The list of contacts or the keypad is shown. Dial a number or select a contact to call. The first contact is put on hold while the phone dials and connects to the second. Touch the [icon] icon. A three-way conference call is created, as shown in **Figure 9**.

Note: Up to six lines may be included in a conference call.

Figure 9: Three-Way Conference Call

13. Making a Call Over Wi-Fi (T-Mobile Only)

You can make calls using your Wi-Fi connection if you do not have any service, or to avoid using up your minutes. Calls over Wi-Fi connection will often be clearer and less prone to being dropped as well. To make a call using Wi-Fi, you must first turn on the feature. To turn on Wi-Fi Calling:

1. Touch the icon. The Settings screen appears, as shown in **Figure 10**.
2. Scroll down and touch **Phone**. The Phone Settings screen appears, as shown in **Figure 11**.
3. Touch **Wi-Fi Calling**. The Wi-Fi Calling settings appear, as shown in **Figure 12**.

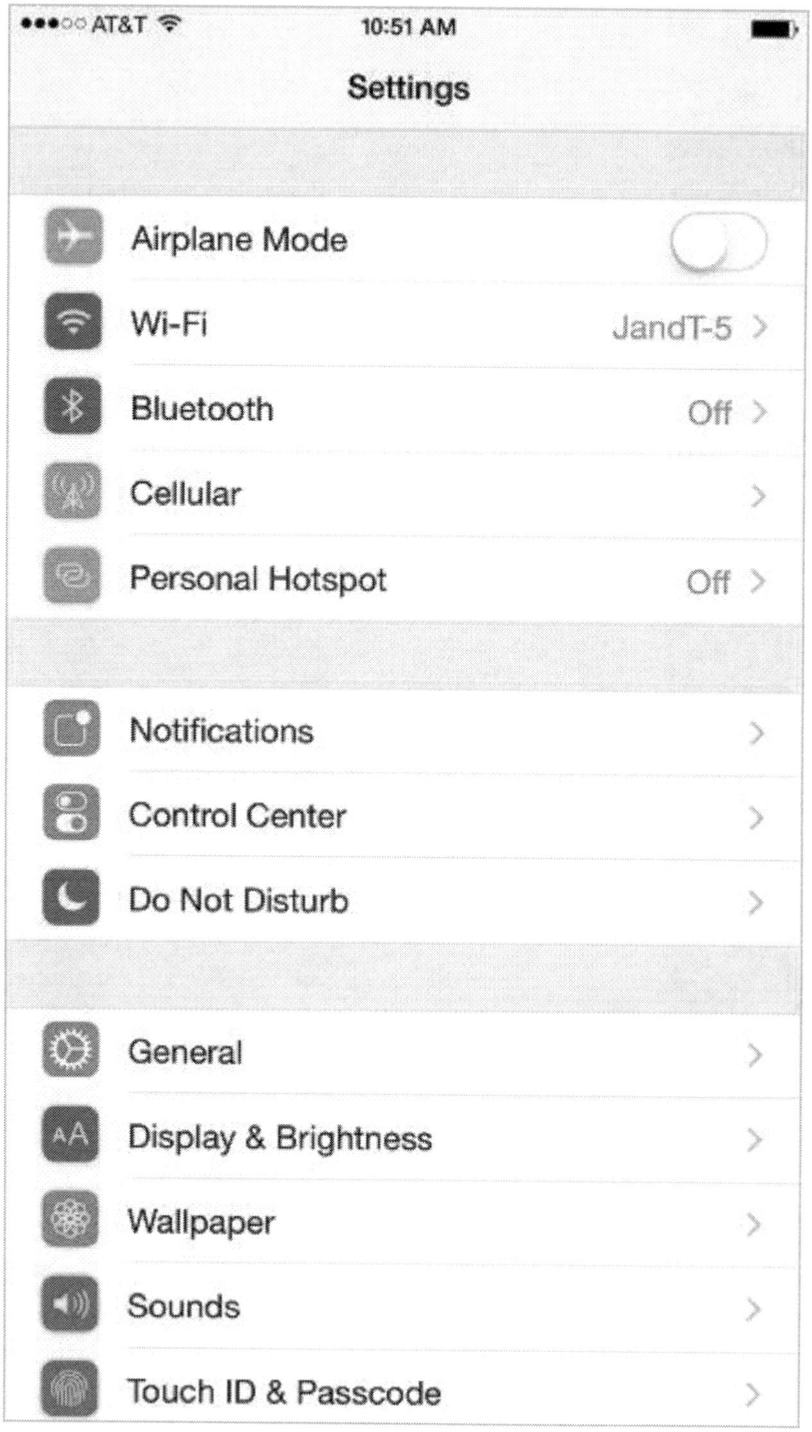

Figure 10: Settings Screen

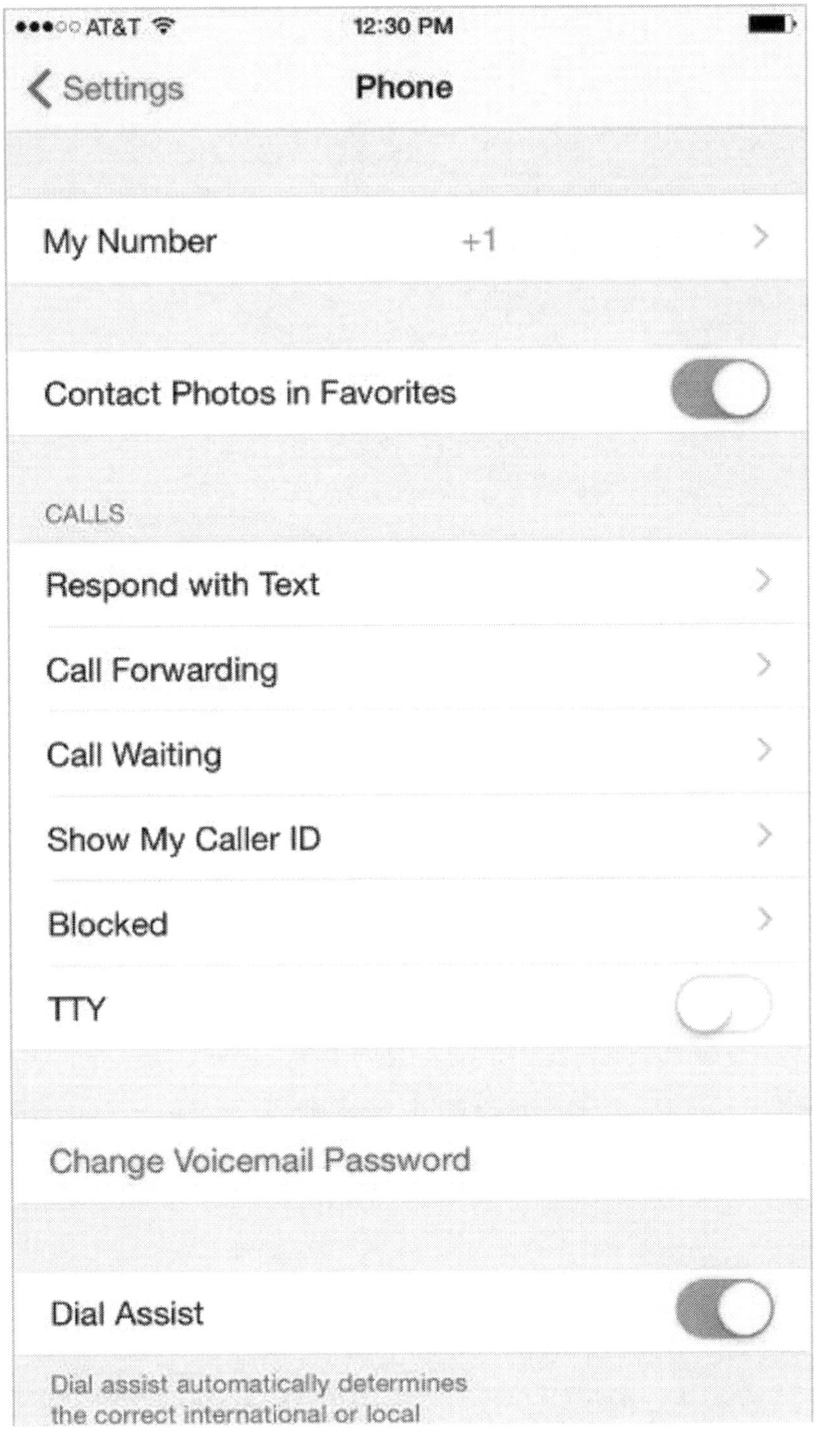

Figure 11: Phone Settings Screen

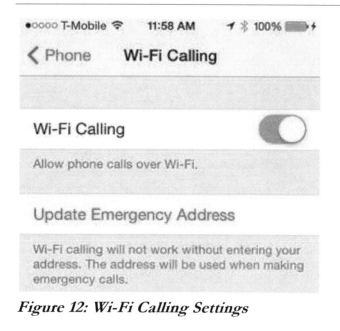

Figure 12: Wi-Fi Calling Settings

14. Starting a Facetime Call

You can place a video call to another iPhone, iPad, Mac, or iPod (third generation and higher). Facetime does not require a Wi-Fi connection. You can place and receive calls using a 4G connection (provided that you have at least one bar of service). However, using Wi-Fi may still provide a better video calling experience. Refer to **Using Wi-Fi** to learn how to turn on Wi-Fi. To place a Facetime call:

1. Touch the icon on the Home screen. The keypad appears.
2. Touch **Contacts** at the bottom of the screen. The Phonebook appears.
3. Touch the name of a contact. The Contact Information screen appears.
4. Touch the icon to place a FaceTime call. A high-pitched beeping sound plays until the call connects.
5. Touch the button at any time to switch cameras, as outlined in **Figure 13**. Using this feature, you can either show your contact what you are seeing or show them your face.

The phone can also receive FaceTime calls. To receive an incoming FaceTime call, touch **Accept**.

Note: You cannot place a FaceTime call to a device that is not compatible with FaceTime. If the contact's device cannot use FaceTime, the icon does not appear on the Contact Information screen.

Figure 13: Switch Camera Icon

Managing Contacts

Table of Contents

1. Adding a New Contact

The phone can store phone numbers, email addresses, and other Contact Information in the phonebook. To add a new contact to the phonebook:

Note: For some unexplained reason, Apple has decided to place the Contacts icon in the Extras folder by default. If you cannot find it, look in that folder.

1. Touch the icon on the Home screen. The phonebook appears.
2. Touch the button at the top of the screen. The New Contact screen appears, as shown in **Figure 1**.
3. Touch **First**. The keyboard appears. Enter the first name of the contact.
4. Touch **Last**. Enter the last name of the contact.
5. Touch any empty field to enter the desired information, and then touch **Done** in the upper right-hand corner of the screen. The contact's information is stored.

Note: Refer to "Tips and Tricks" *on page 358* *to learn how to add an extension after the contact's phone number.*

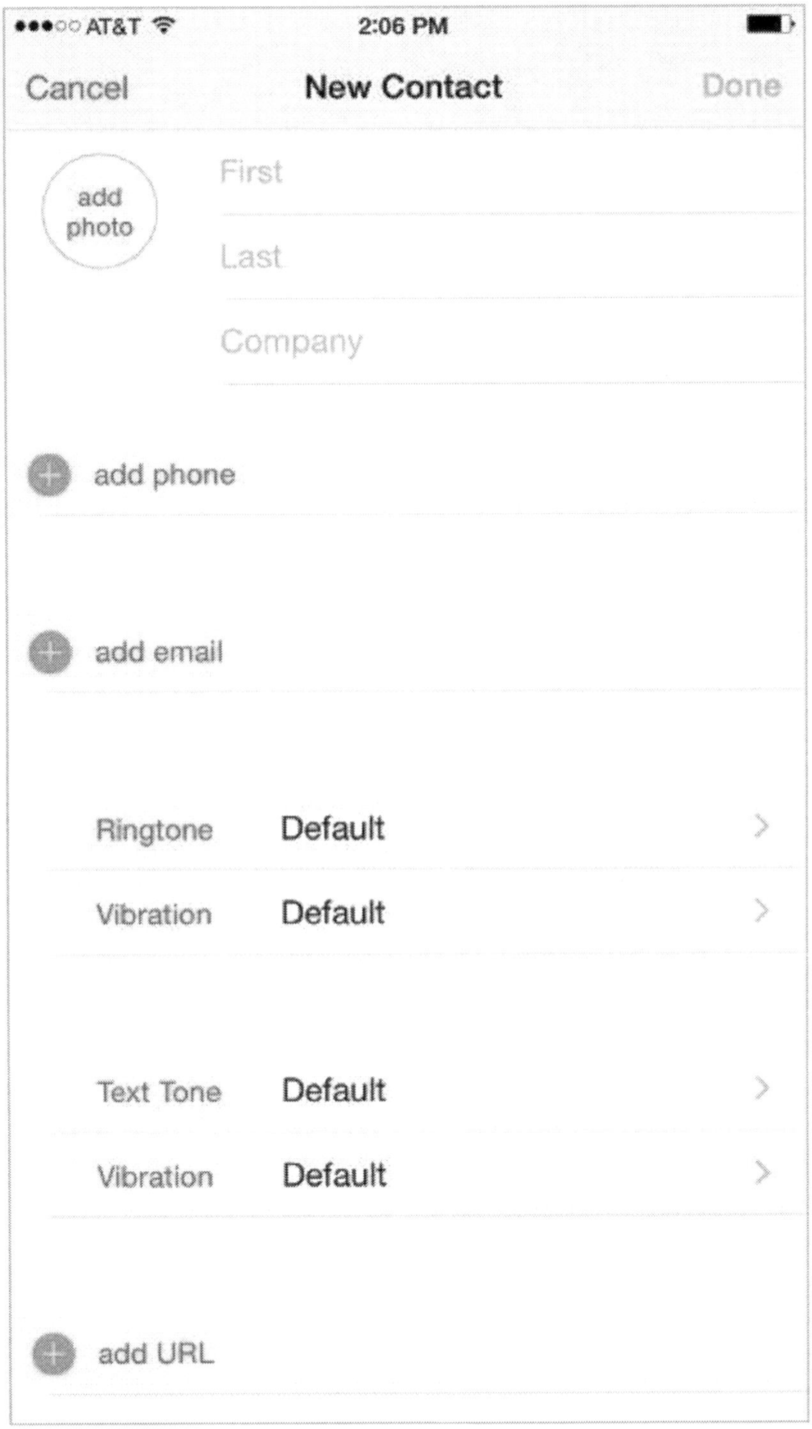

Figure 1: New Contact Screen

2. Finding a Contact

After adding contacts to your phone's phonebook, you may search for them. To find a stored contact:

1. Touch the icon on the Home screen. The phonebook appears.
2. Touch **Search** at the top of the screen. The keyboard appears.
3. Start typing the name of a contact. Contact matches appear as you type, as shown in **Figure 2**.
4. Touch a match. The Contact Info screen appears, as shown in **Figure 3**.

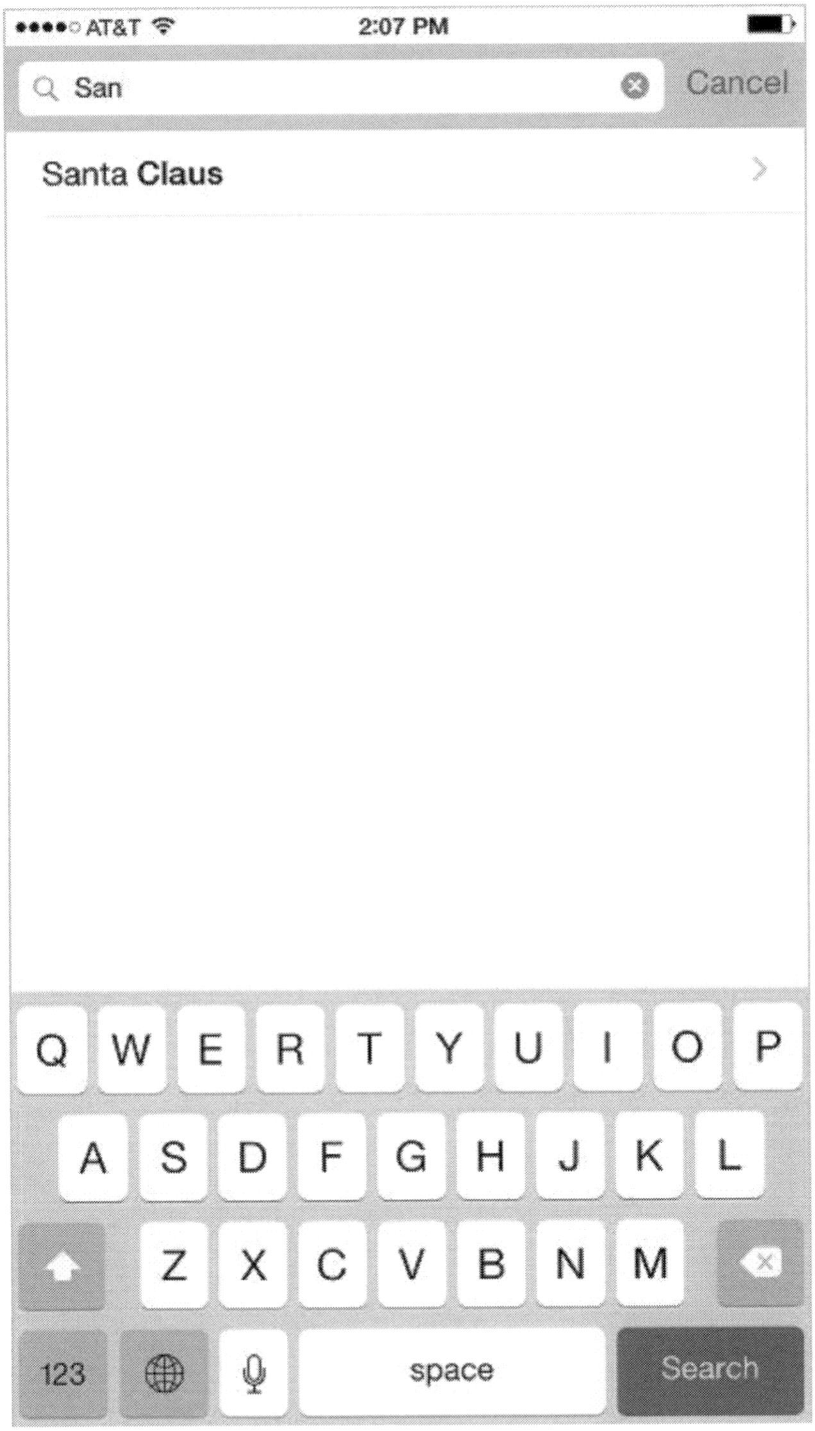

Figure 2: Contact Matches

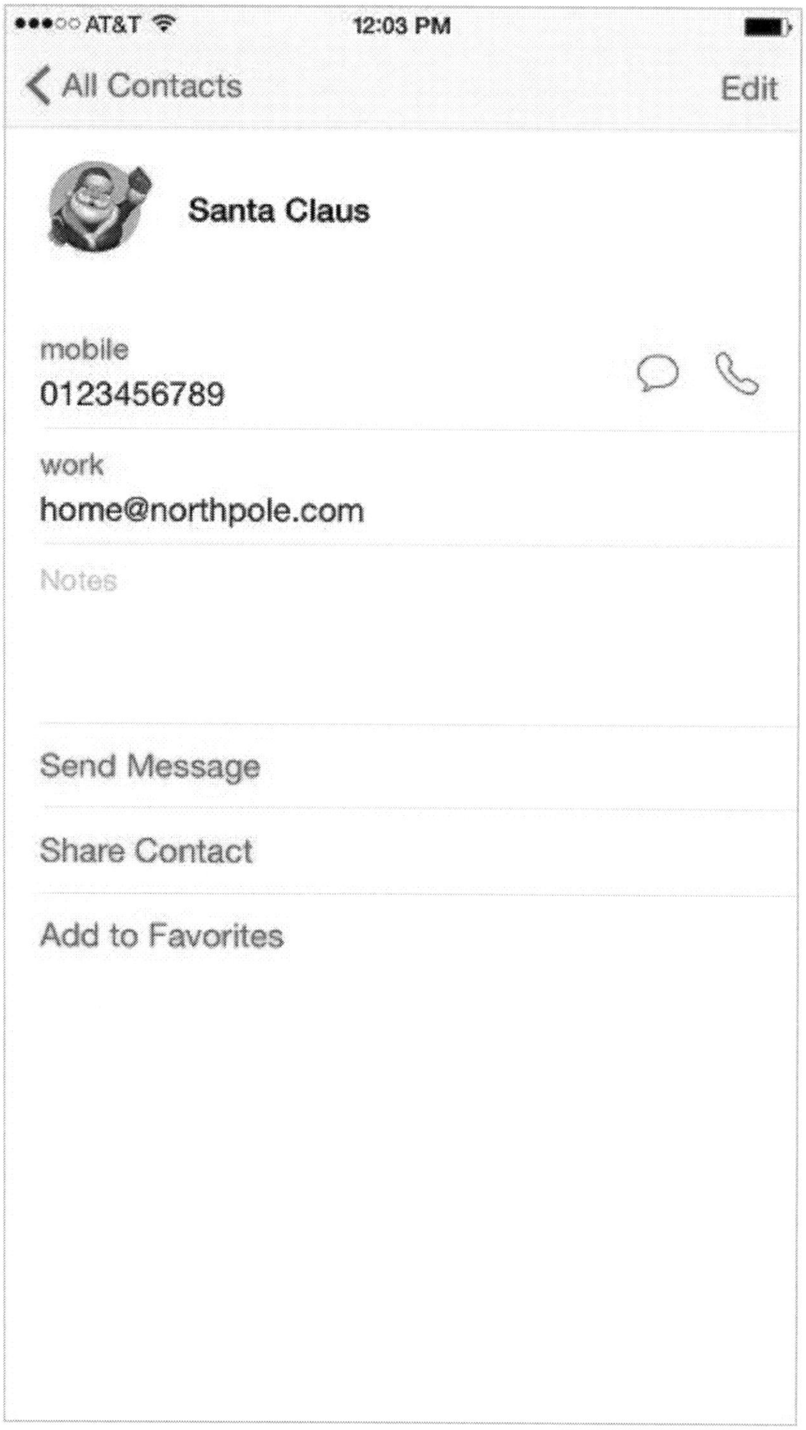

Figure 3: Contact Info Screen

3. Deleting a Contact

You may delete contact information from your phonebook in order to free up space, or for organizational purposes. To delete unwanted contact information:

Warning: There is no way to restore contact information after it has been deleted.

1. Touch the [icon] icon on the Home screen. The phonebook appears. If a list of all contacts does not appear, touch **All Contacts** in the upper left-hand corner of the screen to view the list.
2. Find and touch the name of the contact that you wish to delete. The Contact Info screen appears. Refer to *"Finding a Contact"* on page 60 to learn how to search for a contact.
3. Touch **Edit** at the top of the screen. The Contact Information Editing screen appears.
4. Scroll down, and touch **Delete Contact** at the bottom of the screen, as shown in **Figure 4**. A Confirmation menu appears.
5. Touch **Delete Contact** again. The contact's information is deleted, and will no longer appear in your phonebook.

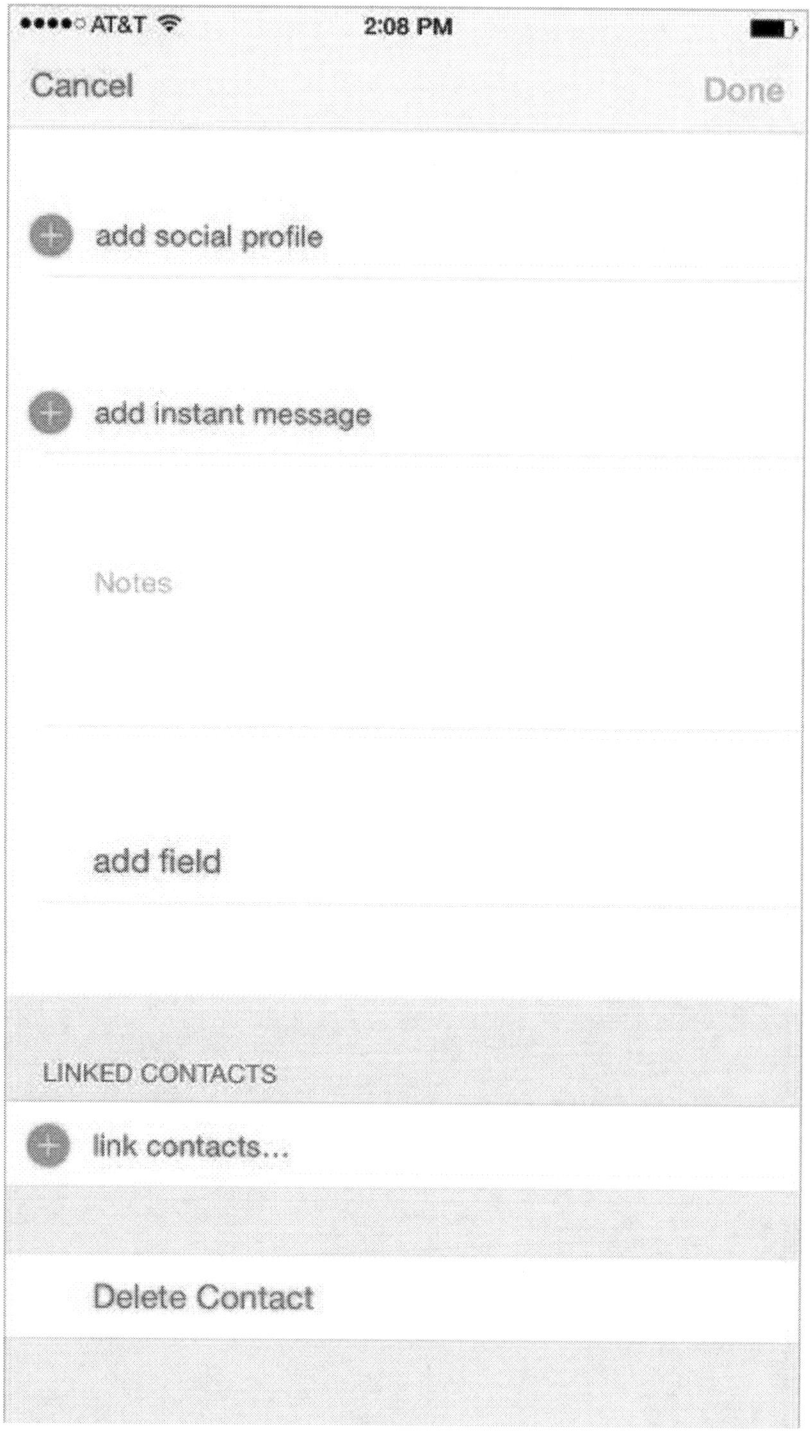

Figure 4: Delete Contact Screen

4. Editing Contact Information

After adding contacts to your phonebook, you may edit them at any time. To edit an existing contact's information:

1. Touch the ![icon] icon on the Home screen. The phonebook appears. If a list of all contacts does not appear, touch **All Contacts** in the upper left-hand corner of the screen to view the list.
2. Find and touch a contact's name. The Contact Info screen appears. Refer to *"Finding a Contact"* on page 60 to learn how to search for a contact.
3. Touch **Edit** at the top of the screen. The Contact Editing screen appears.
4. Touch a field to edit the corresponding information. Touch **Done** at the top of the screen when you are finished. The contact's information is updated.

5. Sharing a Contact's Information

To share a contact's information with someone else:

1. Touch the ![icon] icon. The phonebook appears. If a list of all contacts does not appear, touch **All Contacts** in the upper left-hand corner of the screen to view the list.
2. Find and touch a contact's name. The Contact Info screen appears. Refer to *"Finding a Contact"* on page 60 to learn how.
3. Touch **Share Contact** at the bottom of the contact's information. The Sharing Options menu appears at the bottom of the screen, as shown in **Figure 5**.
4. Follow the steps in the appropriate section below to email or text the contact's information:

To send the contact's information via email:

1. Touch the ![icon] icon in the Sharing Options menu. The New Email screen appears, as shown in **Figure 6**. Choose one of the following options for entering the email address:
2. Start typing the name of the contact with whom you wish to share the information. The matching contacts appear. Touch the contact's name. The contact's email address is added.
3. Enter the email address from scratch. To use a number, touch the **123** button at the bottom left of the screen. When done, touch the **return**button in the lower right-hand corner of the screen. Enter more addresses if needed.

4. Touch the ⊕ icon to select contacts from your phonebook, or enter as many email addresses as you wish.

5. Enter an optional subject by touching **Subject**, and touch **CC** to add other addresses to which to send the information.

6. Touch **Send** at the top of the screen. The contact's information is sent to the selected email addresses.

To send a contact's information via multimedia message, touch the ⬤ icon in the Sharing Options menu. The New Message screen appears, as shown in **Figure 7**. Enter the phone number or phone numbers, and touch **Send**. The contact's information is sent. There are three methods for entering the phone number:

- Start typing the name of the contact with whom you wish to share the information. Matching contacts appear. Touch the contact's name. The contact's number is added.

- Type the phone number from scratch. To use numbers, touch the **123** button at the bottom left of the screen. When done, touch the **return** button in the lower right-hand corner of the screen.

- Touch the ⊕ icon to select one or more contacts from the phonebook.

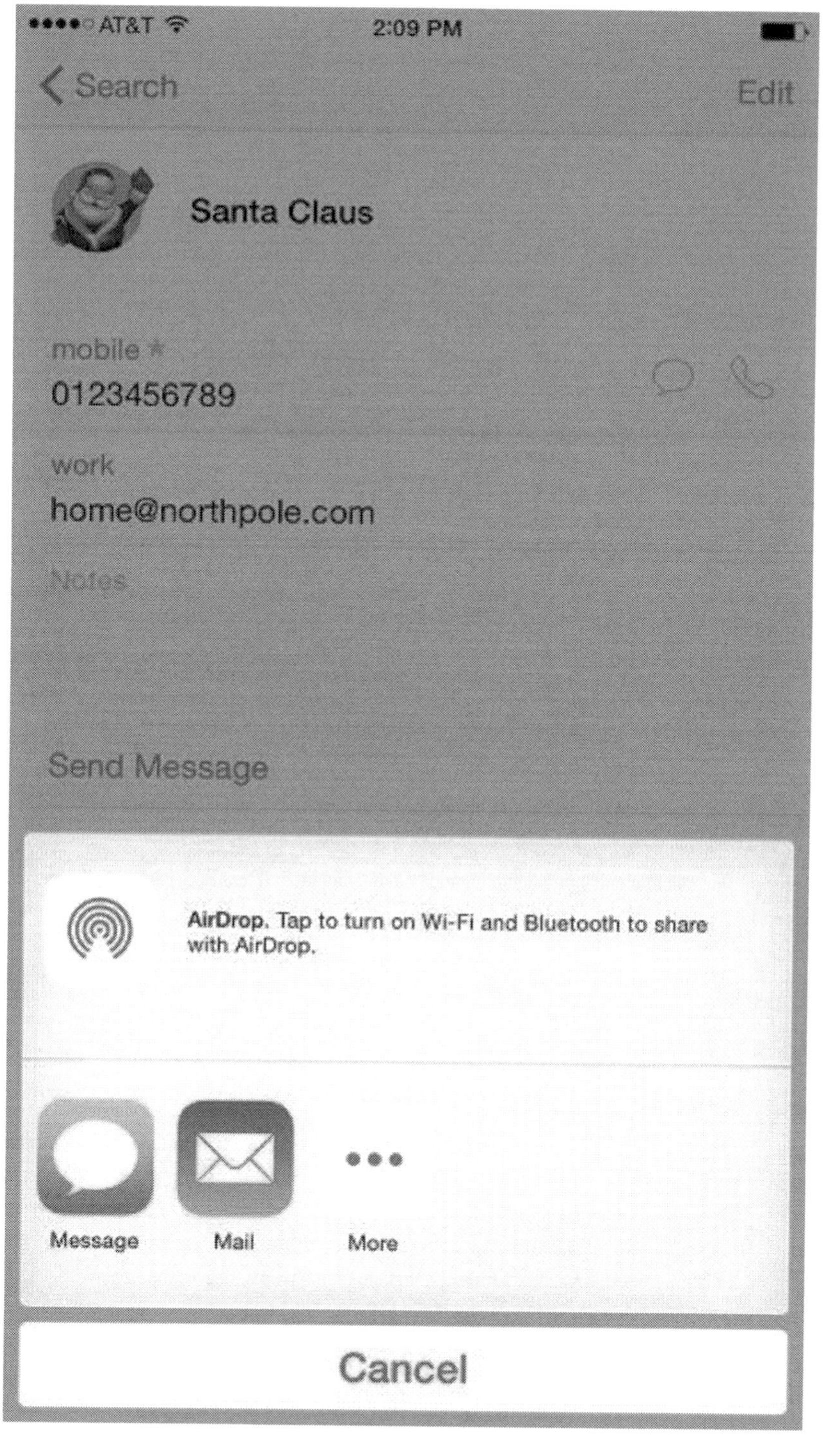

Figure 5: Sharing Options Menu

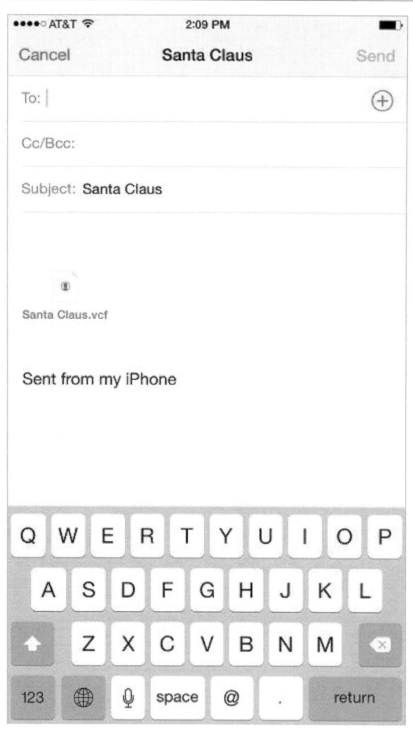

Figure 6: New Email Screen

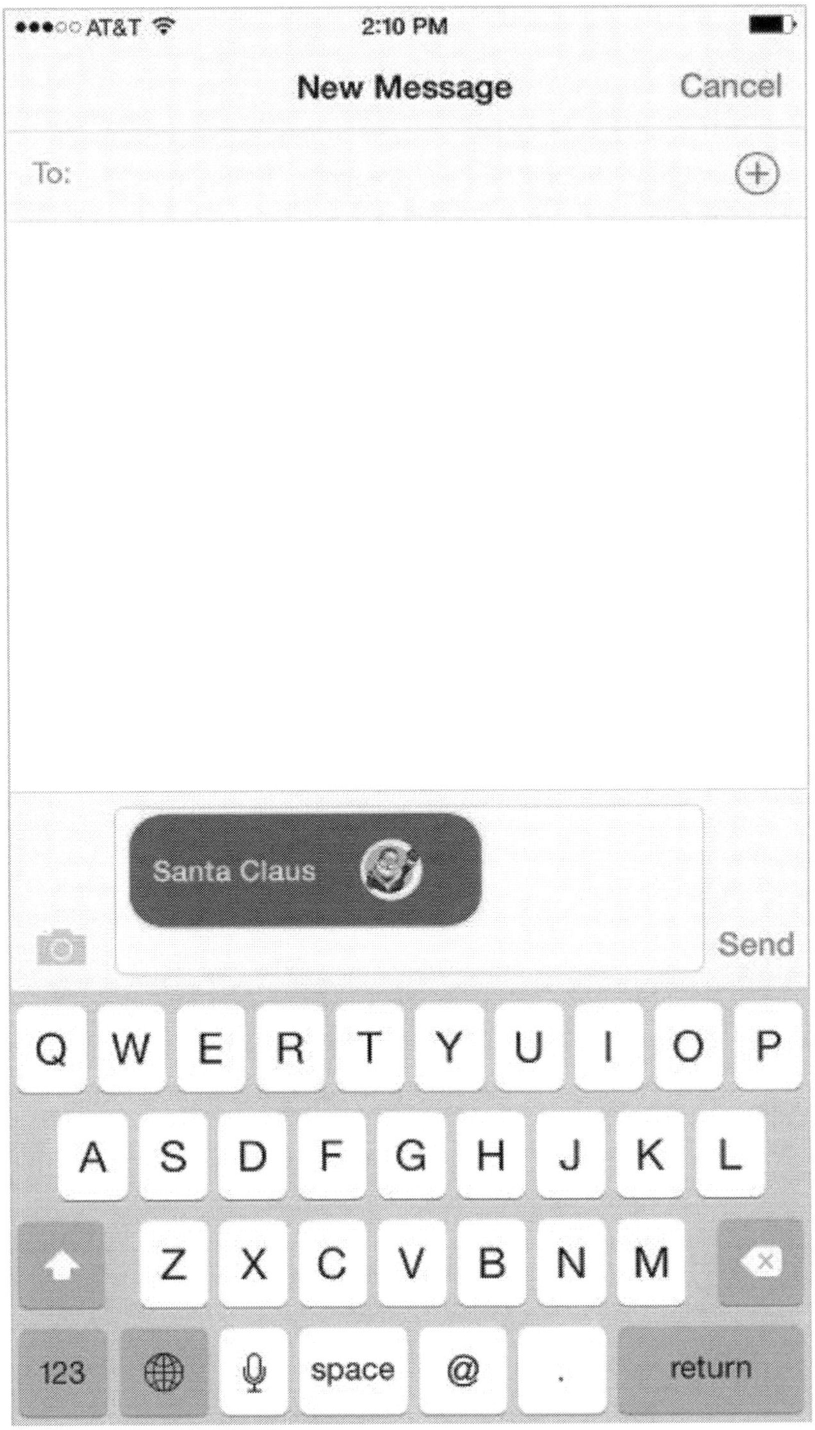

Figure 7: New Message Screen

6. Viewing Recent Contacts

Any contacts that you have recently called or messaged may be viewed in the multitasking menu. To bring up the multitasking menu and view recent contacts, press the **Home** button twice quickly. The Multitasking menu appears, as shown in **Figure 8**. The recent contacts are shown at the top of the screen. To view your favorites, touch the top of the screen and slide your finger to the right.

Figure 8: Multitasking Menu

7. Changing the Contact Sort Order

By default, the phone sorts the contacts in the phonebook by last name. For instance, if the names Jane Doe and John Johnson are in the phonebook, John Johnson would come after Jane Doe because 'J' comes after 'D' in the English alphabet. To change the sort order:

1. Touch the icon. The Settings screen appears, as shown in **Figure 9**.
2. Scroll down, and touch **Mail, Contacts, Calendars**. The Mail, Contacts, Calendars screen appears, as shown in **Figure 10**.
3. Scroll down, and touch **Sort Order** at the bottom of the screen. The Sort Order screen appears, as shown in **Figure 11**.
4. Touch **First, Last**. A check mark appears to the right of the option, and the contacts will be sorted by first name.
5. Touch **Last, First**. A check mark appears to the right of the option, and the contacts will be sorted by last name.

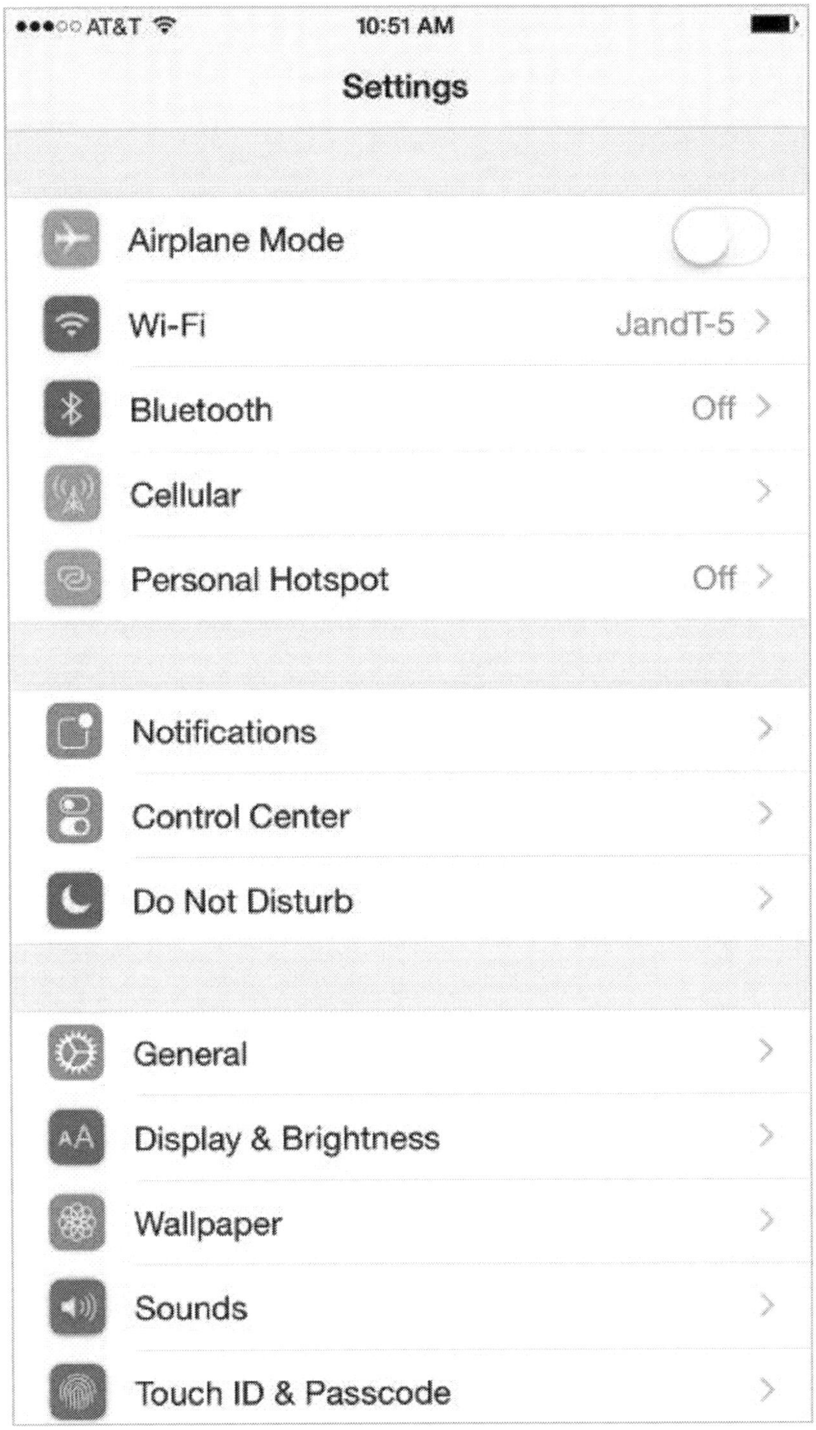

●●●○○ AT&T 📶 10:51 AM ▬▶

Settings

✈️ Airplane Mode ⬜

📶 Wi-Fi JandT-5 ›

❄️ Bluetooth Off ›

📡 Cellular ›

🔗 Personal Hotspot Off ›

🔲 Notifications ›

🎚️ Control Center ›

🌙 Do Not Disturb ›

⚙️ General ›

🔠 Display & Brightness ›

🌸 Wallpaper ›

🔊 Sounds ›

👆 Touch ID & Passcode ›

Figure 9: Settings Screen

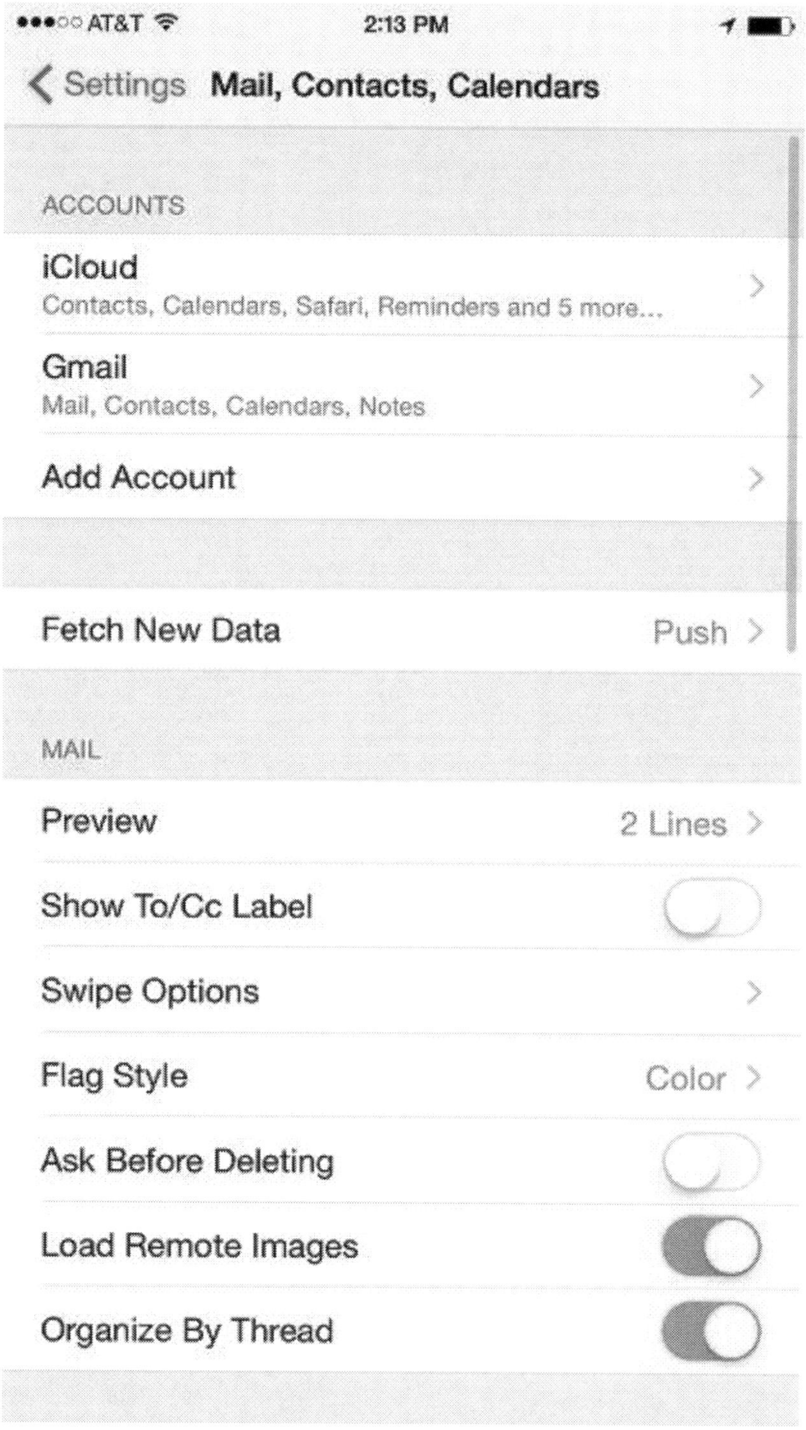

Figure 10: Mail, Contacts, Calendars Screen

Figure 11: Sort Order Screen

8. Viewing the Phonebook in Landscape

The iPhone 6 and 6 Plus have the ability to display the phonebook in landscape view. This view allows you to view the list of contacts on the left, and the information of the currently selected contact on the right. To view the phonebook in landscape view, you must first set the Display Zoom to 'Standard'. If your phone is already is in 'Standard' zoom, just hold your phone horizontally while it is upright. The Landscape Phonebook appears, as shown in **Figure 12**. Otherwise, refer to *"Setting the Display Zoom"* on page 308 to learn how.

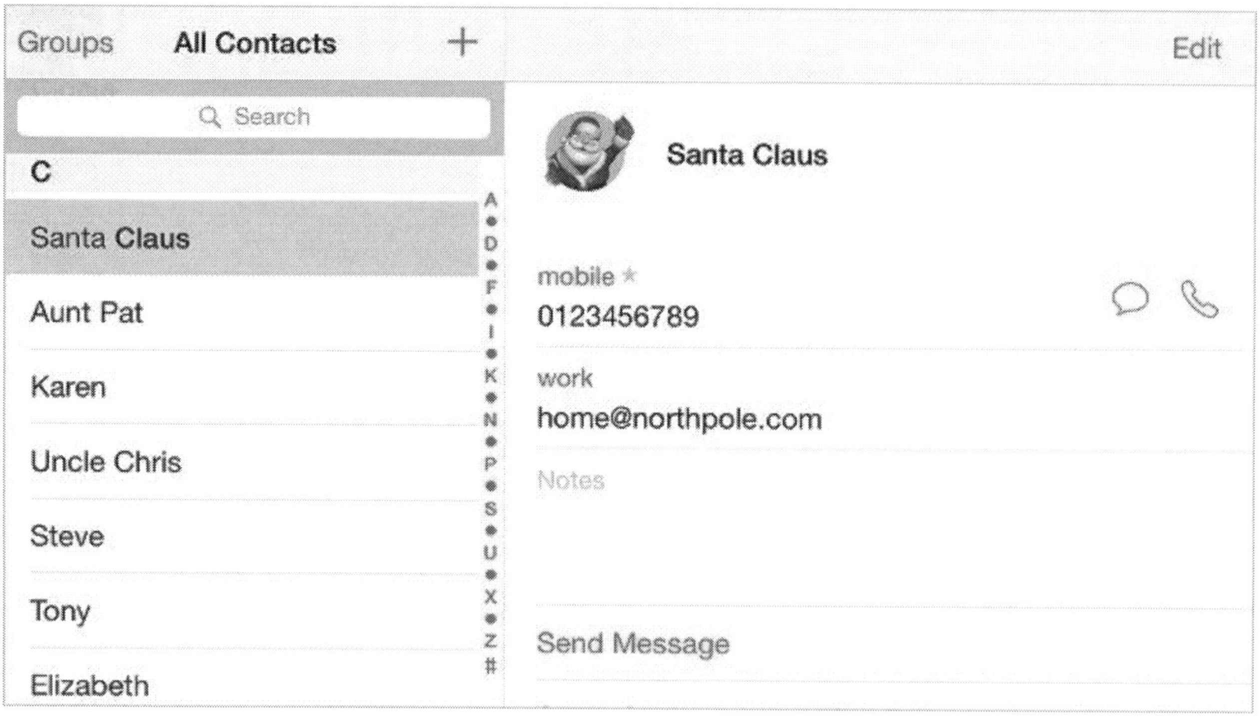

Figure 12: Landscape Phonebook

Text Messaging

Table of Contents

1. Composing a New Text Message

The phone can send text messages to other mobile phones, tablets, and Macs. To compose a new message:

- Touch the icon on the Home screen. The Messages screen appears, as shown in **Figure 1**.
- Touch the icon at the top of the screen. The New Message screen appears, as shown in **Figure 2**.
- Enter the phone number of the recipient. There are three options for entering this information:
- Start typing the name of the contact. Matching contacts appear as you type. Touch the contact's name. The contact's number is added.

- Enter the phone number from scratch.

- Touch the button to select a contact from the Phonebook. Add as many numbers as desired.

- Touch the text field. The cursor starts flashing at the beginning of the field.
- Enter your message. If you begin to type a word incorrectly, the phone may give you a

    suggestion. To accept the suggestion, touch **Space**. To reject it, touch the key.
- Touch **Send** when finished. The message is sent. Your message is shown in a blue (or green) bubble on the right side of the screen, as shown in **Figure 3** (the image may vary slightly on the iPad). All text messages are shown in conversation view.

To send a new message to someone you have already texted:

1. Touch the icon on the Home screen. The Messages screen appears.
2. Touch the name or number of the recipient. The Conversation screen appears. If the name is not in the list, try scrolling down by touching the screen and moving your finger up. If you cannot find the name, you may have deleted your conversation with that contact.
3. Touch the text field. The cursor starts flashing, and a keyboard is shown.
4. Enter the message and then touch **Send**. The message is sent. The most recent message is shown in a blue bubble (iMessage) or green bubble (regular text message) at the bottom right of the conversation. Touch the screen and move your finger down to scroll through older messages.

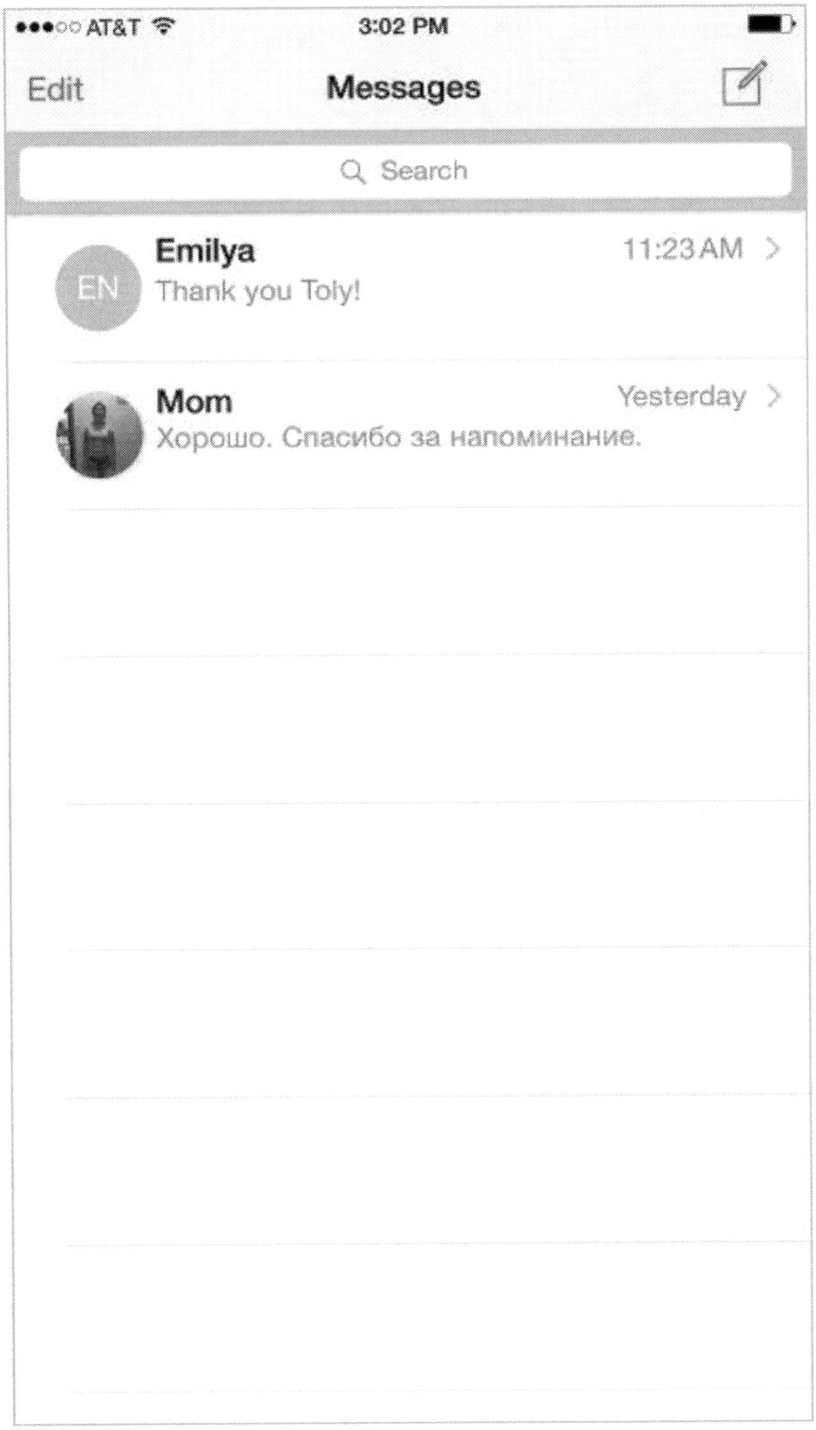

Figure 1: Messages Screen

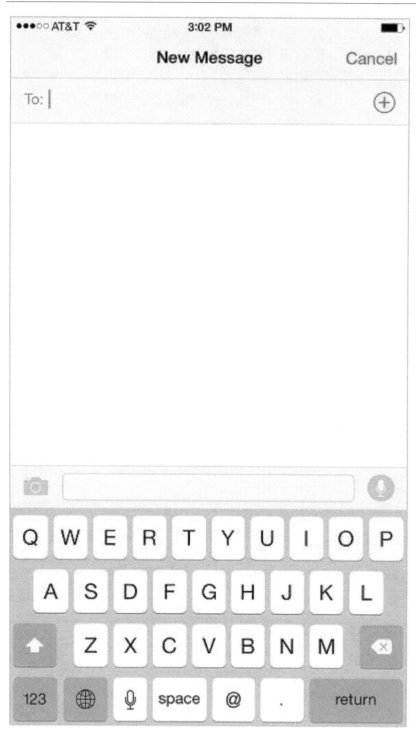

Figure 2: New Message Screen

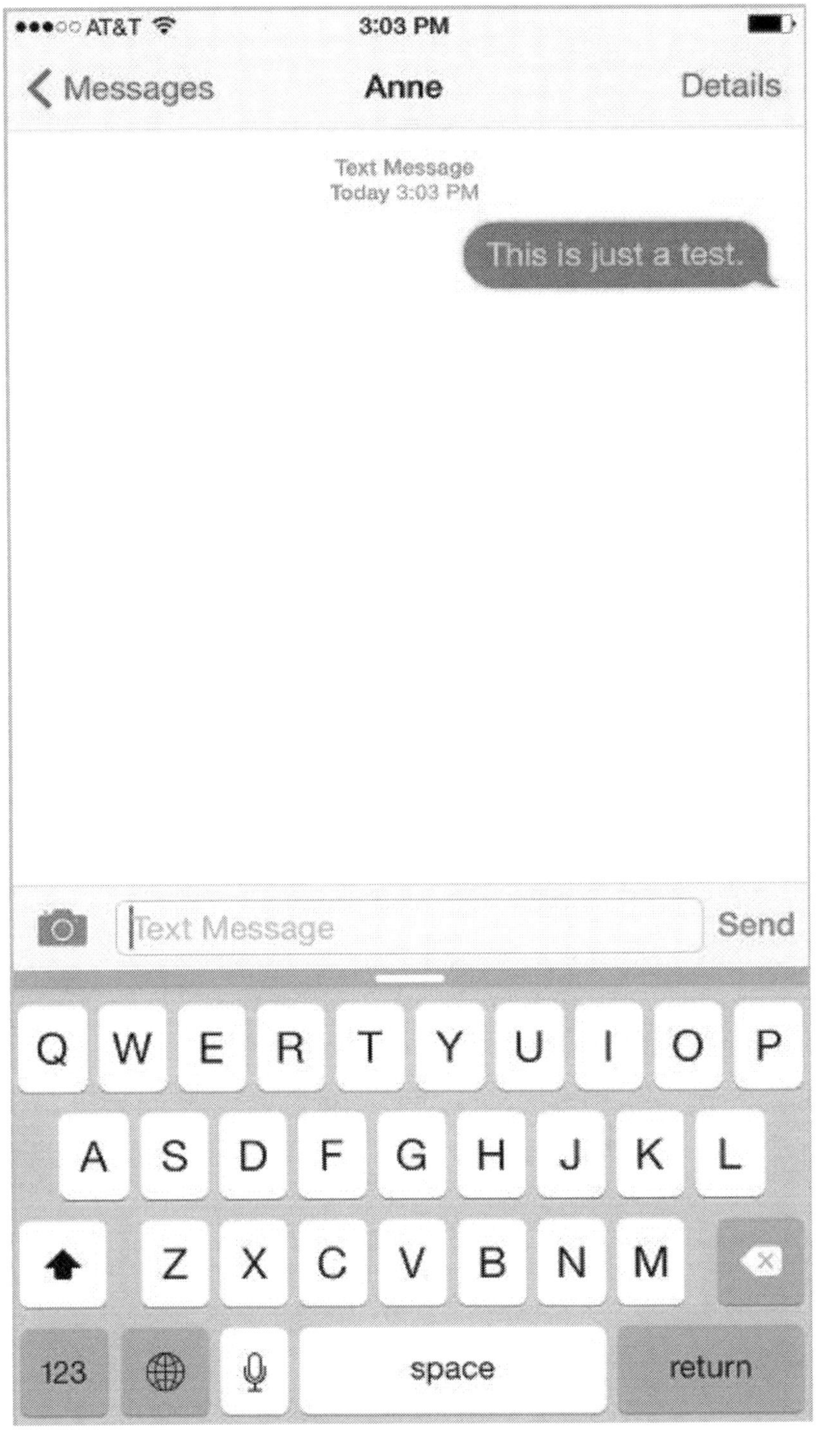

Figure 3: Your Message in a Green Bubble (iMessage)

2. Copying, Cutting, and Pasting Text

The phone allows you to copy or cut text from one location and paste it to another. Copying leaves the text in its current location and allows you to paste it elsewhere. Cutting deletes the text from its current location and allows you to paste it elsewhere. To cut, copy, and paste text:

1. Touch and hold text in a text field, or in a conversation. The Select menu appears above the text, as shown in **Figure 4**. Refer to *"Composing a New Text Message"* on page 77 to learn how to compose a text.
2. Touch **Select All**. All of the text is selected. To select a single word, touch **Select**. Blue dots appear around the word or phrase.
3. Touch and hold one of the blue dots and drag it in any direction. The text between the dots is highlighted and a text menu appears, as shown in **Figure 5**.
4. Touch **Cut** or **Copy**. The corresponding action is taken, and the text is ready to be pasted.
5. Touch and hold any empty text field, and then touch **Paste**. The text is inserted.

Note: Refer to **Tips and Tricks** *to learn more about editing text.*

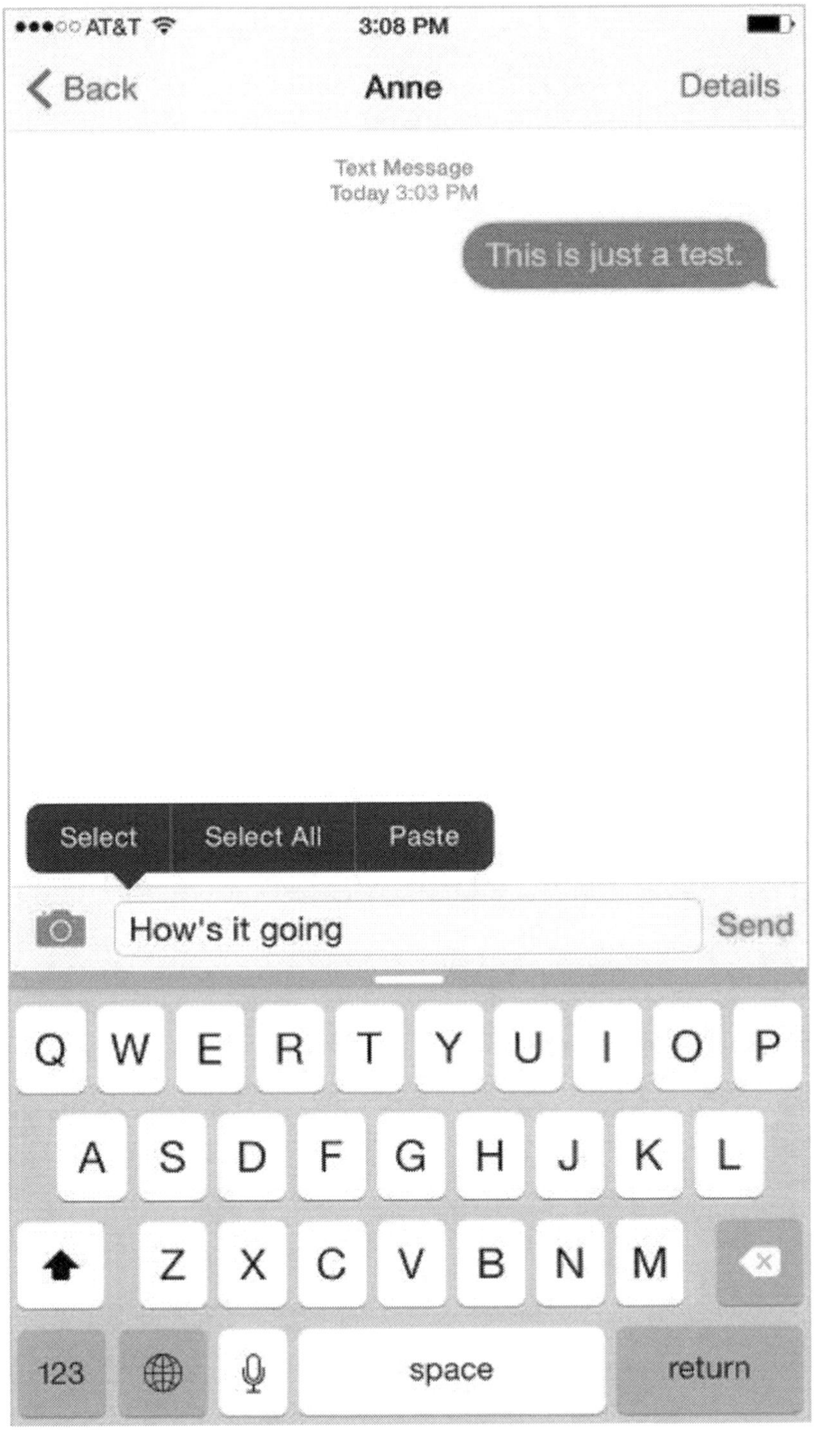

Figure 4: Select Menu

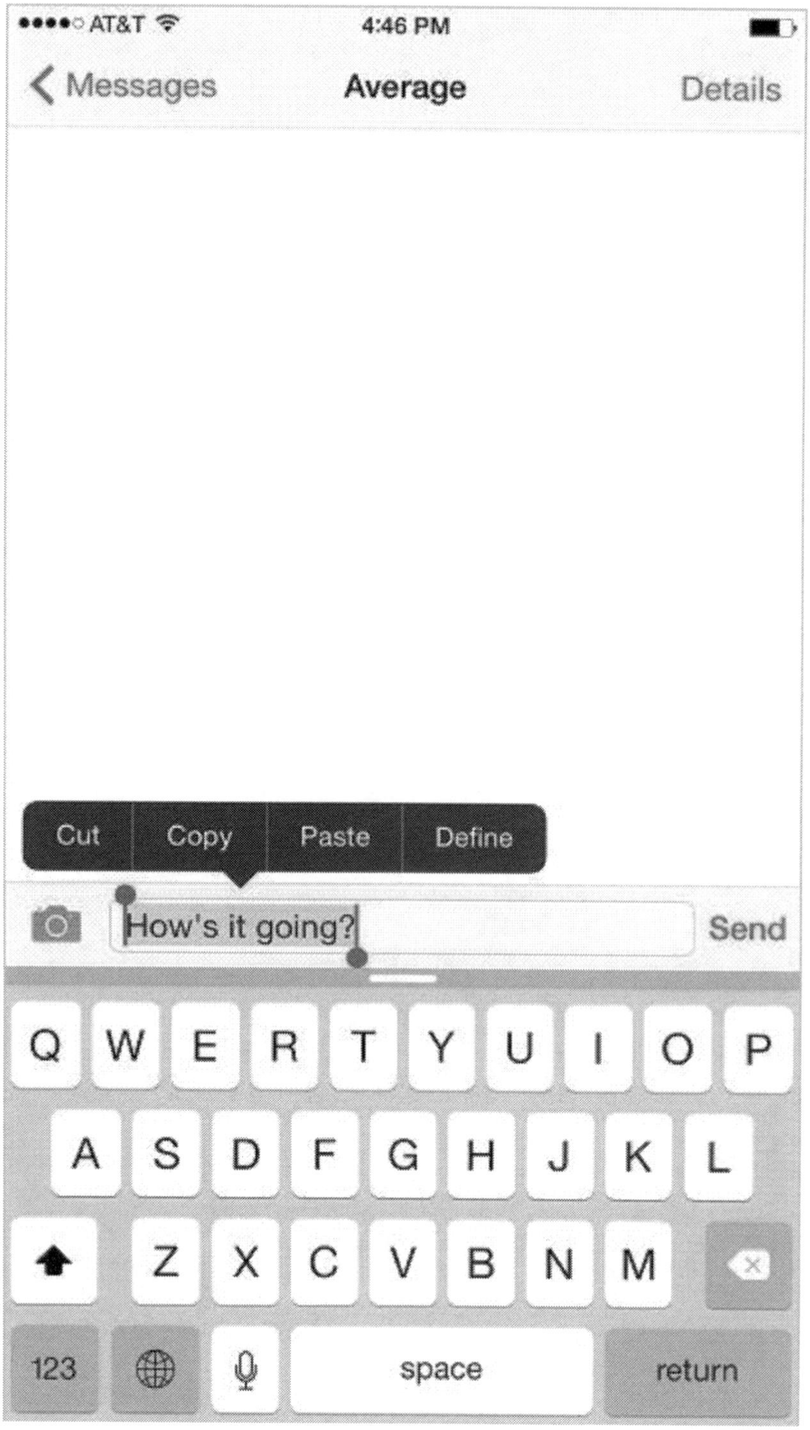

Figure 5: Text Menu

3. Using the Spell Check Feature

The phone will make suggestions for words that are spelled incorrectly. Touch a suggestion to substitute the word immediately. If auto-correction is enabled, the phone will automatically replace common typos. Over time, the phone will learn your most commonly typed words, even names and slang. Refer to *"Adjusting Language and Keyboard Settings"* on page 260 to learn more about auto-correction.

4. Receiving a Text Message

The phone can receive text messages from any other mobile phone. When the phone receives a text, it vibrates once or plays a sound, depending on the settings. The New Message notification appears on the Lock screen, as shown in **Figure 6**, on the Home screen, as shown in **Figure 7**, or in the Notification Bar at the top of the screen, as outlined in **Figure 8**. Whether the notification appears in the Notification Bar or on the Home screen depends on your settings. Use the following tips when receiving text messages:

- Slide the [icon] icon to the right on the Lock screen to open the text message.
- Slide the Notification Bar down while running an application. The Quick Message Reply window appears, as shown in **Figure 9**. To reply without opening the Messages application, enter a reply and touch **Send**.

- The [icon] icon next to the [icon] icon on the Home screen indicates that there is one unread message. This number changes depending on the number of unread messages. The number in the red circle will not disappear until the message is read. Touch the [icon] icon to view the message.

If the New Message notification appears on the Home screen, or while you are using an application:

- Touch **Reply** to send a quick text back to the contact without opening the Messages application.
- Touch **Close** to reply later.

Note: Refer to "Composing a New Text Message" *on page 77* *to learn more about sending text messages.*

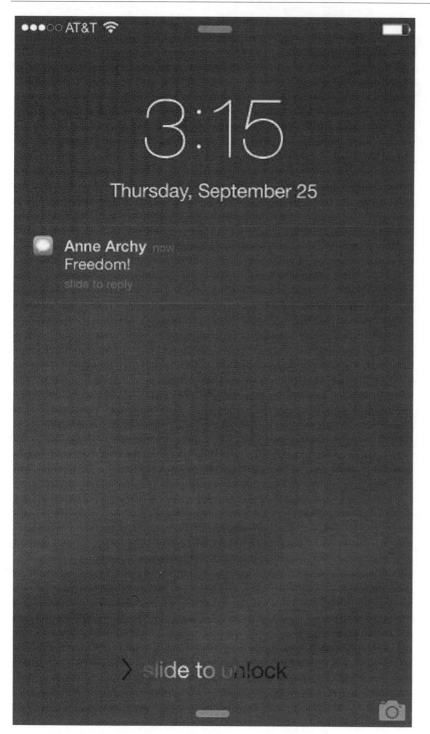

Figure 6: New Message Notification on the Lock Screen

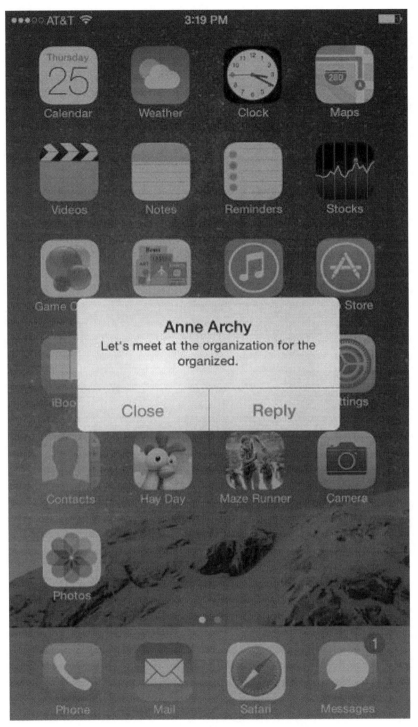

Figure 7: New Message Notification on the Home Screen

Figure 8: New Message Notification in the Notification Bar

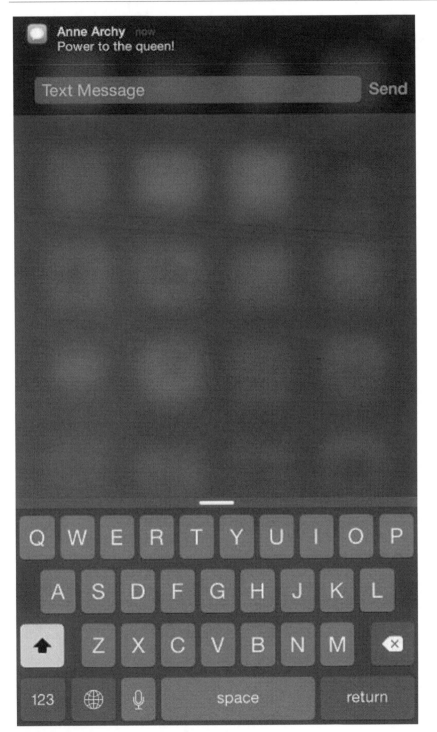

Figure 9: Quick Message Reply Window

5. Reading a Stored Text Message

You may read any text messages that you have received, provided that you have not deleted them. To read stored text messages:

1. Touch the ⬜ icon on the Home screen. The Messages screen appears. The phone organizes conversations based on the date the last message in the conversation was sent or received, with the most recent conversation at the top of the list.
2. Touch the name of a contact to view the conversation. The Conversation screen appears.
3. Touch the screen, and move your finger up or down to scroll through the conversation. The most recent messages appear at the bottom.

6. Forwarding a Text Message

Forwarding a message copies the contents of the original message when you wish to send it to a new recipient. You may wish to forward a text message to save yourself some time entering the same message. To forward a text message:

1. Touch the ⬜ icon on the Home screen. The Messages screen appears, displaying each sender's name on the left and the date of the message on the right.
2. Touch the conversation that contains the message(s) that you wish to forward. The Conversation screen appears.
3. Touch and hold a message in the conversation. The Message menu appears above the message.
4. Touch **More**. A blue check mark appears next to the message, as shown in **Figure 10**.
5. Touch the ⇗ button at the bottom of the screen. The New Message screen appears, with the selected message copied into the text field.
6. Start typing the name of a contact or touch the ⊕ icon to select a number from the Phonebook. The contact is added to the Addressee list.
7. Touch **Send**. The message is forwarded to the contacts in the 'To:' field.

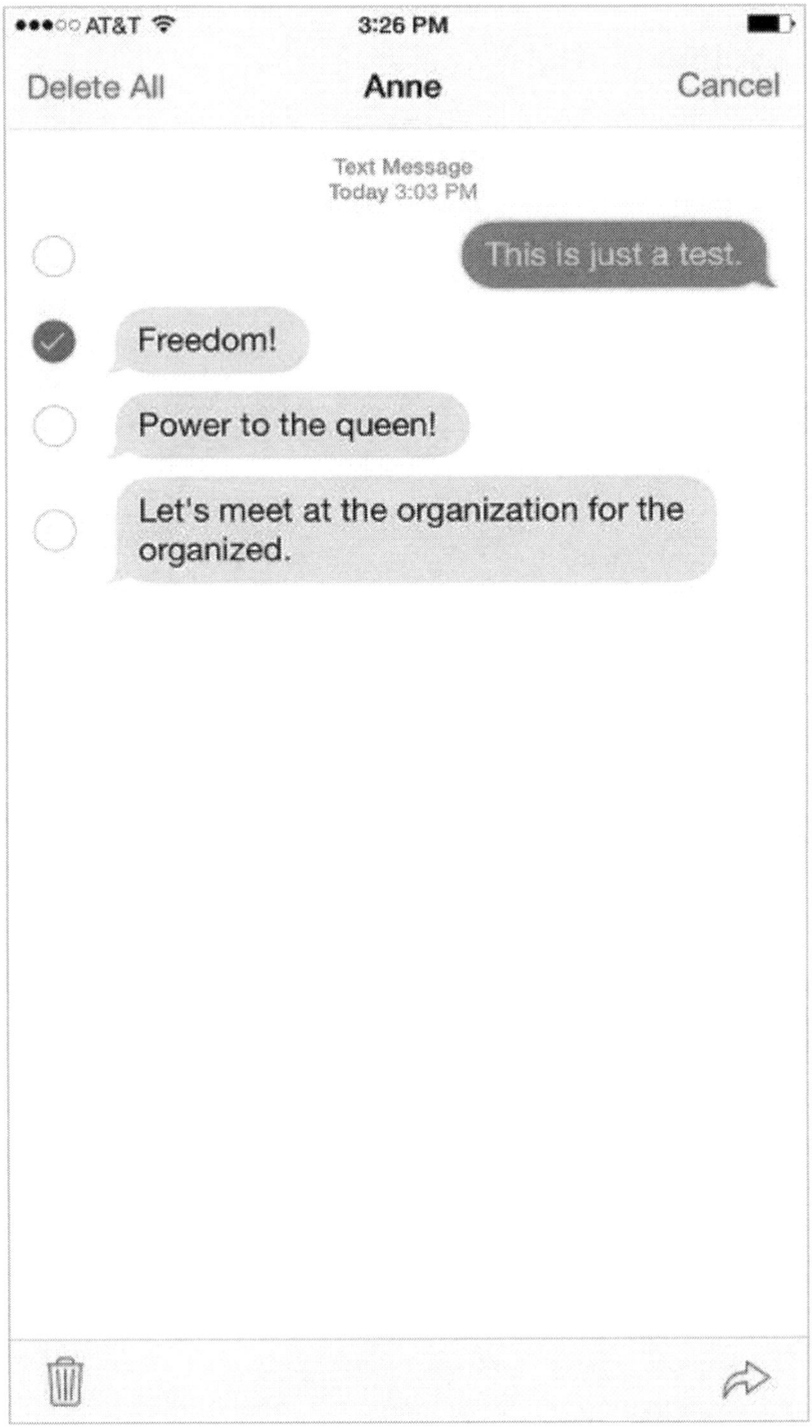

Figure 10: Selected Messages

7. Calling the Sender from within a Text

After receiving a text message from a contact, you may call that person without ever exiting the text message. To call someone from whom you have received a text message:

1. Touch the icon on the Home screen. The Messages screen appears. The phone organizes conversations based on the date the last message in the conversation was sent or received, with the most recent conversation at the top of the list.
2. Touch the conversation that contains the message(s) from the sender that you wish to call. The Conversation screen appears.
3. Touch **Details** at the top of the screen. The Conversation Details screen appears, as shown in **Figure 11**.
4. Touch the icon. The phone places the call.

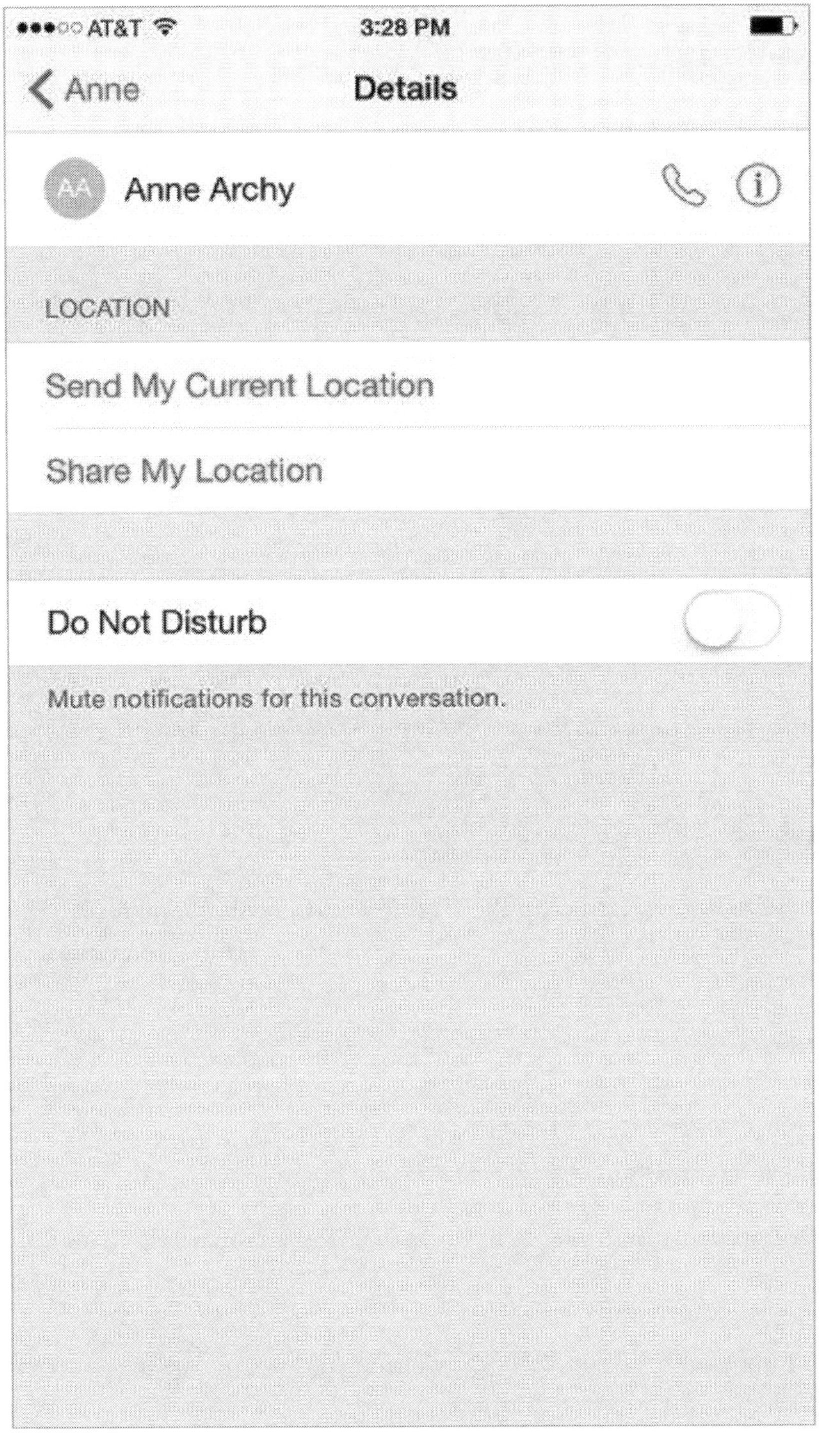

Figure 11: Conversation Details Screen

8. Viewing Sender Information from within a Text

If you have stored a contact's information in the Phonebook, you may view it at any time without leaving a text conversation between the two of you. To view the information of a contact who sent you a message:

1. Touch the [icon] icon on the Home screen. The Messages screen appears.
2. Touch a conversation. The Conversation screen appears.
3. Touch the screen and move your finger down until the top of the conversation appears.
4. Touch **Details** at the top of the screen. The Conversation Details screen appears.
5. Touch the (i) icon. The Contact Information screen appears.

9. Deleting a Text Message

The phone can delete separate text messages or an entire conversation, which is a series of text messages between you and a contact.

Warning: Once deleted, text messages cannot be restored.

To delete an entire conversation, touch the conversation on the Conversation screen, and slide your finger to the left. 'Delete' appears on the right side of the screen. Touch **Delete**. The conversation is deleted.
To delete a separate text message:

1. Touch the [icon] icon on the Home screen. The Messages screen appears.
2. Touch and hold a message in a conversation. The message menu appears.
3. Touch **More**. Touch any other messages that you wish to delete. A mark appears next to each selected message.
4. Touch the [trash icon] icon at the bottom of the screen. A confirmation dialog appears.
5. Touch **Delete Message**. The selected messages are deleted.

10. Adding Texted Phone Numbers to the Phonebook

A phone number sent via text message can be added to your Phonebook immediately. To add a texted phone number to your Phonebook:

1. Touch the icon on the Home screen. The Messages screen appears.
2. Touch a conversation. The Conversation screen appears.
3. Touch and hold the phone number in the conversation. The Phone Number menu appears, as shown in **Figure 12**. On an iPad, the Phone Number menu appears above the phone number.
4. Touch **Add to Contacts**. The Info screen appears.
5. Touch **Create New Contact** or **Add to Existing Contact**. If you touched 'Create New Contact', the New Contact screen appears, with the phone number field filled in, as shown in **Figure 13**. If you touched 'Add to Existing Contact' the Phonebook appears, allowing you to select a contact to whom you wish to attach the number.
6. Touch **First** and enter a first name. Touch **Last** and enter a last name. Touch **Done** at the top of the screen. The contact is added to your Phonebook.

Figure 12: Phone Number Menu

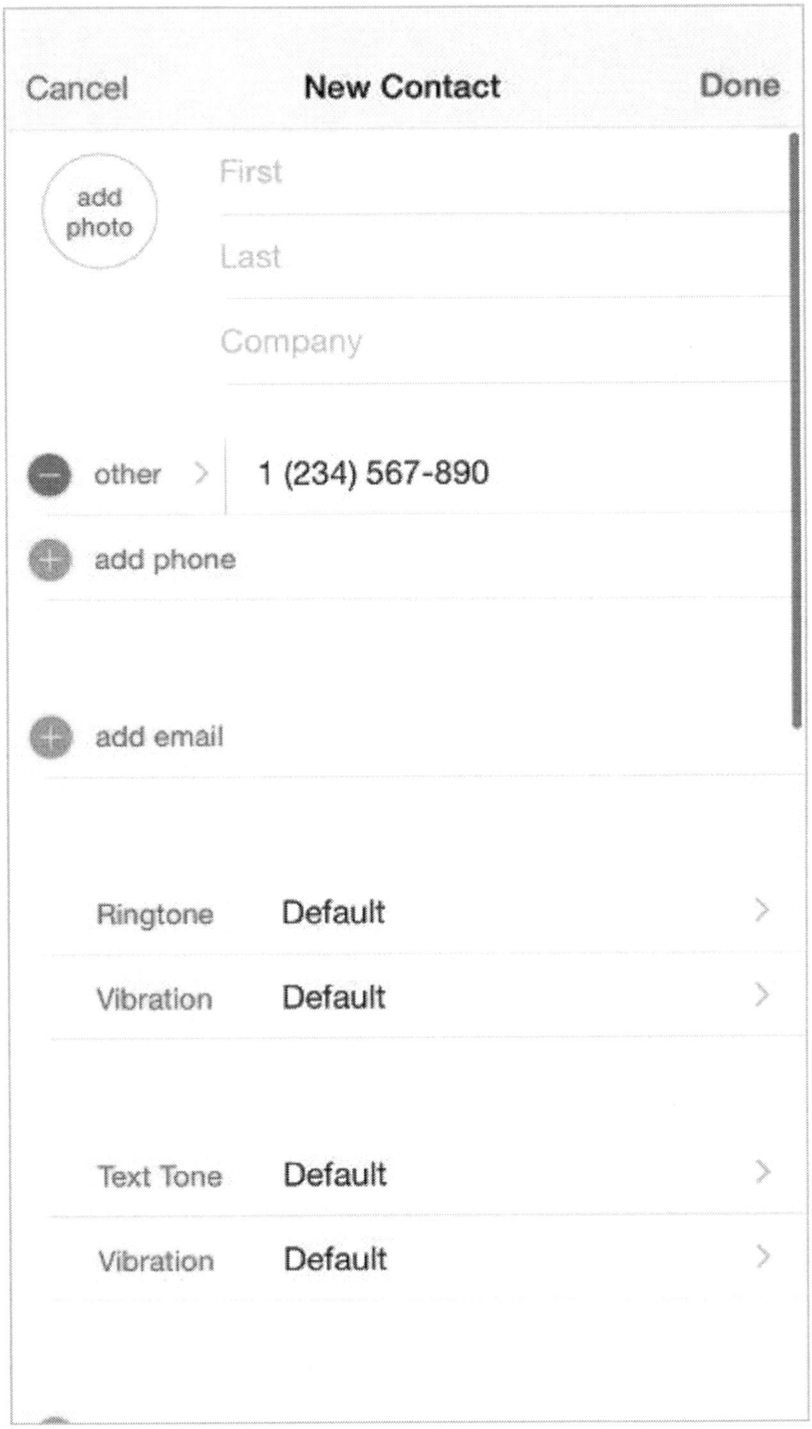

Cancel   **New Contact**   Done

add
photo

First

Last

Company

other   >   1 (234) 567-890

add phone

add email

Ringtone   Default   >

Vibration   Default   >

Text Tone   Default   >

Vibration   Default   >

Figure 13: New Contact Screen

11. Sending a Picture Message

You may attach a picture to any text message that you send.

To send a picture message:

1. Touch the ⬜ icon on the Home screen. The Messages screen appears.
2. Touch the ⬜ icon. The New Message screen appears.
3. Touch the 📷 button to the left of the text field. The Photo Attachment menu appears, as shown in **Figure 14**.
4. Follow the steps in one of the sections below to either attach an existing picture or take a picture to send:

To attach an existing picture to the text message:

- Touch **Photo Library**. A list of Photo Albums appears, as shown in **Figure 15**.
- Touch a photo album. The photo album opens.
- Touch a photo. The preview of the photo appears.
- Touch **Choose**. The photo is attached to the text message. Alternatively, touch **Cancel** to select a different photo.

To take a picture and attach it to the text message:

1. Touch **Take Photo or Video**. The camera turns on, as shown in **Figure 16**.
2. Touch the ⬜ button at the bottom of the screen. The photo is captured and a preview of the photo appears.
3. Touch **Use Photo** to use the photo in the message, or touch **Retake** to discard the picture and take another one. The photo is attached. Alternatively, touch **Cancel** while the camera is turned on to return to the conversation without taking a picture.
4. Touch **Send**. The picture message is sent.

Note: Up to nine photos may be sent in a picture message.

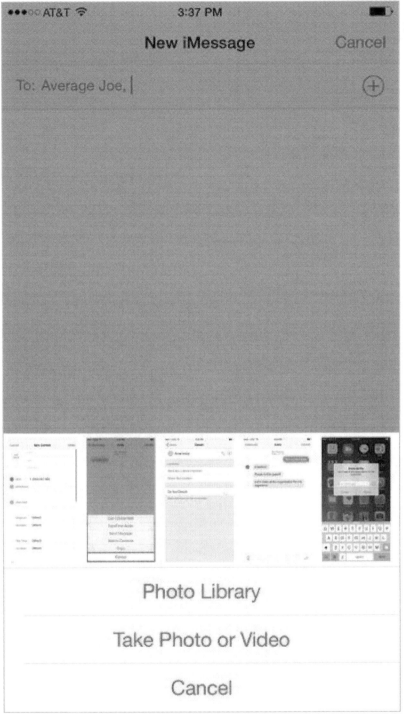

Figure 14: Photo Attachment Menu

Figure 15: List of Photo Albums

Figure 16: Camera Turned On

12. Leaving a Group Conversation (iMessage Only)

You may remove yourself from a group conversation if you no longer wish to participate. Once removed, you will not receive any further messages in that conversation. To leave a group conversation:

1. Touch **Details** at the top of the conversation. The Conversation details appear.
2. Touch **Leave this Conversation**. A confirmation dialog appears.
3. Touch **Leave this Conversation** again. You are removed from the conversation.

13. Naming a Conversation (iMessage Only)

In order to find it more quickly and easily, you may name a conversation with a group. The title of the conversation will show up on the phone of everyone involved in the conversation. To name a conversation:

1. Touch **Details** in the upper right-hand corner of the conversation. The Conversation details appear.
2. Touch **Subject**. The virtual keyboard appears, and you may now enter a title.
3. Enter the title of the conversation. The conversation is renamed.

14. Adding a Voice Message to a Conversation (iMessage Only)

You may add a short voice message to a text message or conversation. This feature only works when using iMessage. If you send a text message to someone who does not use an iPhone, or has not registered for iMessage, this feature will not work. To add a voice message to an iMessage:

1. Touch and hold the ![microphone icon] icon to the right of the text field. The microphone turns on.

2. Speak the voice message that you would like to attach. When you are finished, release the ![microphone icon] icon. The voice message is recorded, as shown in **Figure 17**.

3. Touch the ![up arrow icon] icon. The voice message is sent. Alternatively, touch the ![play icon] icon to preview the voice message, or touch the ![x icon] icon if you would like to discard the voice message.

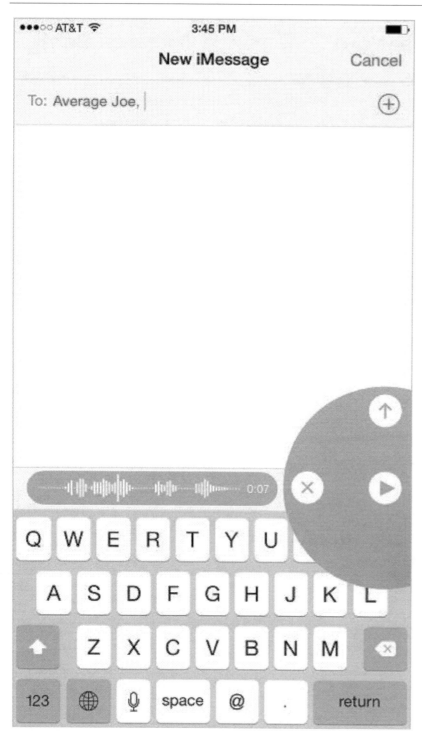

Figure 17: Recorded Voice Message

15. Quickly Adding a Video or Photo to a Conversation (iMessage Only)

You may quickly add a video to a conversation if you are on the go. To add a video to a conversation:

1. Touch and hold the 📷 icon, and drag your finger up. The camera turns on.

2. Drag your finger over the 📷 icon until it turns orange, and release the screen. The camera captures a picture, and immediately sends it to the recipient.

3. You may also drag your finger over, and hold the ⚪ icon to record a quick video. Release the ⚪ icon when you have finished recording. Touch the ↑ icon to send the video. Alternatively, touch the ▶ icon to preview the video, or touch the ✕ icon if you would like to discard the video.

16. Sharing Your Location in a Conversation

You may choose to share your location with a contact or a number of participants in a conversation. To share your location for a specified amount of time:

1. Touch **Details** in the upper right-hand corner of the conversation. The Conversation details appear.
2. Touch **Share My Location**. The Location Sharing menu appears, as shown in **Figure 18**.
3. Touch one of the following options to share your location for the corresponding amount of time: **Share for One Hour**, **Share Until End of Day**, or **Share Indefinitely**. You location is shared. The last option will allow you to share your location until you touch **Stop Sharing My Location** on the Conversation Details screen.

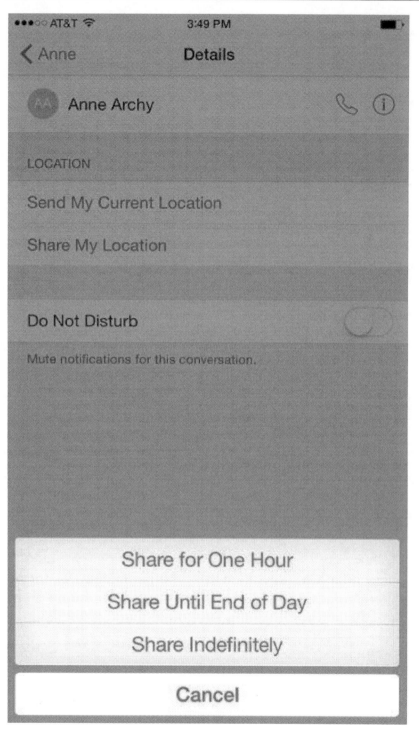

Figure 18: Location Sharing Menu

17. Viewing All Attachments in a Conversation

The Messaging application provides a convenient way to view all of the pictures, videos, and voice messages attached to a conversation in one neat list. To view all attachments in a conversation, touch **Details** at the top of a conversation. The Conversation details appear, and the list of attachments is shown at the bottom of the screen. To save one of the attachments in the list to a photo album:

1. Touch the attachment that you want to save. The attachment appears in full screen.
2. Touch the center of the screen. The Attachment menu appears.

3. Touch the ⬆️ icon at the top of the screen, if it is a photo, or at the bottom of the screen, if it is a video, or if there are two or more attachments. The Save Photo menu appears, as shown in **Figure 19**, or the Save Video menu appears, as shown in **Figure 20**.

4. Touch the ⬇️ icon. The attachment is saved to the Recently Added album on your phone.

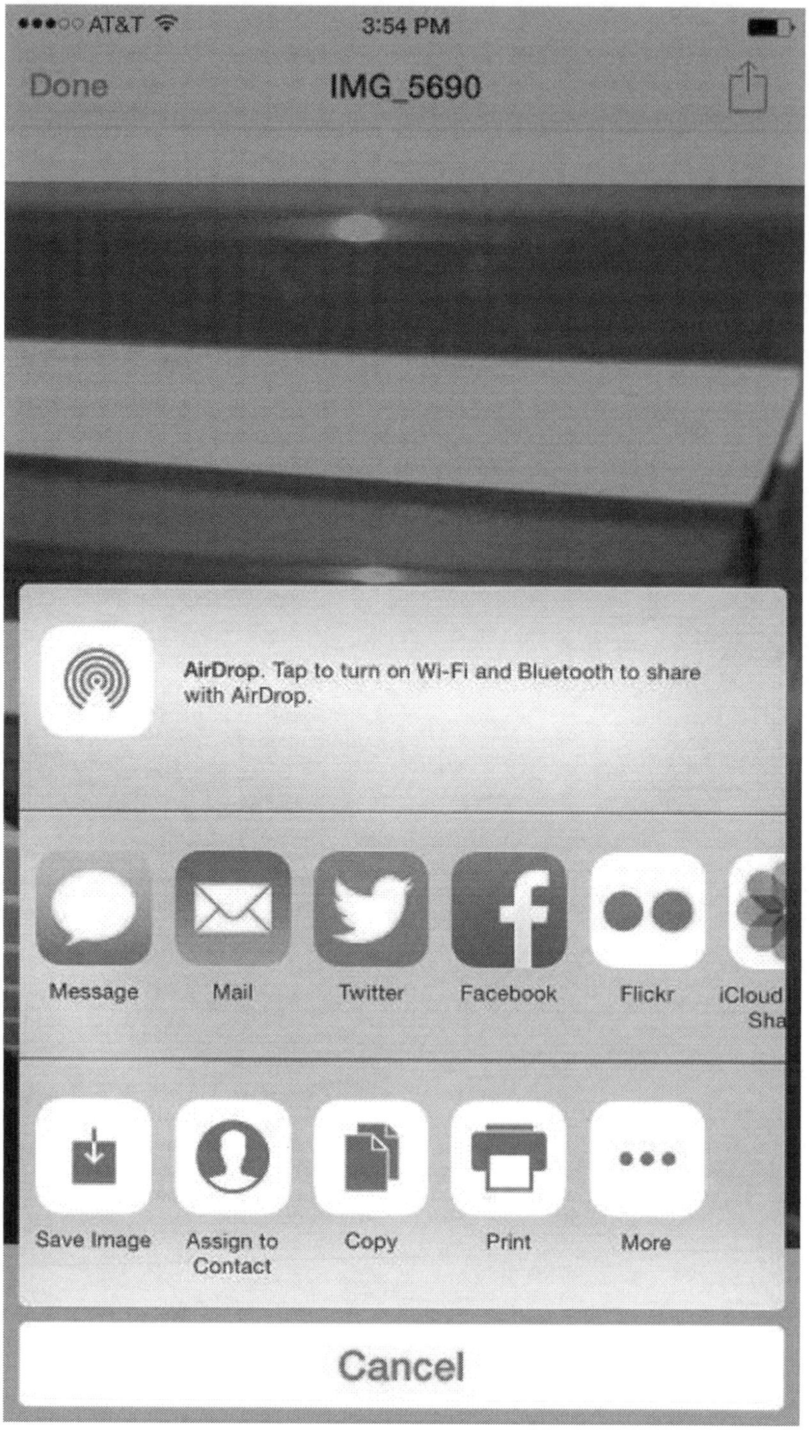

Figure 19: Save Photo Menu

Figure 20: Save Video Menu

18. Viewing the Messages Screen in Landscape

The iPhone 6 and 6 Plus have the ability to display the Messages screen in landscape view. This view allows you to view the list of conversations on the left, and the list of messages of the currently selected conversation on the right. To view the Messages screen in landscape view, you must first set the Display Zoom to 'Standard'. If your phone is already is in 'Standard' zoom, just hold your phone horizontally while it is upright. The Landscape Messages screen appears, as shown in **Figure 21**. Otherwise, refer to *"Setting the Display Zoom"* on page 260 to learn how.

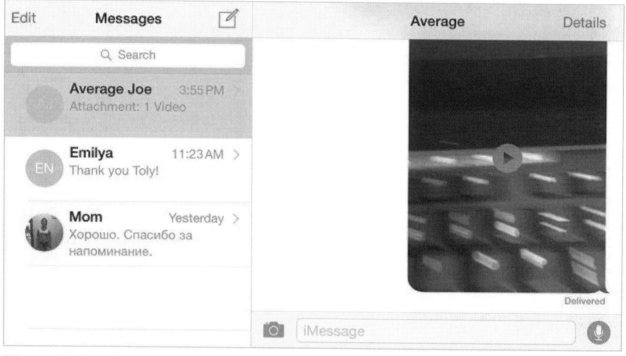

Figure 21: Landscape Messages Screen

Using the Safari Web Browser

Table of Contents

1. Navigating to a Website

You can surf the web using your phone. To navigate to a website using the web address:

1. Touch the icon on the Home screen. The Safari Web browser opens.
2. Touch the Address bar at the top of the screen, as outlined in **Figure 1**. The keyboard appears. If you do not see the Address bar, touch the screen and move your finger down to scroll up.
3. Touch the web address at the top of the screen. button. The address field is erased.
4. Enter a web address and touch **Go**. Safari navigates to the website.
5. Touch the button. Safari navigates to the previous web page.
6. Touch the button. Safari navigates to the next web page.

Figure 1: Address Bar in Safari

2. Adding and Viewing Bookmarks

The phone can store favorite websites as Bookmarks to allow you to access them faster in the future. To add a Bookmark in Safari:

1. 1. Touch the icon on the Home screen. The Safari browser opens.
2. Navigate to a website. Refer to *"Navigating to a Website"* on page 111 to learn how.
3. Touch the button at the bottom of the screen. The Bookmark menu appears, as shown in **Figure 2**.
4. Touch the icon. The Add Bookmark window appears, as shown in **Figure 3**.
5. Enter a name for the bookmark and touch **Save** in the top right-hand corner of the screen. The website is added to the Bookmarks.
6. To view saved Bookmarks, touch the icon in the Safari browser. The icon is located at the top of the screen on an iPad, or at the bottom of the screen on an iPhone. The Bookmarks screen appears, as shown in **Figure 4**. Touch a bookmark. Safari navigates to the indicated website.

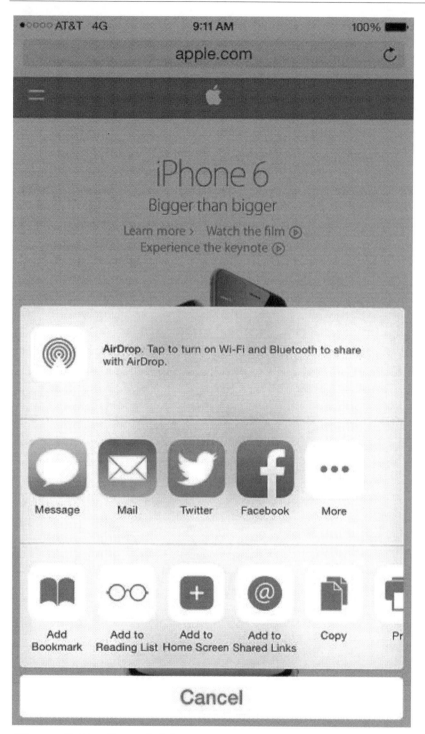

Figure 2: Bookmark Menu

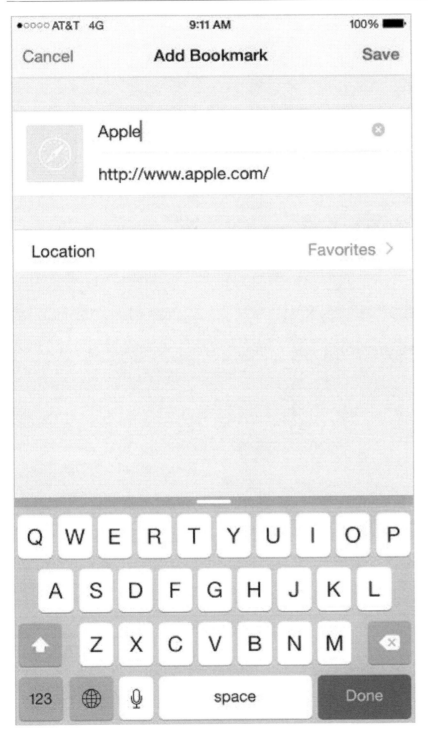

Figure 3: Add Bookmark Window

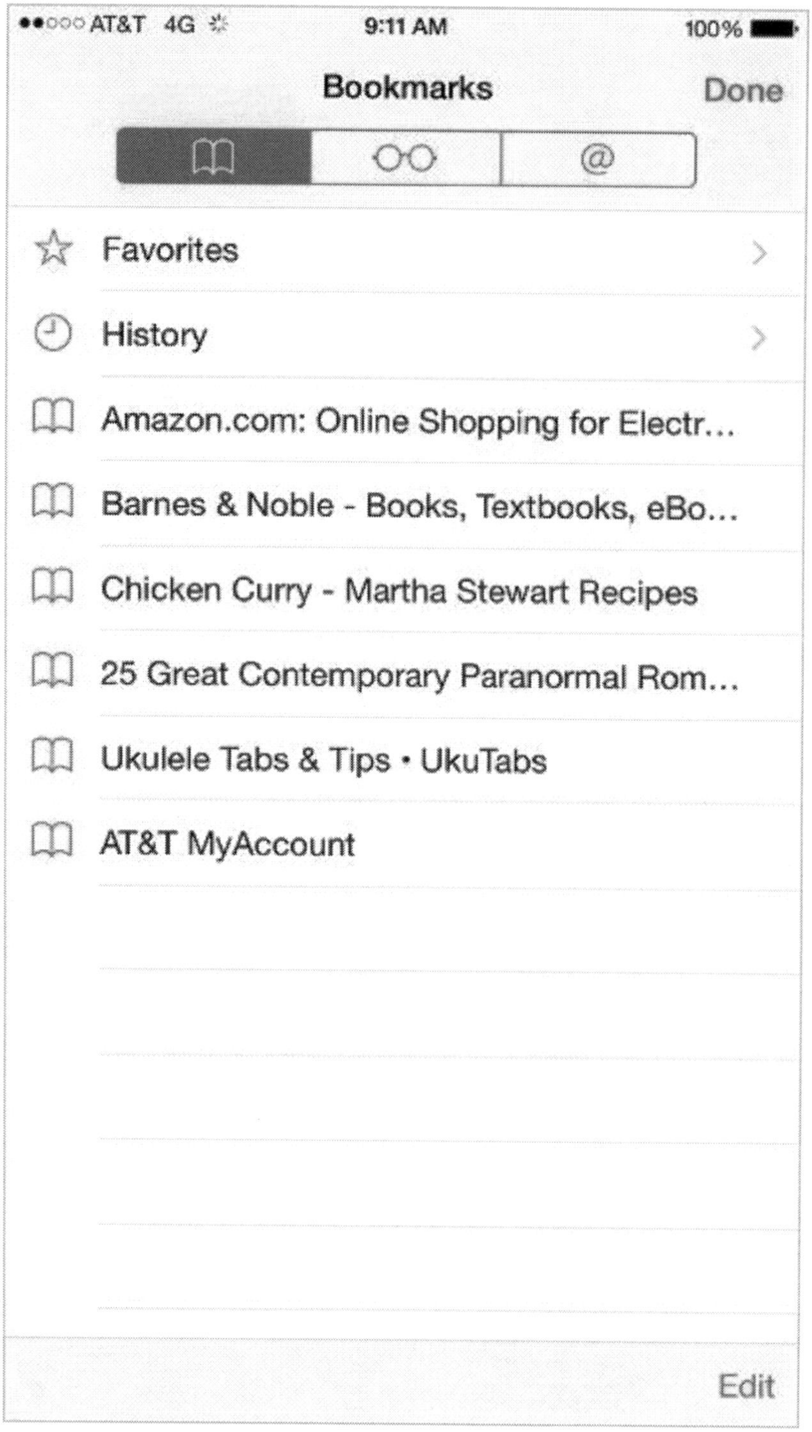

●●○○○ AT&T 4G ☼   9:11 AM   100% ▬

Bookmarks   Done

| 📖 | ◯◯ | @ |

☆   Favorites   ›

🕘   History   ›

📖   Amazon.com: Online Shopping for Electr...

📖   Barnes & Noble - Books, Textbooks, eBo...

📖   Chicken Curry - Martha Stewart Recipes

📖   25 Great Contemporary Paranormal Rom...

📖   Ukulele Tabs & Tips • UkuTabs

📖   AT&T MyAccount

             Edit

Figure 4: Bookmarks Screen

3. Adding a Bookmark to the Home Screen

Bookmarks can be added to the Home screen; they will then appear like application icons. To add a bookmark to the Home screen as an icon:

1. Touch the ⊘ icon on the Home screen. The Safari browser opens.
2. Navigate to a website. Refer to *"Navigating to a Website"* on page 111 to learn how.
3. Touch the ⬆ button at the bottom of the screen. The Bookmark menu appears.
4. Touch the ➕ icon. The Add to Home window appears, as shown in **Figure 5**.
5. Enter a name for the bookmark and touch **Add**. The bookmark is added to the Home screen.

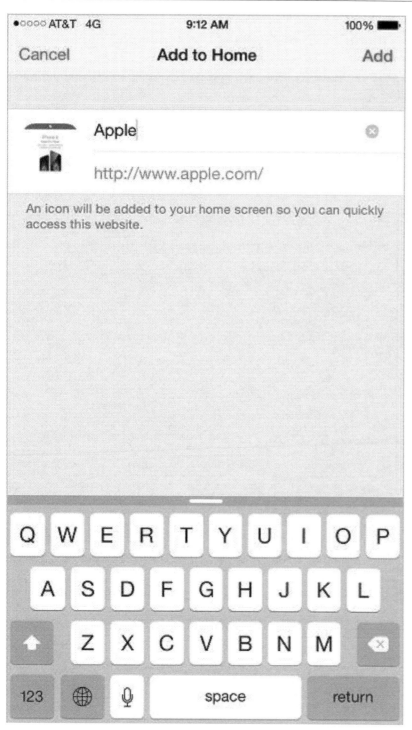

Figure 5: Add to Home Window

4. Managing Open Browser Tabs

The Safari Web browser supports up to 36 open browser tabs. This feature is analogous to tabbed browsing in a browser like Mozilla Firefox or Google Chrome. Use the following tips when working with browser tabs:

- To view the open Safari tabs, touch the ⎙ button in Safari. The ⎙ icon is located at the top of the screen on an iPad, or at the bottom of the screen on an iPhone. The open Safari tabs appear, as shown in **Figure 6**. Touch the screen and flick your finger up or down to view other open tabs. While viewing the open Safari tabs:

- To open a new browser tabs, touch the ➕ button.
- To close a tab, touch the tab and move it to the left. You can also touch **Done** to return to the tab that you were just viewing.
- To reorder the tabs, touch and hold a tab, and move it up or down.
- Rotate the phone to view the classic tabs, as they appear on a computer browser, as shown in **Figure 7**.

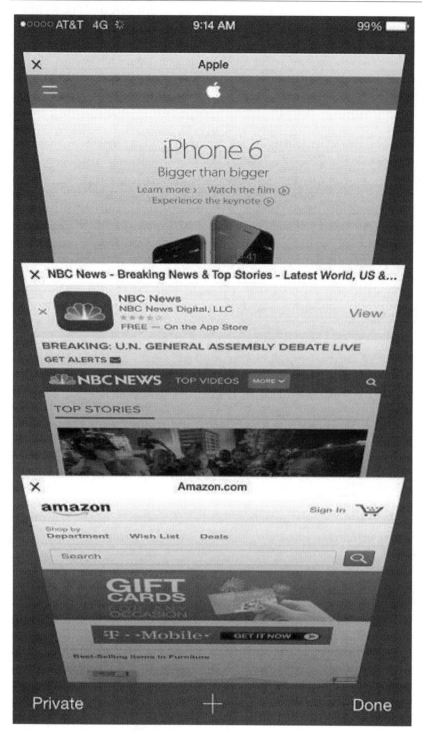

Figure 6: Open Safari Tabs

Figure 7: Classic Safari Tabs

5. Blocking Pop-Up Windows

Some websites may have pop-up windows that interfere with browsing the internet. By default, pop-ups are already blocked. To block pop-ups:

1. Touch the ⚙ icon on the Home screen. The Settings screen appears, as shown in **Figure 8**.
2. Scroll down and touch **Safari**. The Safari Settings screen appears, as shown in **Figure 9**.
3. Touch the ⬯ switch next to 'Block Pop-Ups'. Pop-ups will now be blocked.
4. Touch the ⬮ switch next to 'Block Pop-Ups'. Pop-ups will now be allowed.

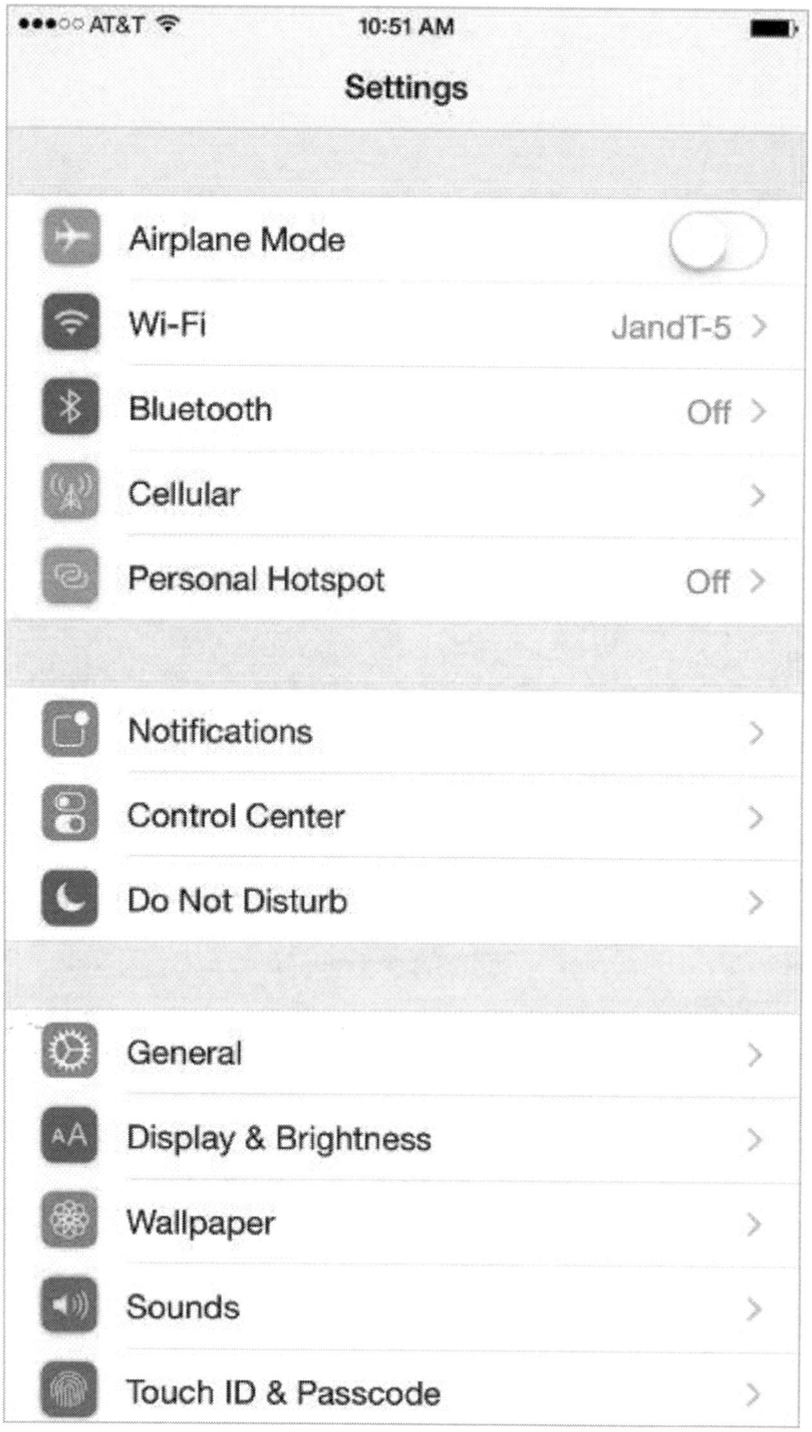

Figure 8: Settings Screen

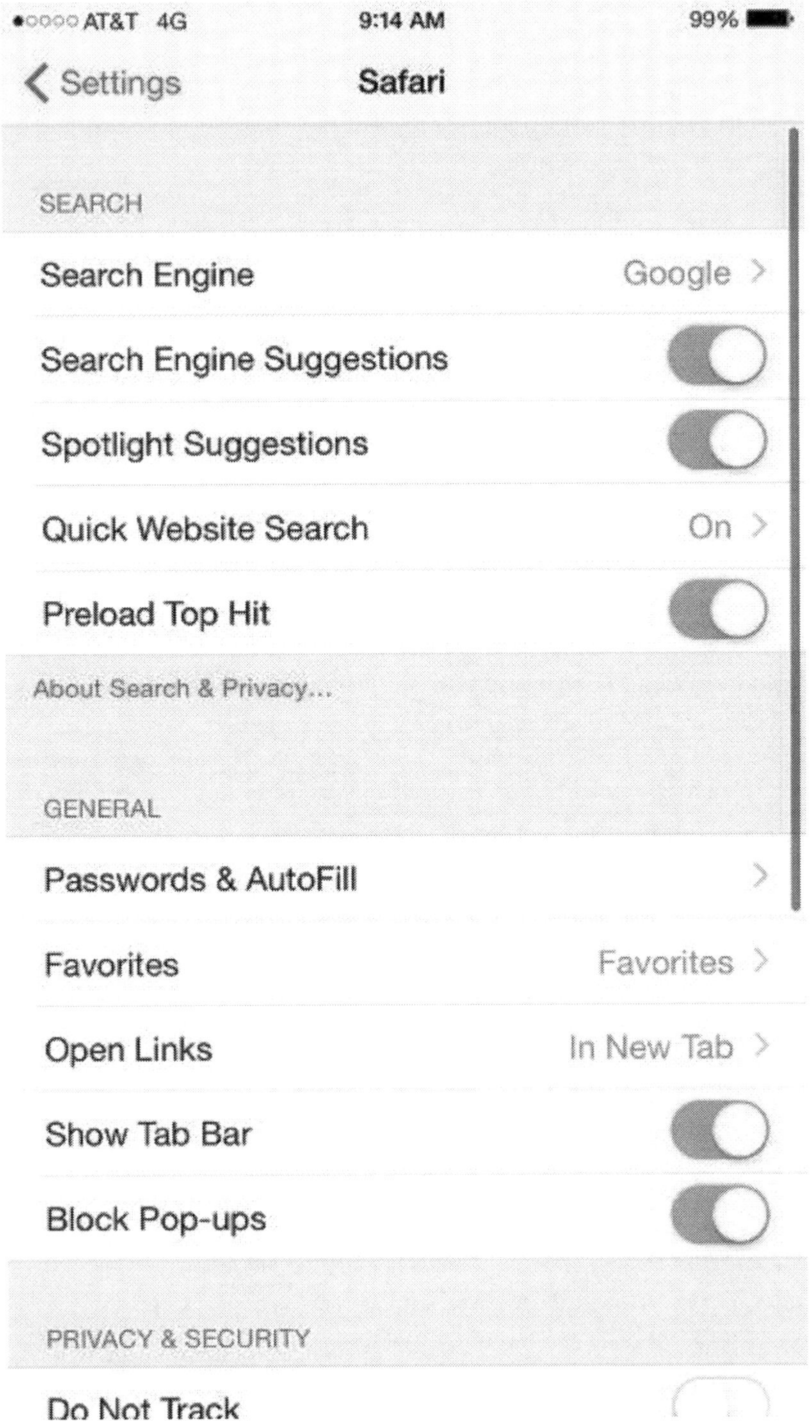

Figure 9: Safari Settings Screen

6. Changing the Search Engine

Google, Yahoo, or Bing can be set as the default search engine in Safari. When you get your new iPhone 6, the default search engine is set to Google. The Address bar at the top of the screen also acts as a search field in Safari. To change the default search engine:

1. Touch the ⊚ icon on the Home screen. The Settings screen appears.
2. Touch **Safari**. The Safari Settings screen appears.
3. Touch **Search Engine**. A list of search engines appears.
4. Touch the preferred search engine. The default search engine is set, and its name will now appear in the empty search field.

7. Clearing the History and Browsing Data

The phone can clear the list of recently visited websites, known as the History, as well as other data, such as saved passwords, known as Cookies. The phone can also delete data from previously visited websites, known as the Cache. To delete all of these items:

1. Touch the ⊚ icon on the Home screen. The Settings screen appears.
2. Touch **Safari**. The Safari Settings screen appears.
3. Touch **Clear History and Website Data**. A confirmation dialog appears.
4. Touch **Clear History and Data** (or touch **Clear**, if using an iPad). The selected data is deleted and the option is grayed out on the Safari Settings screen.

8. Viewing an Article in Reader Mode

The Safari browser can display certain news articles in Reader Mode, which allows you to read them like a book with no images or links. To view an article in Reader Mode, touch the ☰ button in the address bar (when available), as outlined in **Figure 10**. Reader Mode turns on, as shown in **Figure 11**. When Reader Mode is available, "Reader Mode Available" briefly appears in the address bar when the page has finished loading.

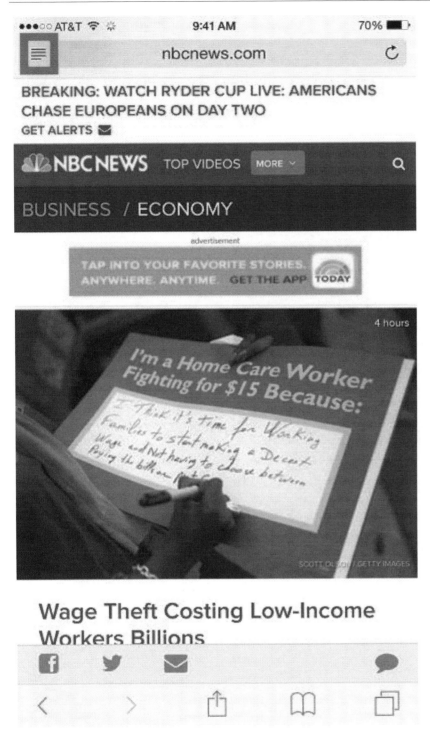

Figure 10: Reader Button in the Address Bar

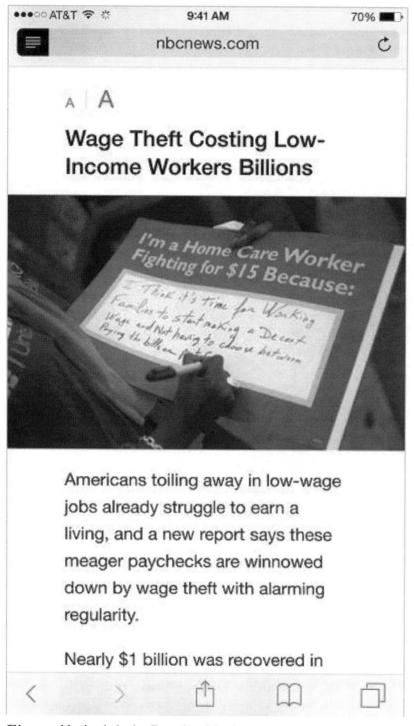

Figure 11: Article in Reader Mode

9. Turning Private Browsing On or Off

In order to preserve privacy, the Safari Web browser allows you to surf the internet without saving the History or any other data showing that you have visited a particular website. To open a private tab:

1. Touch the [icon] button. The open browser tabs appear.
2. Touch **Private**. Private Mode is turned on.
3. Touch the [icon] icon to open a new private tab.
4. When you are ready to exit private mode, touch the [icon] button, and then touch **Private** again.

10. Setting Up the AutoFill Feature

Safari can automatically fill in personal information, such as passwords and credit card information, to save you time when filling forms or shopping online. To set up the AutoFill feature:

1. Touch the [icon] icon on the Home screen. The Settings screen appears.
2. Touch **Safari**. The Safari Settings screen appears.
3. Touch **Passwords & AutoFill**. The Passwords & Autofill screen appears, as shown in **Figure 12**.
4. Touch one of the following [switch] switches turn on the corresponding AutoFill:

- **Use Contact Info** - Enables the use of contact information when filling in forms. The Phonebook appears. Touch the name of a contact to use the contact information to fill in forms. It is recommended that you create a contact entry for yourself and use it for this feature.
- **Names and Passwords** - Enables the use of saved names and passwords. You will be given the option to set up a security lock in order to keep your private information safe. Websites will give you the option to save your username and password. You can also touch the [switch] switch next to 'Always Allow' to save passwords even for websites that will never save your password otherwise.
- **Credit Cards** - Enables the use of saved credit card information. You will be given the option to set up a security lock in order to keep your private information safe. Touch **Saved Credit Cards**, and then touch **Add Credit Card** to add a new credit card.

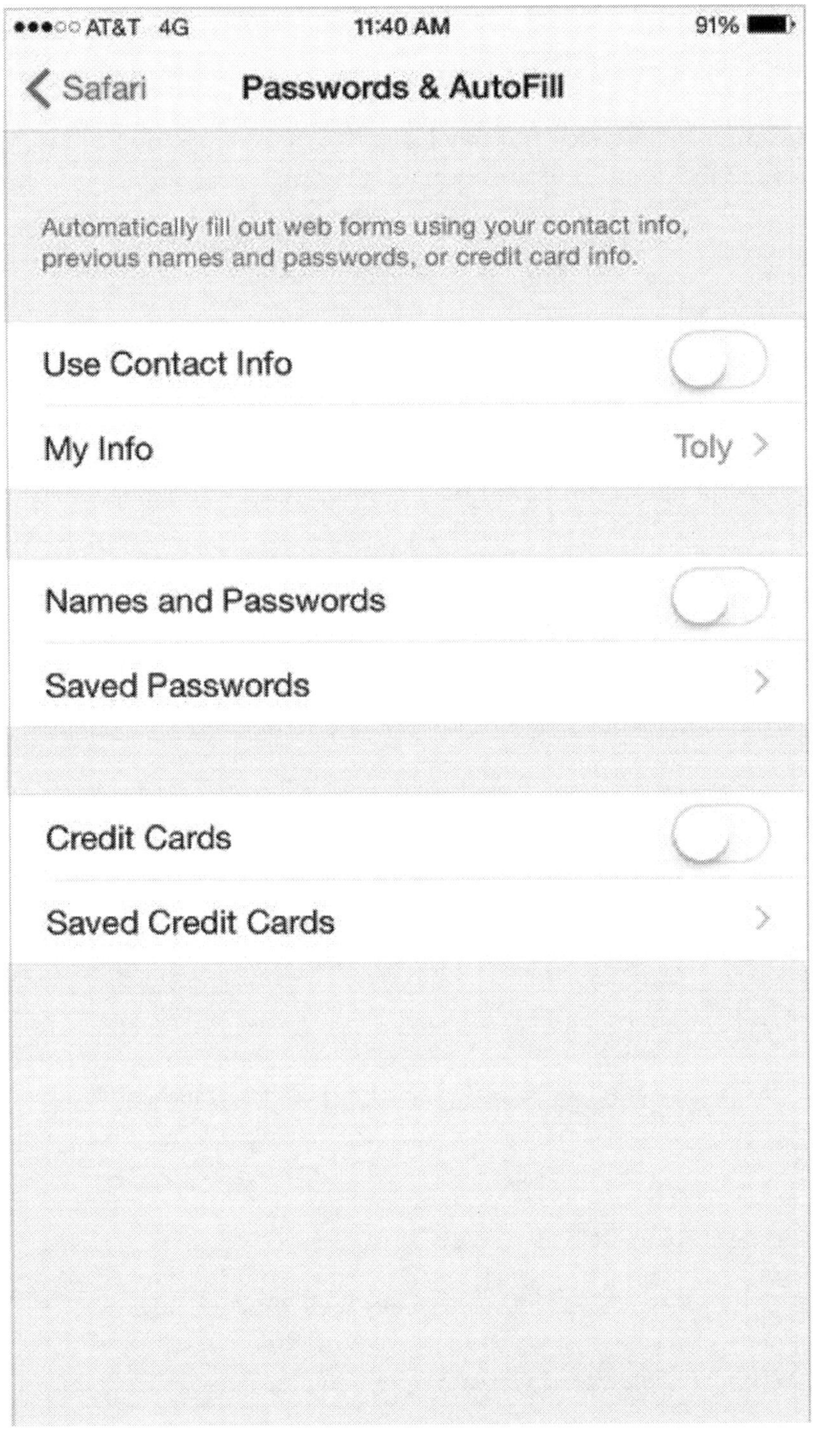

Figure 12: Passwords & Autofill Screen

11. Customizing the Smart Search Field

The address bar in the Safari browser can act as a search field that assists you by matching your search terms while you type. To customize the smart search field:

1. Touch the ⚙ icon on the Home screen. The Settings screen appears.
2. Touch **Safari**. The Safari Settings screen appears.
3. Touch one of the following ⬭ switches to turn on the corresponding smart search feature:

   - **Search Engine Suggestions** - Enables search term matching to assist you when performing a search.
   - **Preload Top Hit** - Automatically loads the most popular search result when you perform a search. The web page is loaded in the background before you even touch the link.
   - **Spotlight Suggestions** - Allows you to search the web using Spotlight search, which can be accessed by touching the center of the Home screen and sliding your finger down.

*Note: Refer to **Changing the Search Engine** to learn how to customize the search engine in Safari.*

12. Viewing Recently Closed Tabs

The Safari browser saves a history of all browser tabs that were recently closed. To view all recently closed browser tabs:

1. Touch the 🧭 icon on the Home screen. The Safari Web browser opens.
2. Touch and hold the ➕ icon. A list of recently closed browser tabs appears, as shown in **Figure 13**.
3. Touch one of the websites in the list. The selected website opens in a new tab.

●●●○○ AT&T 4G   11:41 AM   91% ■■■▶

Recently Closed Tabs   Done

Apple
apple.com

Amazon.com
amazon.com

Pomir Grill | Afghanistan Cuisine
pomirgrill.com

Figure 13: List of Recently Closed Tabs

13. Scanning a Credit Card Using the Phone's Camera

When you wish to use a credit card to purchase a product online, you have the option to use your phone's camera to scan the card. To scan a credit card using the camera:

1. Navigate to the website where you wish to enter the credit card number. Refer to *"Navigating to a Website"* on page 111 to learn how.
2. Touch the credit card field on the page. The virtual keyboard appears.
3. Touch **Scan Credit Card** above the keyboard. The camera turns on. If the Camera Access dialog appears, touch **OK** to allows Safari to use the camera.
4. Align the credit card with the white frame on the screen. The camera reads the credit card number, and enters it in the field.

Note: You will still need use the keyboard to enter the expiration date and security code (on the back of your card).

Managing Photos and Videos

Table of Contents

1. Taking a Picture

The iPhone 6 has built-in rear-facing and front-facing cameras. To take a picture, touch the
icon on the Home screen. The camera turns on, as shown in **Figure 1**. Use the following tips when taking a picture:

- Touch **Square** to take a square picture. Touch **Photo** to activate the default camera.
- Touch the button in the upper right-hand corner of the screen at any time to switch between the cameras.
- Touch the button to take a picture. The picture is captured, and is automatically stored in the 'Recently Added' album. If the surroundings are too dark, refer to *"Using the Flash"* on page 136 for help.

Note: Refer to "Tips and Tricks" *on page 358 to learn how to take a picture directly from the Lock screen.*

Figure 1: Camera Turned On

2. Capturing a Video

The phone have a built-in camcorder that can shoot HD video. To capture a video:

1. Touch the icon. The camera turns on.
2. Touch **Video**, or move your finger to the right until 'Video' appears in orange. The camcorder turns on.
3. Touch the button. The camera begins to record.
4. Touch the button. The camera stops recording and the video is automatically saved to the 'Videos' and 'Recently Added' albums.

Note: Touch the thumbnail in the bottom left-hand corner of the screen to preview the video.

3. Using the Digital Zoom

While taking pictures or capturing video, use the camera's built-in Digital Zoom feature if the subject of the photo is far away. The Digital Zoom will not work when recording videos. To zoom in before taking a photo, touch the screen with two fingers and move them apart. The appears at the bottom of the screen, and the camera zooms in. To zoom out before taking a photo, touch the screen with two fingers apart and bring them together. The appears at the bottom of the screen, and the camera zooms out.

Note: Because of its digital nature, the zoom function will not provide the best resolution, and the image may look fuzzy. Try to be as close as possible to the subject of the photo.

4. Using the Flash

iPhones have a built-in LED flash that can be used along with the rear-facing camera. When shooting a video with the flash turned on, it will remain on throughout the movie. To use the flash:

1. Make sure the camera is turned on and the rear camera is activated. Refer to *"Taking a Picture"* on page 133 to learn how.

2. Touch the ⚡ icon in the upper-left hand corner of the screen. The ⚡ Auto   On   Off menu appears.

3. Touch **On**. The flash is turned on, and will be used when taking a picture or capturing a video.

4. Touch **Off.** The flash is turned off, and will never be used.

5. Touch **Auto**. The flash will be used as needed, as determined by the phone's light sensor.

5. Focusing on a Part of the Screen

While taking pictures, the camera can focus on a particular object or area on the screen. This will adjust the lighting and other elements to make the object or area stand out in the picture. To focus on a specific part of the screen, just touch that area. A yellow box appears and the camera focuses.

6. Browsing Photos

After taking photos on your phone, or transferring them from your computer, you may view them at any time. To view saved photos:

1. Touch the ![icon] icon on the Home screen. The Photos application opens.
2. Touch **Albums** at the bottom of the screen. A list of photo albums appears, as shown in **Figure 2** . The photos that you have taken using the phone are in an album called 'Recently Added'.
3. Touch an album. The photos in the album appear.
4. Touch a photo. The photo appears in full screen.
5. Use the following tips when viewing photos:

   - Touch a photo with your thumb and forefinger and move the two fingers apart to zoom in on it. The zoom will center where your fingers were joined.
   - Touch the screen twice quickly to zoom out completely. Touch the photo with your thumb and forefinger spread apart and move the fingers together while touching the photo to zoom out gradually. Move your fingers apart to zoom in.

   - Touch the ![button] button at the top of the screen while viewing a photo to return to album view. If the ![button] button is not shown, touch the photo once to make the photo menus appear at the top and bottom of the screen.

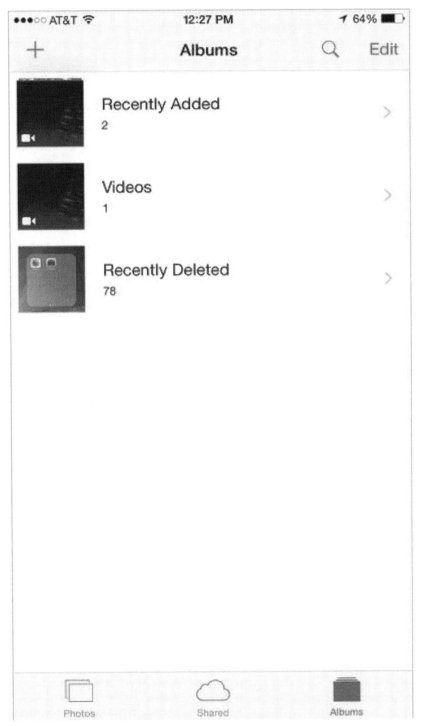

Figure 2: List of Photo Albums

7. Editing a Photo

The iPhone 6 provides advanced photo-editing tools. To edit a photo:

1. Touch the icon at the Home screen. The Photos application opens.
2. Touch **Albums** in the bottom right-hand corner of the screen. A list of photo albums appears.
3. Touch an album. The photos in the album appear.
4. Touch a photo. The photo appears in full screen.
5. Touch **Edit** at the top of the screen. The Photo Editing menu appears, as shown in **Figure 3**.
6. Touch one of the following icons to edit the photo:

- Enhances the quality of the photo. Touch **Done** to save the changes.

- Allows you to crop or rotate the photo. Touch the corners of the photo and drag the selected portion, as shown in **Figure 4**. Touch **Done** at the bottom of the screen to save the crop. Repeat steps 1-6 above, and touch **Revert** to return the photo to its original appearance. You may also touch the icon to rotate the photo.

- Allows you to add a color effect, such as Mono (grayscale) or Instant (Polaroid) to the photo.

- Allows you to customize the appearance of the photo by adjusting the amount of light, color, and tone in the photo. These settings are for advanced users only.

- Removes red-eye from the photo. Touch each red eye in the photo and then touch **Done** to save the changes. This icon only appears if one or more faces are detected in the photo.

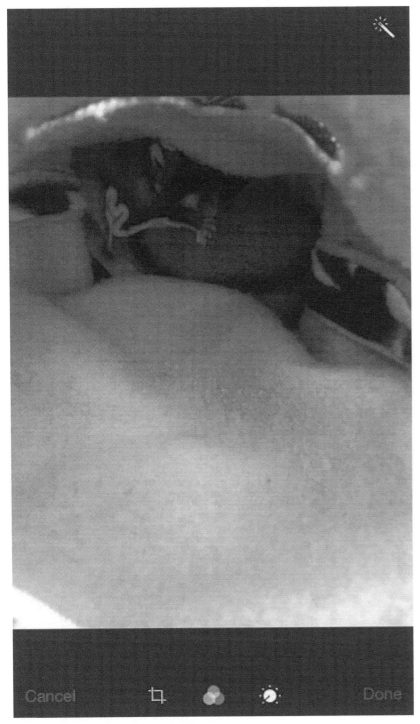

Figure 3: Photo Editing Menu

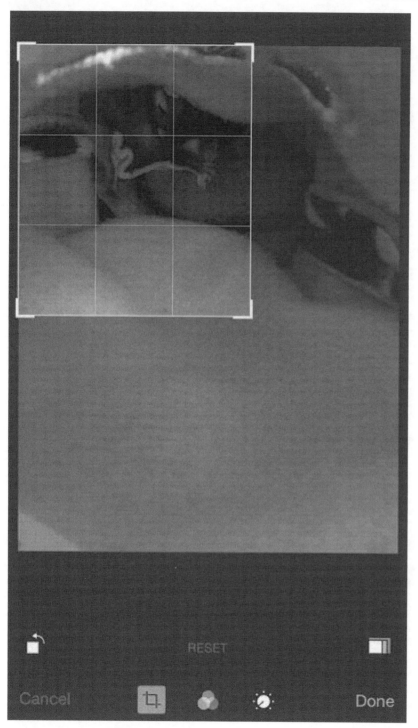

Figure 4: Cropping a Photo

8. Deleting a Photo

You may delete unwanted pictures from your phone to free up memory. To delete a photo:

Warning: Once a picture is deleted, there is no way to restore it. Deleting a picture removes it from all albums.

1. Touch the ![icon] icon. The Photos application opens.
2. Touch **Albums** at the bottom of the screen. A list of photo albums appears.
3. Touch an album. The photos contained in the album appear.
4. Touch a photo. The photo appears in full screen view.
5. Touch the ![trash] button at the of the screen. A confirmation dialog appears.
6. Touch **Delete Photo**. The photo is deleted from all albums on the phone. You may also delete several pictures at a time, by touching **Select** at the top of an album, and then selecting each photo that you wish to delete. Follow steps 5-6 to delete the selected photos.

Note: Refer to "Recovering Deleted Photos" *on page 154 to learn how to recover deleted photos within 30 days of deleting them.*

9. Creating a Photo Album

You can create a photo album right on your phone. To create a photo album:

1. Touch the ![icon] icon. The Photos application opens.
2. Touch **Albums** at the bottom of the screen. A list of photo albums appears.
3. Touch the ![plus] button at the top of the screen. The New Album window appears, as shown in **Figure 5**.
4. Enter a name for the album and touch **Save**. The new photo album is created, and you can now choose photos to add to it.
5. Touch a photo album, and then touch photos to add them. Touch a photo a second time to deselect it. Touch **Albums** at the bottom of the screen at any time to return to the album list.
6. Touch **Done** at the top of the screen. The selected photos are added to the new photo album.

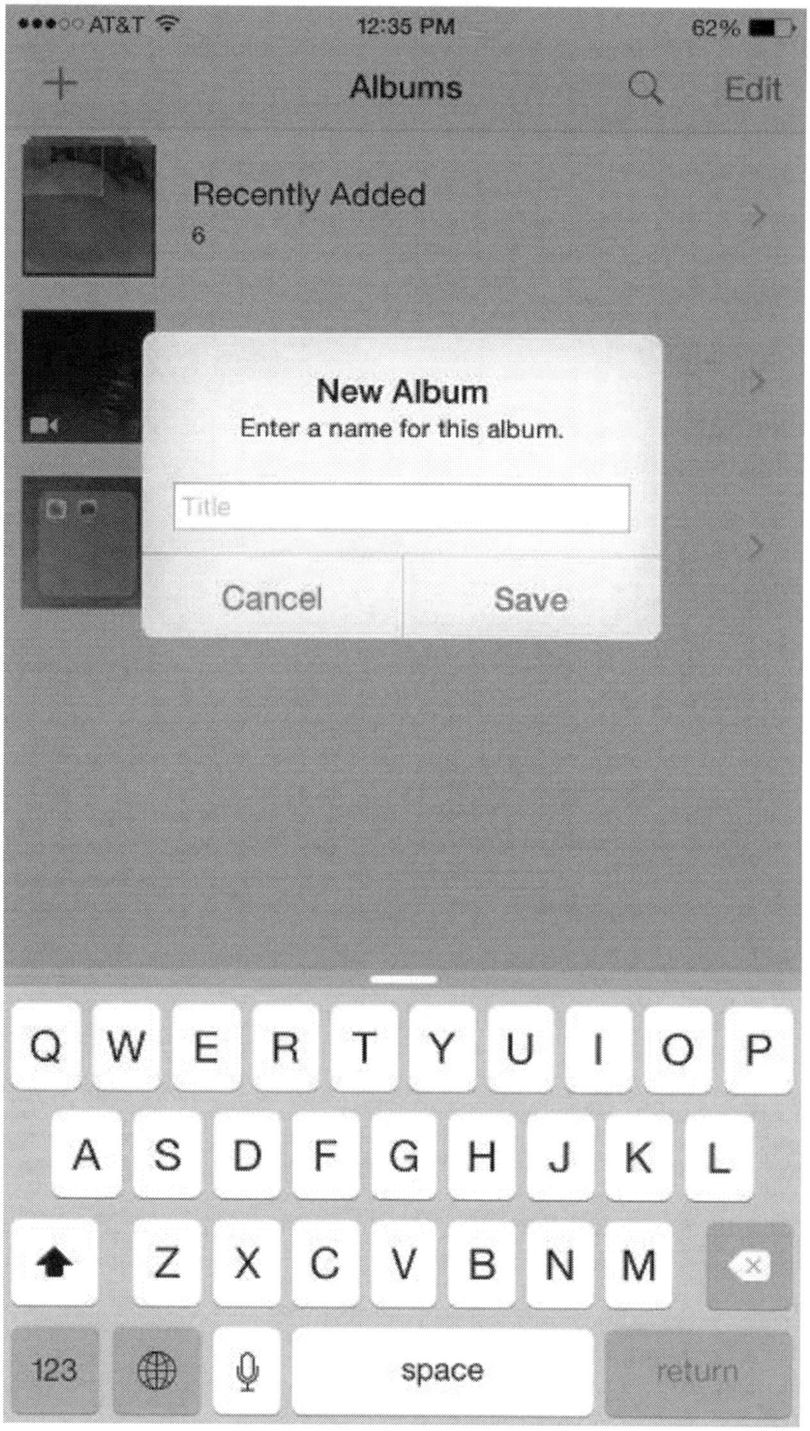

Figure 5: New Album Window

10. Editing a Photo Album

Photo albums stored on the phone can be edited right from your phone. Refer to **Creating a Photo Album** to learn how to make a new photo album using your phone.

To edit the name of a photo album:

1. Touch the ![icon] icon. The Photos application opens.
2. Touch **Albums** at the bottom of the screen. A list of photo albums appears.
3. Touch **Edit** at the top of the screen. The ![button] button appears next to each album that may be edited.
4. Touch the name of a photo album. The virtual keyboard appears.
5. Enter a new name for the album and touch **Done**. The album is renamed.

To add photos to an album:

1. Touch the ![icon] icon. The Photos application opens.
2. Touch **Albums** at the bottom of the screen. A list of photo albums appears.
3. Touch an album. The photos contained in the album appear.
4. Touch **Select** in the upper right-hand corner of the screen. Photos can now be selected.
5. Touch as many photos as desired. The photos are selected, and ![icon] icons appear on the thumbnails, as shown in **Figure 6**.
6. Touch **Add To**. A list of photo albums appears. You cannot add photos to any album that is grayed out.
7. Touch the name of a photo album. The selected photos are added to the album.

Note: Adding photos to an album does not remove them from the original album.

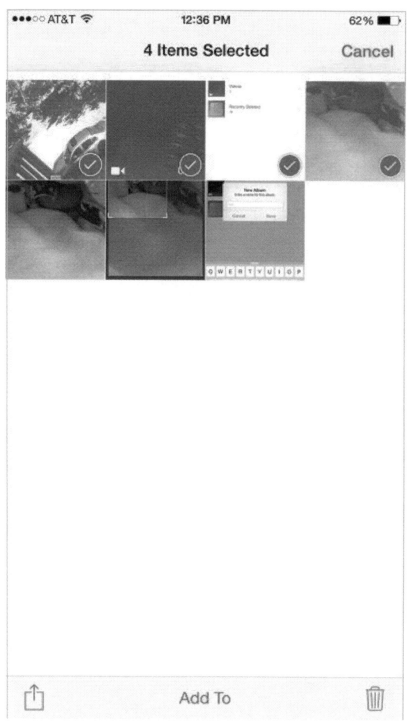

Figure 6: Selected Photos

11. Deleting a Photo Album

Photo albums stored on the phone can be deleted right from your phone. To delete a photo album:

Warning: When an album is deleted from the phone, any photos that are stored in other albums will remain on the phone. Make sure any photos that you wish to keep are stored in another album. Refer to **Editing a Photo Album** *to learn how to add photos to an album.*

1. Touch the ![icon] icon. The Photos application opens.
2. Touch **Albums** at the bottom of the screen. A list of photo albums appears.
3. Touch **Edit** at the top of the screen. The ![button] button appears next to each album that may be deleted. Some albums cannot be deleted.
4. Touch the ![button] button next to an album. 'Delete' appears.
5. Touch **Delete**. A confirmation dialog appears.
6. Touch **Delete Album**. The photo album is deleted.

12. Starting a Slideshow

The phone can play a slideshow using the photos in your albums. To begin a slideshow:

1. Touch the ![icon] icon. The Photos application opens.
2. Touch **Albums** at the bottom of the screen. A list of photo albums appears.
3. Touch an album. The photos in the album appear.
4. Touch a photo. The photo appears in full screen.
5. Touch the ![icon] icon at the bottom of the screen. The Photo options appear, as shown in **Figure 7**.
6. Touch **Slideshow** at the top of the screen. The Slideshow Settings screen appears, as shown in **Figure 8**.
7. Touch **Transitions** and select the transition for the slideshow. You may also touch the ![switch] switch to turn on Music from your library.
8. Touch **Start Slideshow**. The slideshow begins.

Figure 7: Photo Options

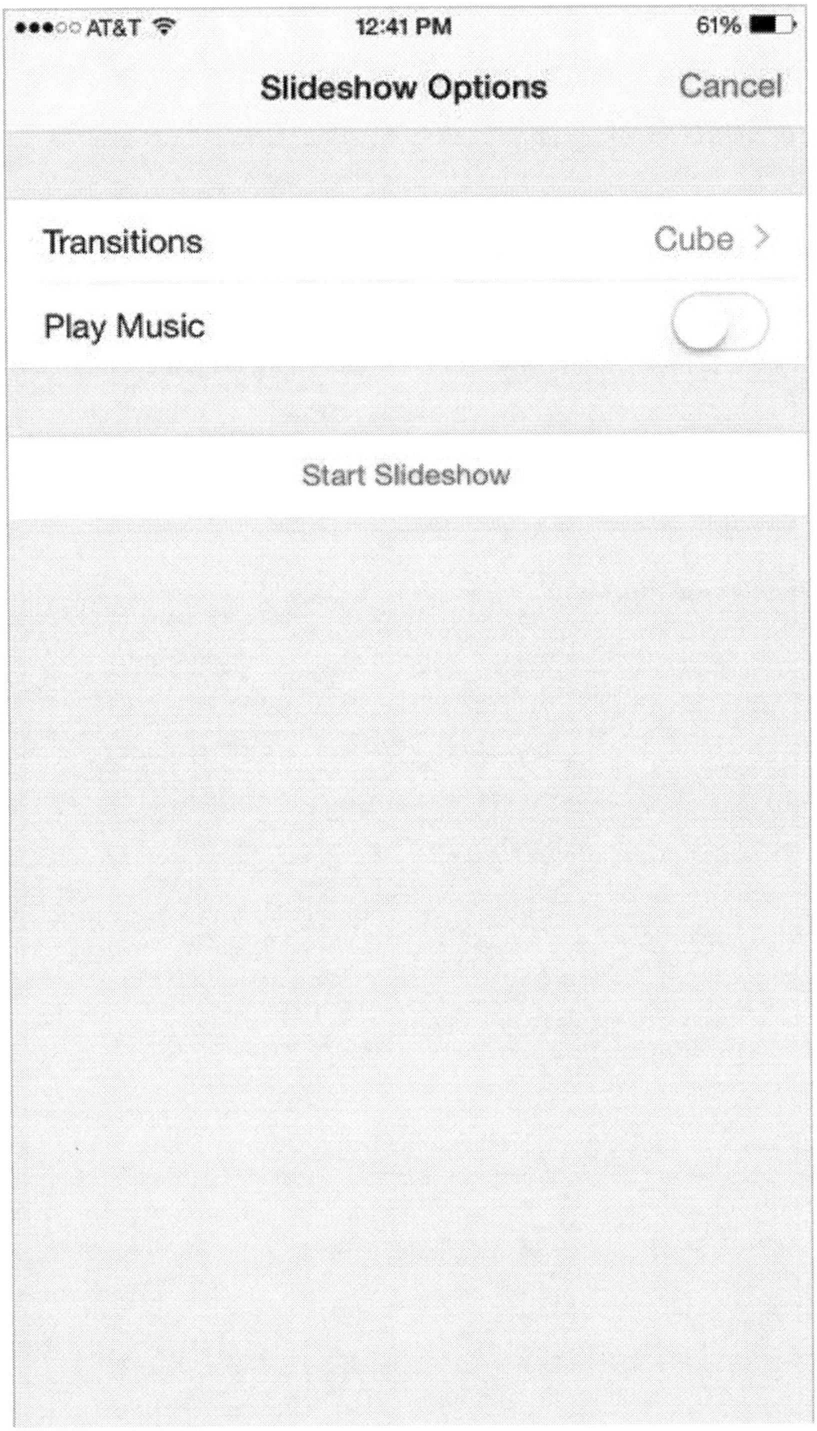

●●●○○ AT&T 📶   12:41 PM   61% ■▭

Slideshow Options   Cancel

Transitions   Cube >

Play Music

Start Slideshow

Figure 8: Slideshow Settings Screen

13. Browsing Photos by Date and Location

The phone can sort photos according to the physical locations where they were taken, as well as the dates on which they were captured. To browse photos by date and location:

1. Touch the icon. The Photos application opens.
2. Touch **Photos** at the bottom of the screen. The Moments screen appears.
3. Touch **Collections** at the top of the screen. A list of albums appears, organized by date and location, as shown in **Figure 9**.
4. Touch an album in any location. The selected album opens.
5. Touch the name of a town. A map appears, showing the locations where photos were taken. Touch **Moments** to return to the photo list.

Note: You may only view pictures sorted by location if you have Location Services turned on. Refer to "Turning Location Services On or Off" *on page 239 to learn more.*

Figure 9: List of Albums Organized by Date and Location

14. Searching for a Photo

Use the Search feature to find a photo more quickly while viewing the Photos application. To search for a photo:

1. Touch the 🔍 icon at the top of the screen while using the Photos application. 'Search Photos' appears.
2. Enter the name of the album, or the location where the photo was taken. You may also search by date.
3. Touch **Search**. A list of matching results appears as you type, as shown in **Figure 10**.

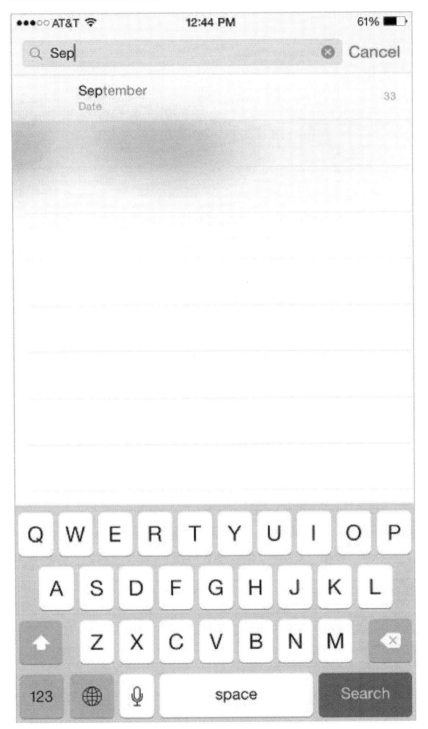

Figure 10: List of Matching Photo Results

15. Recording a Time-Lapse Video

You can record a time-lapse video, which allows you to capture a short video of an event that takes place over a long period of time, such as the budding of a flower. To record a time-lapse video:

1. Touch the icon. The camera turns on.
2. Touch **Time-Lapse**. The time-lapse camcorder turns on.
3. Touch the button. The camcorder begins to record the time-lapse video.
4. Touch the button. The time-lapse video is captured and stored in the 'Time-lapse' album. The Photos application marks every time-lapse video with the icon.

16. Recovering Deleted Photos

You may recover a deleted photo if fewer than 30 days have passed since you deleted it. To recover deleted photos:

1. Touch the icon. The Photos application opens.
2. Touch **Albums** at the bottom of the screen. A list of photo albums appears.
3. Touch the **Recently Deleted** album. The recently deleted photos appear. The number of days on each photo shows the amount of time left before the photo will be permanently deleted.
4. Touch **Select** at the top of the screen, and then touch each photo that you want to recover. The photos are selected, and icons appear on the thumbnails.
5. Touch **Recover** at the bottom of the screen. The selected photos are returned to their original albums.

Using iTunes

Table of Contents

1. Registering with Apple

In order to buy content, you will need to have an iTunes account. Refer to *"Signing In to an iTunes Account"* on page 208 to learn more.

2. Buying Music and Ringtones in iTunes

Music and ringtones can be purchased directly from the phone via iTunes. To buy music using the iTunes application:

1. Touch the ![icon] icon. The iTunes application opens.
2. Touch the ![icon] icon at the bottom of the screen. The iTunes Music Store opens and the new releases are shown.
3. Touch **Genres** at the top of the screen to browse music. A list of Genres appears. You may also search for a specific song or artist by touching **Search**.
4. Touch an album. The Album description appears, as shown in **Figure 1**.
5. Touch the price of the album. 'Buy Album' appears.
6. Touch **Buy Album**. The album is purchased. Touch the price of a song and then touch **Buy Song** to buy a single song.
7. To purchase a ringtone, follow steps 1-3, and then touch the name of the ringtone. Touch **Buy** to purchase the ringtone.

Note: You may need to enter your iTunes password when purchasing music using the phone.

Figure 1: Album Description

3. Buying or Renting Videos in iTunes

Videos can be purchased or rented directly from the phone and viewed using the Videos application. To buy videos using the iTunes application:

1. Touch the [icon] icon. The iTunes application opens.
2. Touch the [icon] icon or the [icon] icon. The iTunes Video Store opens, and the featured videos appear, as shown in **Figure 2** (Movie Store).
3. Touch **Featured**, **Charts**, or **Genres** at the top of the screen to browse videos. Touch a video. The Video description appears, as shown in **Figure 3**.
4. Touch the price of the video. 'Buy Movie', 'Rent Movie', or 'Buy HD Episode' appears, depending on your selection.
5. Touch **Buy NAME**, where NAME refers to the type of video that you are buying. The phone may ask for your iTunes password. The video is purchased or rented, and the download begins.

Note: When renting a video, the video is available for 24 hours once you start watching it. Once 24 hours has passed, you will not be able to resume the video if you pause it.

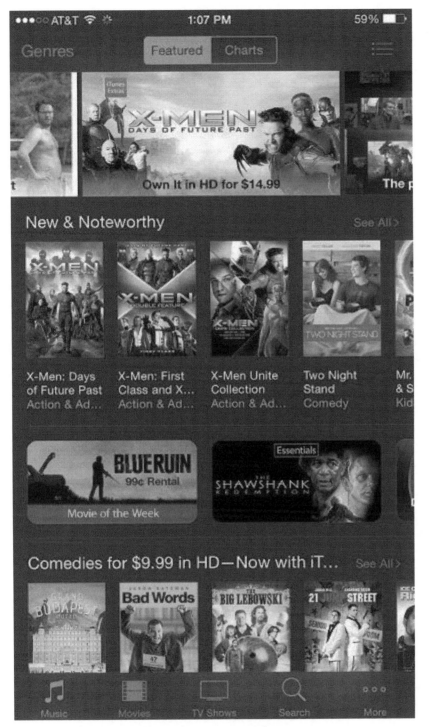

Figure 2: iTunes Video Store (Movies)

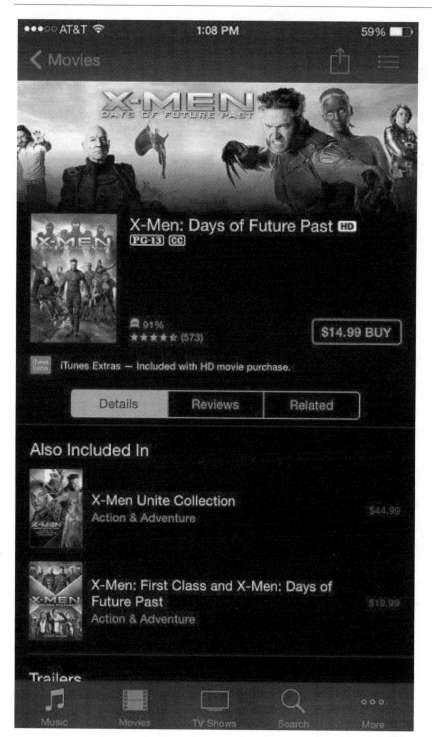

Figure 3: Video Description

4. Searching for Media in iTunes

The phone can search for any media in the iTunes Store. To search for media:

1. Touch the ⬤ icon. The iTunes application opens.
2. Touch the ⬛ icon. 'Search' appears at the top of the screen. Touch the ⬤ button to clear the field, if necessary.
3. Enter the name of an artist, actor, song, or video that you wish to find. Touch **Search**. The matching results appear, organized by the type of media, as shown in **Figure 4**.
4. Touch a song, video, or ringtone. The media description appears.

Note: Refer to "Buying Music and Ringtones in iTunes" *on page 156 or* "Buying or Renting Videos in iTunes" *on page 158 to learn how to purchase media.*

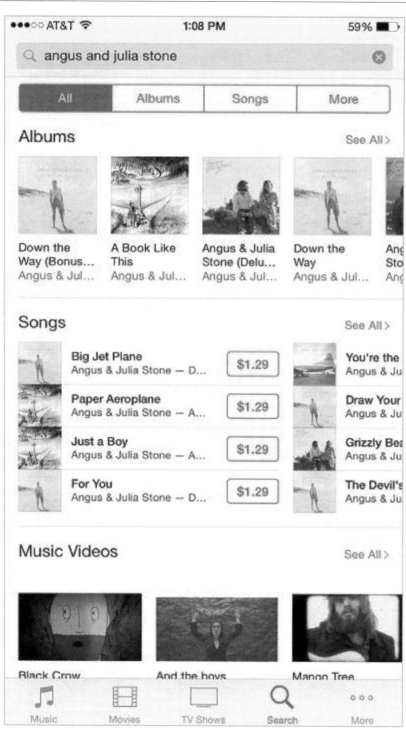

Figure 4: Available Media Results

5. Playing Media

To play media purchased in iTunes on the phone, use the Music Application. To learn how, refer to *"Using the Music Application"* on page 165.

6. Sharing Your iTunes Account with Family

You may allow your friends or family members to purchase content using your iTunes account. Make sure that you trust the people to whom you give access to your iTunes account. To share your iTunes account:

1. Touch the icon. The Settings screen appears, as shown in **Figure 5**.
2. Scroll down and touch **iCloud**. The iCloud Settings appear.
3. Touch **Set Up Family Sharing**. The Family Sharing window appears.
4. Touch **Get Started**. The Family Setup begins.
5. Touch **Continue**. The Purchase Sharing screen appears.
6. Touch **Continue**. The Terms and Conditions appear.
7. Touch **Agree**, and then touch **Agree** again. The Payment Method screen appears.
8. Confirm that your payment method is correct, and touch **Continue**. The Location Sharing screen appears.
9. Touch **Share Your Location** to allow your family members or friends to view your location at all times, or touch **Not Now** to keep your location private. The Family settings appear.
10. Touch **Add Family Member**. The Add Family Member dialog appears.
11. Enter the name or email address of the family member or friend, and touch **Next**. An invitation to use your iTunes account is sent, and your contact may now use your account.

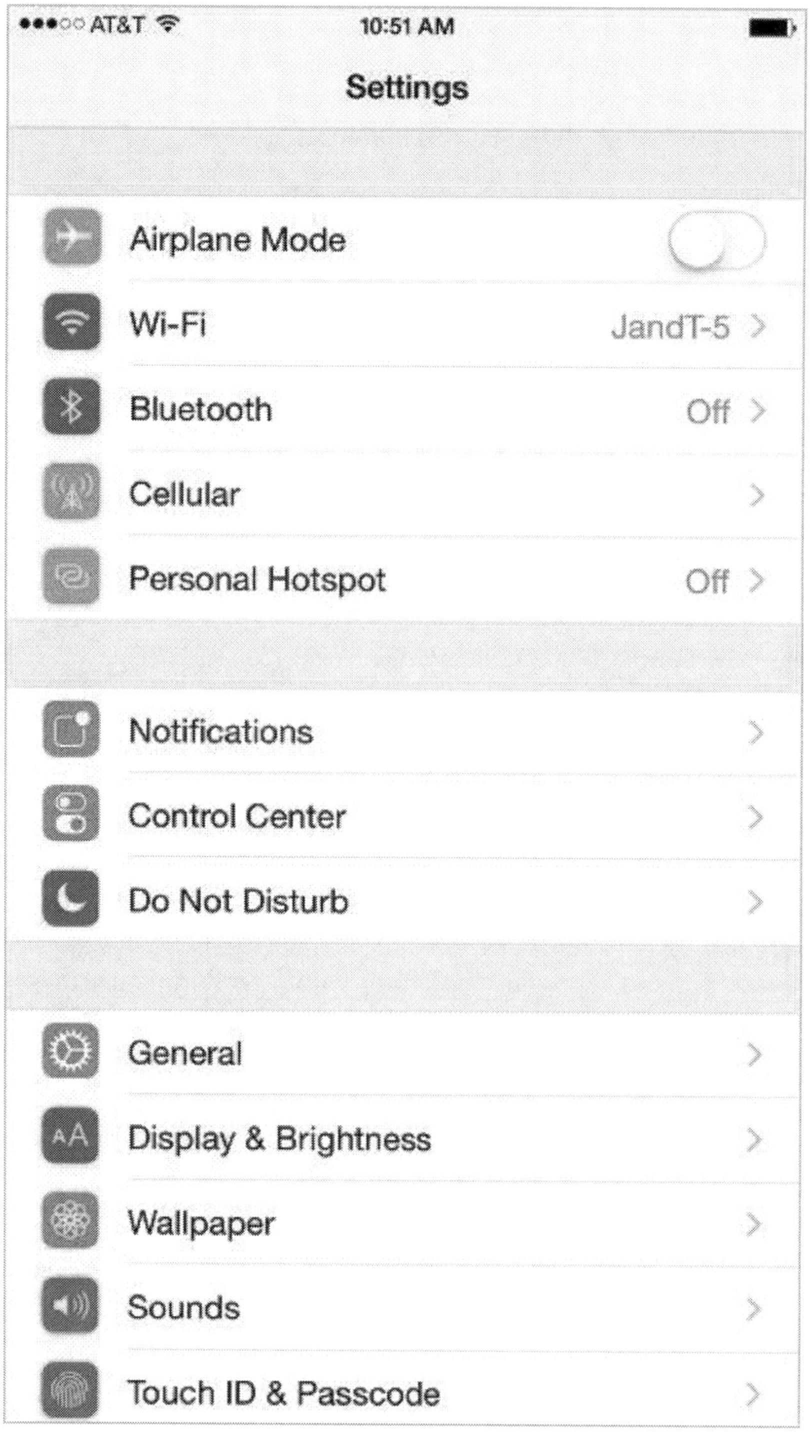

Figure 5: Settings Screen

Using the Music Application

Table of Contents

1. Downloading Media

Use the iTunes Application to download media to the phone. Refer to *"Using iTunes"* on page 155 to learn how.

2. Playing Music

The Music application on the phone can be used to play music. To listen to your music:

1.   Touch the 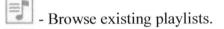 icon. The Music application opens.
2.   Touch one of the following icons at the bottom of the screen to browse music:

    - Browse existing playlists.

    - Browse existing artists.

    - Browse existing songs.

3.   Use the following tips to navigate the Music Application:

- Touch a playlist, artist, or song to play the item. The item plays, as shown in **Figure 1**.
- Tilt the phone horizontally. The album art for the available albums appears, as shown in **Figure 2**.
- After you have exited the Music application, touch the screen at the bottom and drag your finger up to bring up the music controls, as shown in **Figure 3**. Touch the name of the artist to return to the Music application.
- The music controls will also appear on the lock screen, as shown in **Figure 4**.

Figure 1: Music Playing

Figure 2: Album View

Figure 3: Music Controls

Figure 4: Music Controls on the Lock Screen

3. Using Additional Audio Controls

Use the Song Controls to control music while it is playing. Touch one of the following to perform the corresponding function:

◄◄ - Skip to the beginning of the current song or skip to the previous song.

►► - Skip to the next song.

❚❚ - Pause the current song.

► - Resume the current song when it is paused.

≣ - View the current playlist.

Repeat - Repeat the song or artist that is currently playing.

――――――― - Drag the | on the bar at the top of the screen to go to a different part of the song.

Shuffle - Shuffle all songs in the playlist. Touch again to play the songs in order.

Create - Create an iTunes Radio station from the artist or song that is currently playing.

*Note: Touch both **Repeat** and **Shuffle** to play songs continuously in random order. To shuffle and play all songs on the phone, go to the song list and touch **Shuffle**.*

4. Creating a Playlist

Playlists can be created in iTunes. However, the Music application can perform the same function. To create a playlist in the Music application:

1. Touch the [icon] icon in the Music application. The existing playlists appear.
2. Touch **New Playlist**. The New Playlist window appears, as shown in **Figure 5**.
3. Enter the name of the playlist and touch **Save**. A list of the songs on your phone appears, as shown in **Figure 6**.
4. Touch one of the icons at the bottom of the screen to browse music to add to the new playlist. Refer to *"Playing Music"* on page 165 to learn more about finding music in the Music application.
5. Touch a song. The song is grayed out and added to the playlist.
6. Touch **Done**. The playlist is populated with the selected music.

After creating a playlist, you can add or remove music from it. To edit a playlist:

1. Touch the icon in the Music application. The available playlists appear.
2. Touch a playlist. The Playlist screen appears, as shown in **Figure 7**.
3. Touch **Edit**. A button appears next to every song in the playlist.
4. Touch the button next to a song. The song is removed from the playlist.
5. To add songs, touch the button at the top of the screen, and then repeat steps 4 and 5 from the instructions above. The selected songs are added to the playlist.
6. Touch **Done**. The changes to the playlist are saved.

Note: Removing a song from a playlist will not delete it from the Music library.

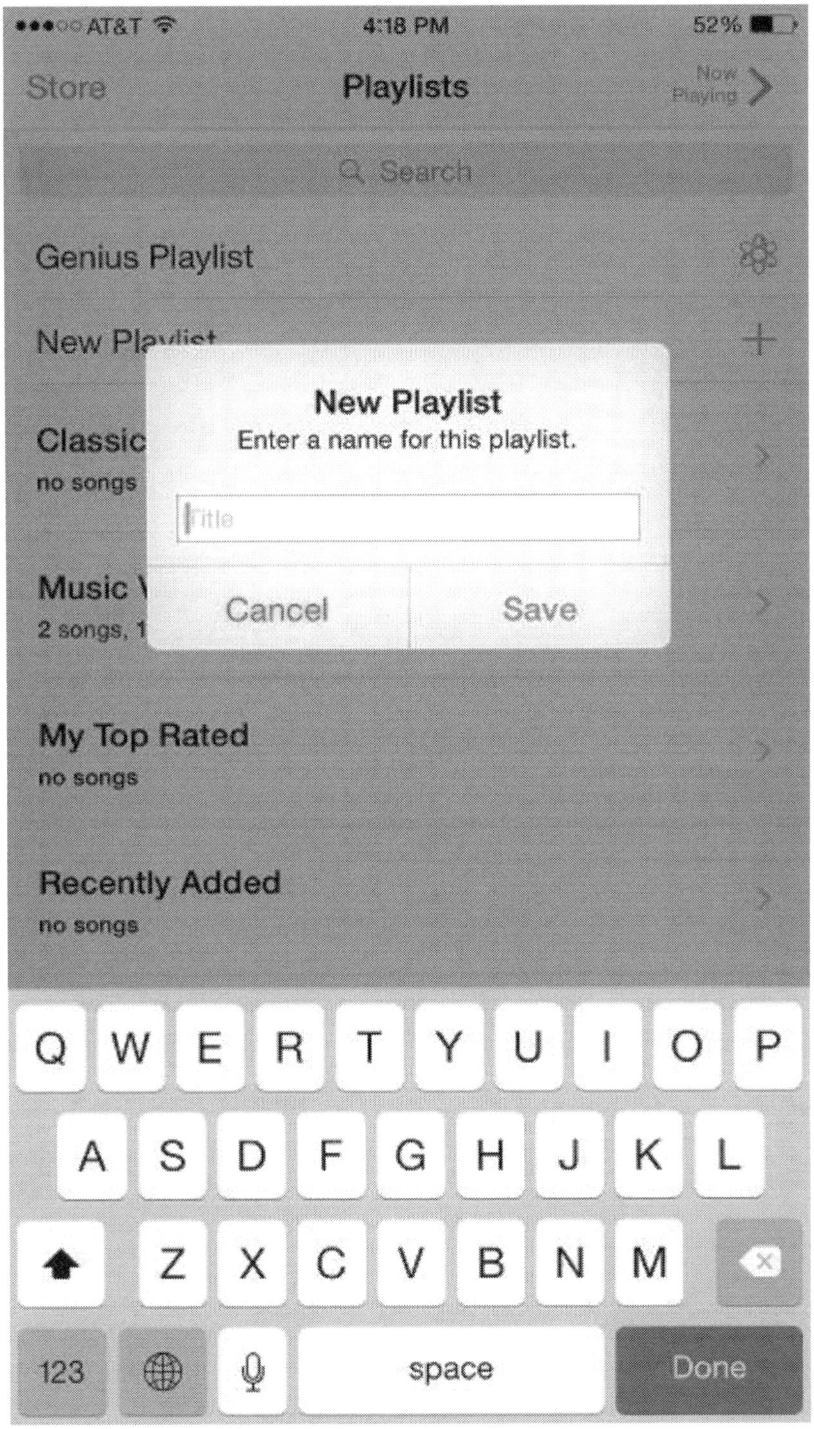

Figure 5: New Playlist Window

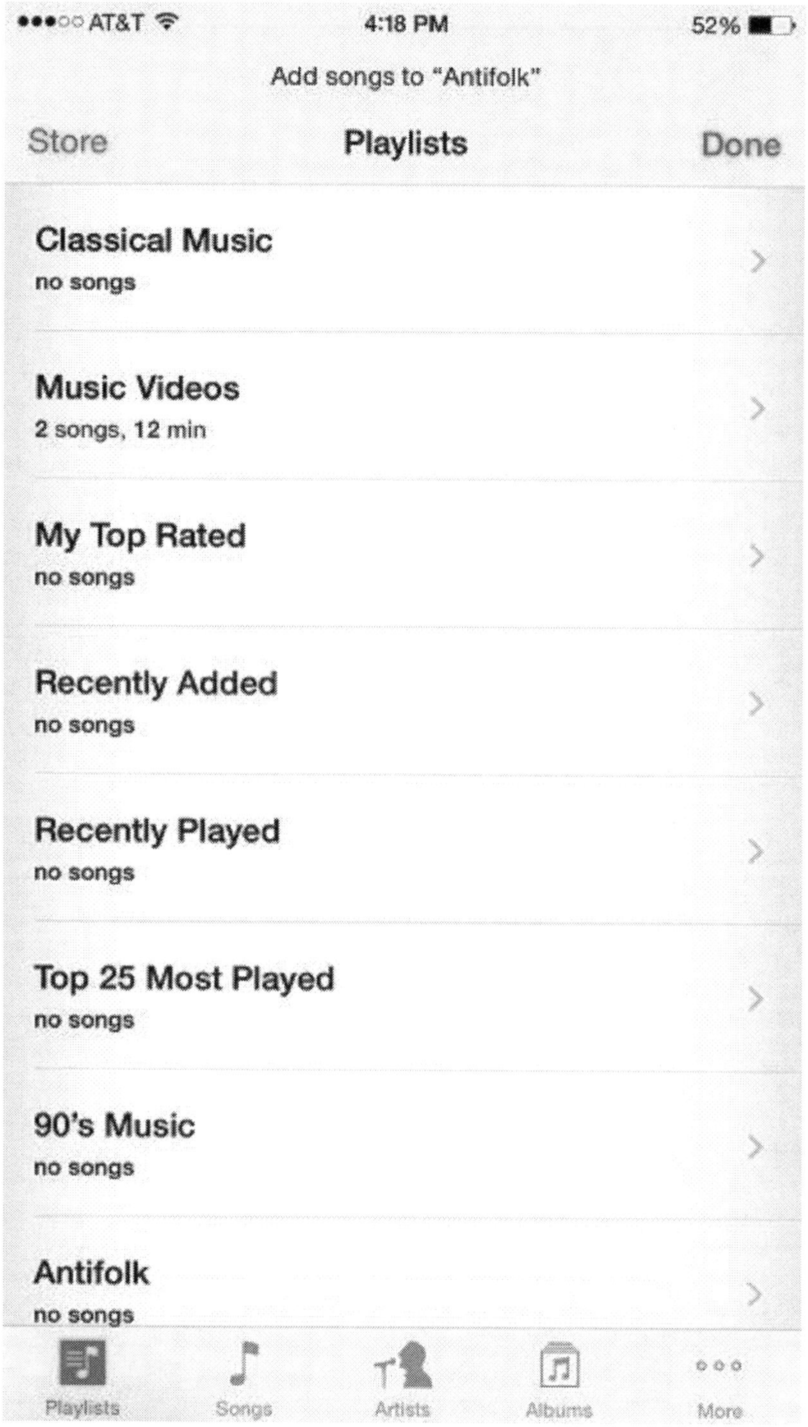

●●●○○ AT&T 🛜   4:18 PM   52% 🔋

Add songs to "Antifolk"

Store   **Playlists**   Done

Classical Music
no songs   ›

Music Videos
2 songs, 12 min   ›

My Top Rated
no songs   ›

Recently Added
no songs   ›

Recently Played
no songs   ›

Top 25 Most Played
no songs   ›

90's Music
no songs   ›

Antifolk
no songs   ›

Playlists   Songs   Artists   Albums   More

Figure 6: List of Songs on Your Phone

Figure 7: Playlist Screen

5. Using the iTunes Radio

The iTunes Radio is a free service that allows you to create personalized stations based on artists, songs, or genres.
To create a new iTunes Radio station:

1. Touch the [icon] icon in the Music application. The iTunes Radio screen appears, as shown in **Figure 8**.

2. Touch the [icon] icon. The New Station screen appears, as shown in **Figure 9**.
3. Touch a genre in the list, or touch the search field at the top of the screen, and enter an artist, genre, or song. A preview of the station begins to play.

4. Touch the [icon] icon next to the station name. The station is added to your stations.

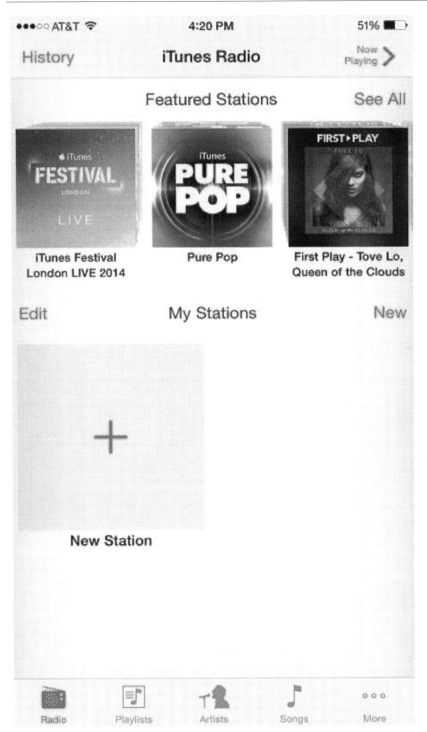

Figure 8: iTunes Radio Screen

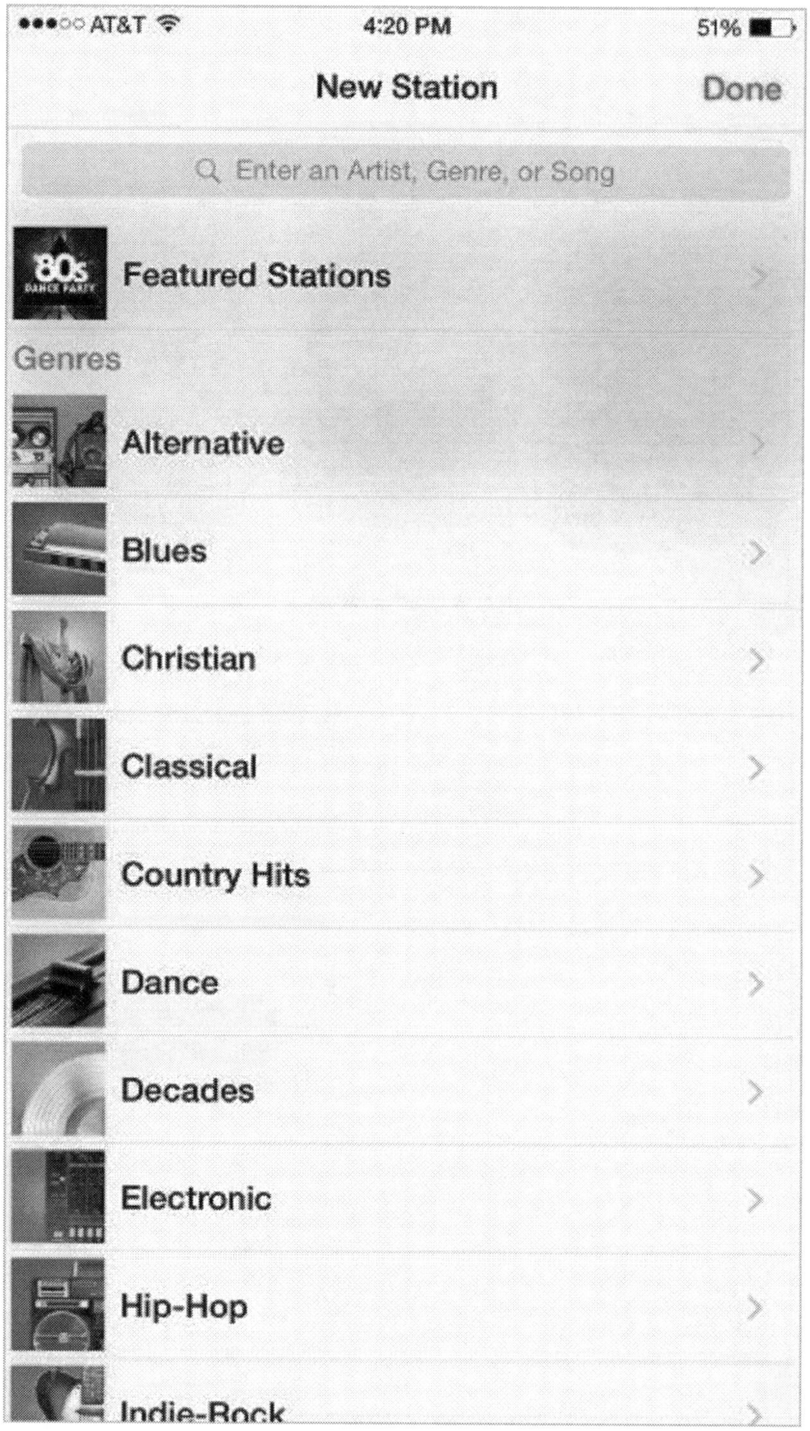

Figure 9: New Station Screen

6. Tips and Shortcuts

Click *"Music Tips and Tricks"* on page 363 to learn how to change the navigation icons in the Music application, delete music right from your phone, and more.

Using the Mail Application

Table of Contents

1. Setting Up the Mail Application

Before the Mail application can be used, at least one account must be set up on your phone. To set up the Mail application:

1. Touch the ⊚ icon. The Settings screen appears, as shown in **Figure 1**.
2. Scroll down and touch **Mail, Contacts, Calendars**. The Mail, Contacts, Calendars screen appears, as shown in **Figure 2**.
3. Touch **Add Account**. The Account Type screen appears, as shown in **Figure 3**.
4. Touch one of the email services in the list to set up an email account. The corresponding email setup screen appears.
5. Enter all of the required information, and touch **Next** at the top of the screen. The email account is added to your phone.

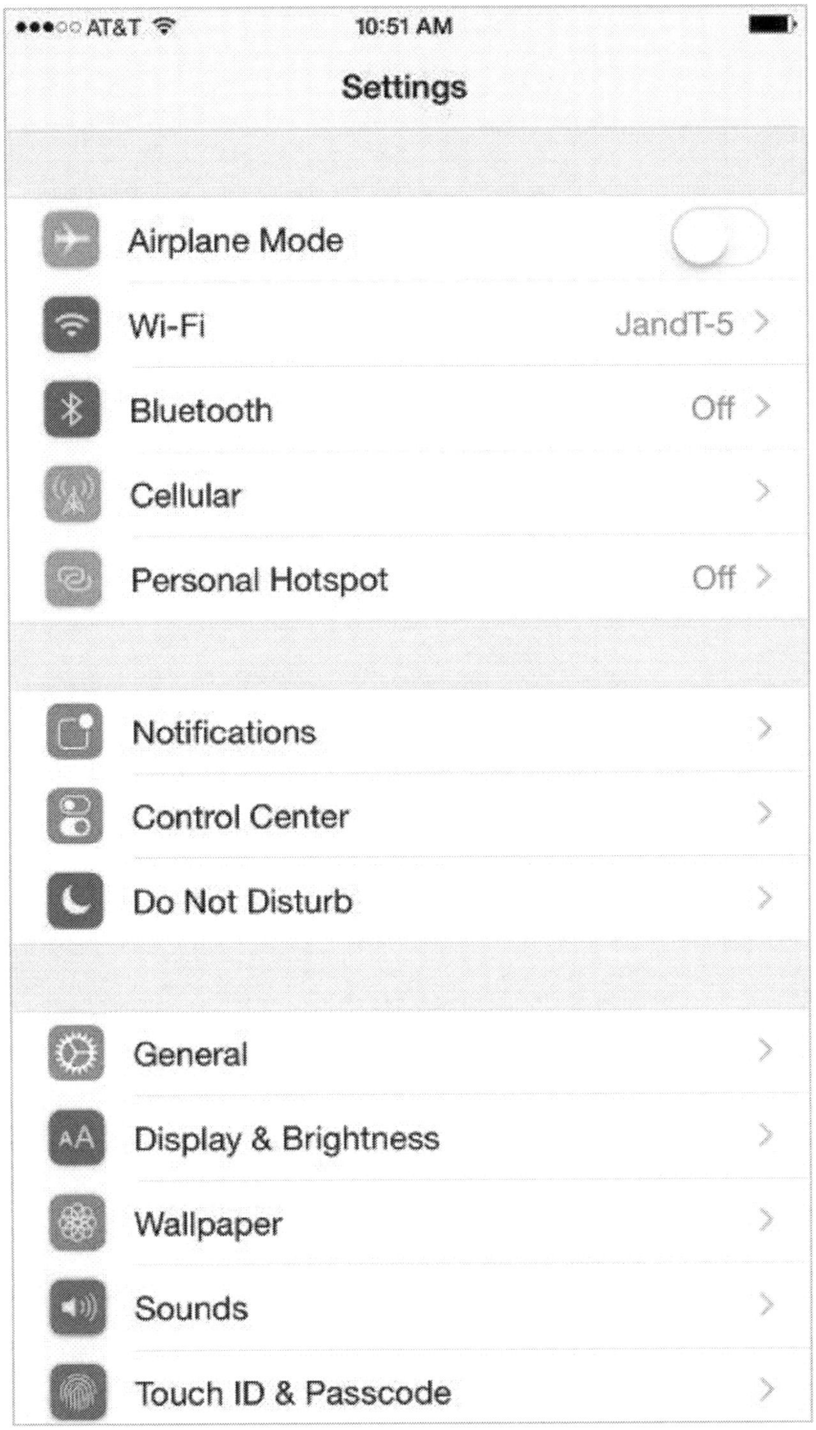

●●●○○ AT&T 🛜   10:51 AM   ▬

Settings

✈ Airplane Mode   ⬭

🛜 Wi-Fi   JandT-5 ›

✳ Bluetooth   Off ›

📶 Cellular   ›

🔗 Personal Hotspot   Off ›

🔔 Notifications   ›

🎛 Control Center   ›

🌙 Do Not Disturb   ›

⚙ General   ›

🅰 Display & Brightness   ›

🌐 Wallpaper   ›

🔊 Sounds   ›

👆 Touch ID & Passcode   ›

Figure 1: Settings Screen

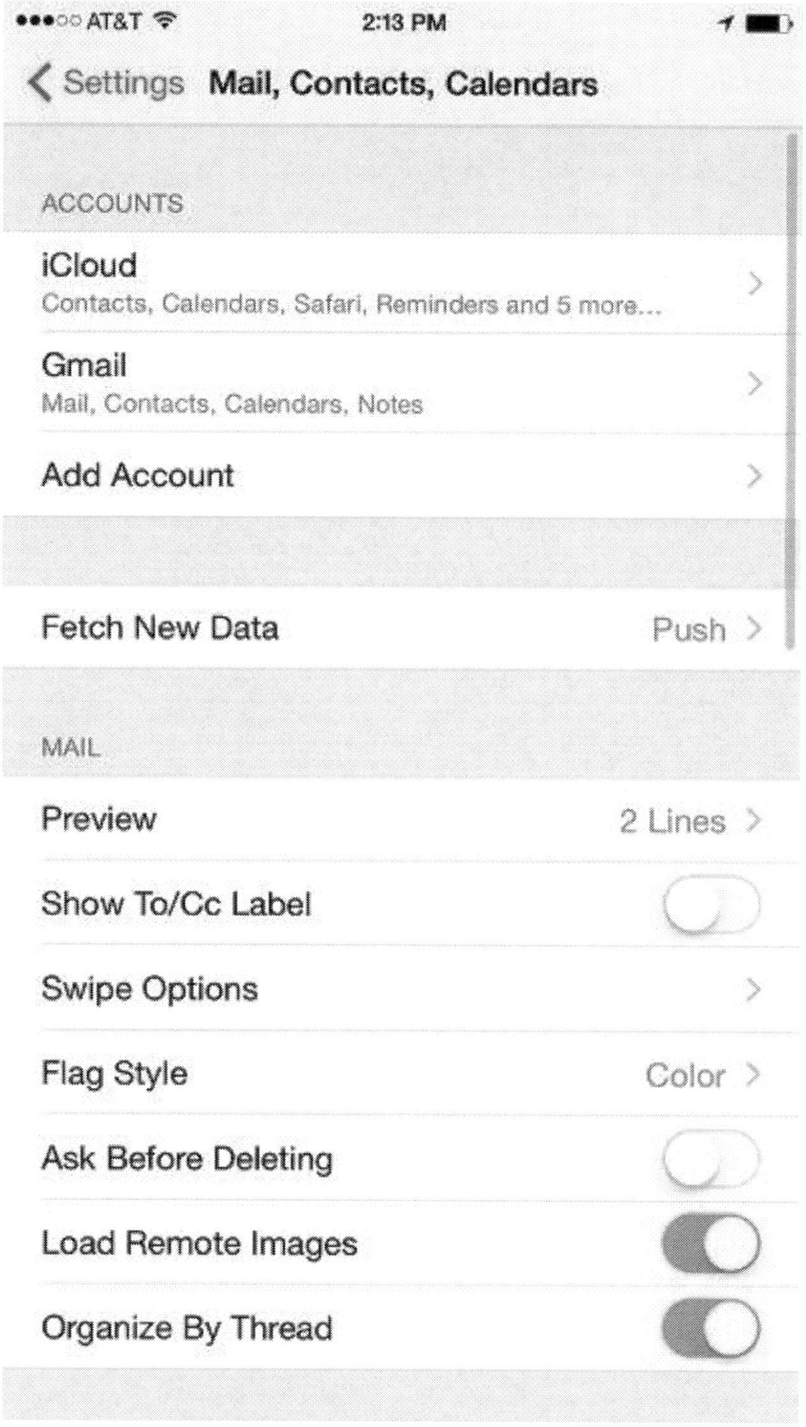

●●●○○ AT&T 📶   2:13 PM   ✈ 🔋

❮ Settings Mail, Contacts, Calendars

ACCOUNTS

iCloud   ❯
Contacts, Calendars, Safari, Reminders and 5 more...

Gmail   ❯
Mail, Contacts, Calendars, Notes

Add Account   ❯

Fetch New Data   Push ❯

MAIL

Preview   2 Lines ❯

Show To/Cc Label   ⬜

Swipe Options   ❯

Flag Style   Color ❯

Ask Before Deleting   ⬜

Load Remote Images   🔘

Organize By Thread   🔘

Figure 2: Mail, Contacts, Calendars Screen

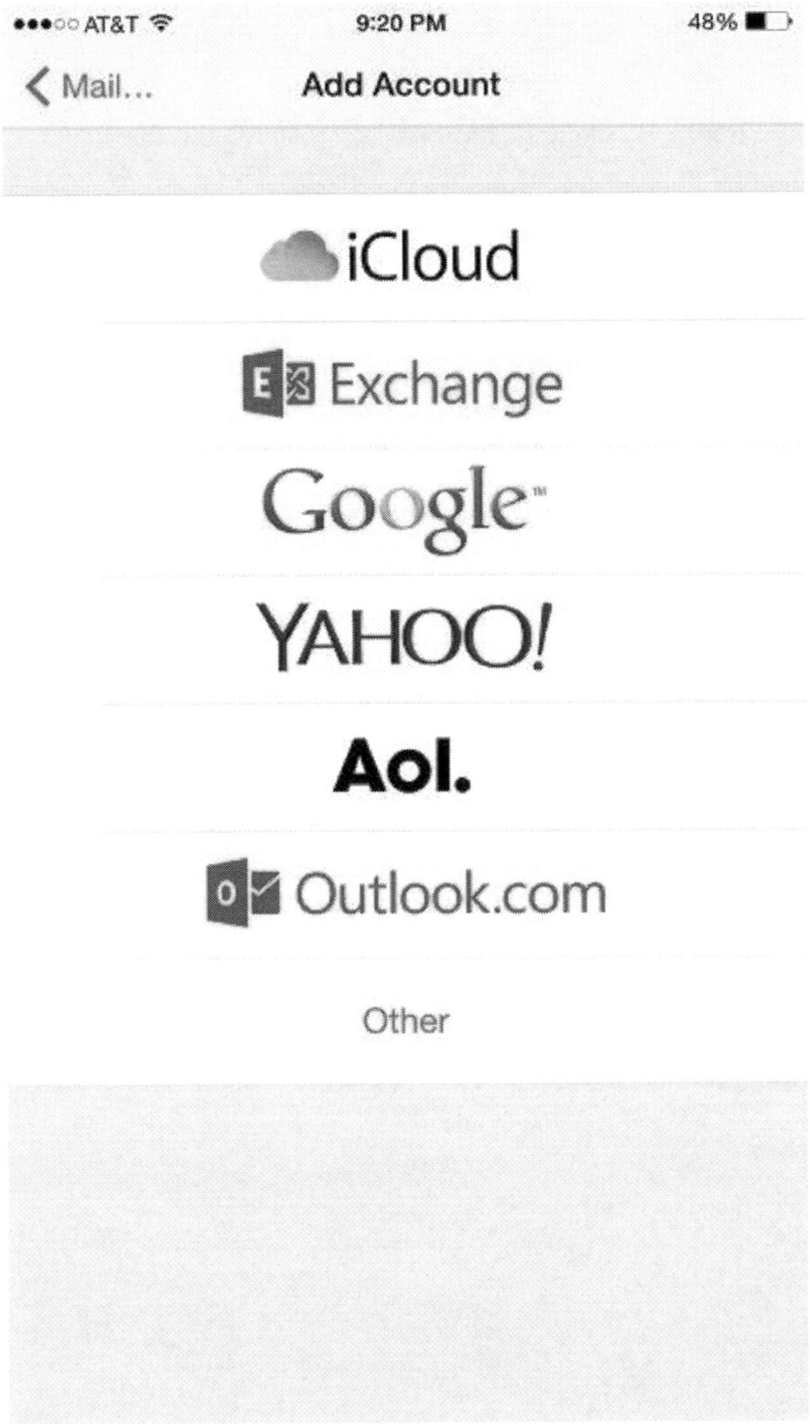

Figure 3: Account Type Screen

2. Reading Email

You can read your email on the phone using the Mail application. Before opening the Mail application, make sure you have set up your email account. Refer to *"Setting Up the Mail Application"* on page 180 to learn how. To read your email:

1. Touch the icon. The Mail application opens, and the Inbox appears, as shown in **Figure 4**. If the emails are not shown, touch **Inbox** at the top of the screen.
2. Touch an email. The email opens.
3. Touch **Inbox** at the top of the screen in an email to return to the list of received emails. Touch **Mailboxes** at the top of the Inbox to return to the list of mailboxes. The mailbox list varies depending on the mail service.

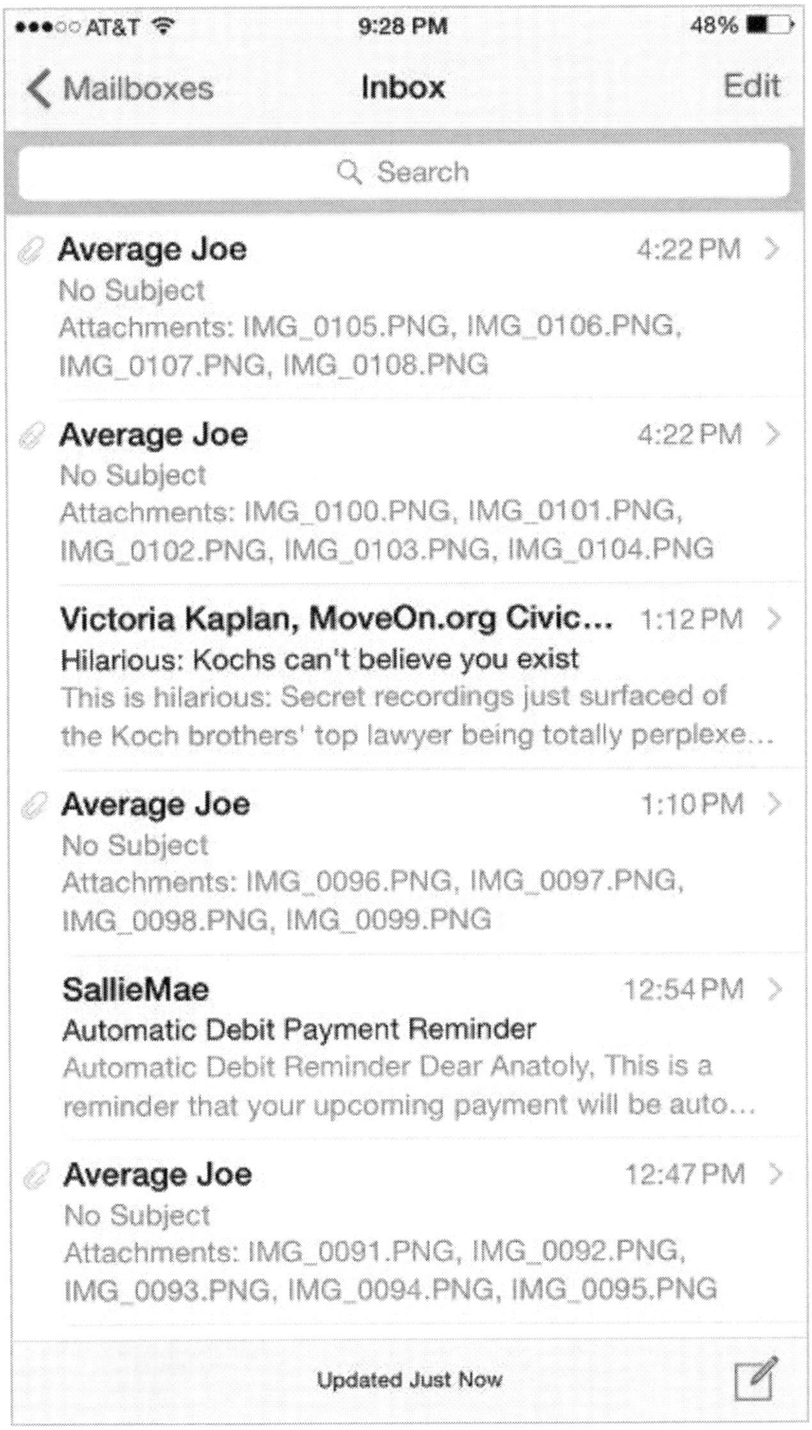

●●●○○ AT&T 📶   9:28 PM   48% ■

⟨ Mailboxes   **Inbox**   Edit

🔍 Search

📎 **Average Joe**   4:22 PM ⟩
No Subject
Attachments: IMG_0105.PNG, IMG_0106.PNG,
IMG_0107.PNG, IMG_0108.PNG

📎 **Average Joe**   4:22 PM ⟩
No Subject
Attachments: IMG_0100.PNG, IMG_0101.PNG,
IMG_0102.PNG, IMG_0103.PNG, IMG_0104.PNG

Victoria Kaplan, MoveOn.org Civic...   1:12 PM ⟩
Hilarious: Kochs can't believe you exist
This is hilarious: Secret recordings just surfaced of
the Koch brothers' top lawyer being totally perplexe...

📎 **Average Joe**   1:10 PM ⟩
No Subject
Attachments: IMG_0096.PNG, IMG_0097.PNG,
IMG_0098.PNG, IMG_0099.PNG

SallieMae   12:54 PM ⟩
Automatic Debit Payment Reminder
Automatic Debit Reminder Dear Anatoly, This is a
reminder that your upcoming payment will be auto...

📎 **Average Joe**   12:47 PM ⟩
No Subject
Attachments: IMG_0091.PNG, IMG_0092.PNG,
IMG_0093.PNG, IMG_0094.PNG, IMG_0095.PNG

Updated Just Now   ✎

Figure 4: Email Inbox

3. Switching Accounts in the Email Application

If you have more than one active email account, you can switch between them, or view all of your email in one Inbox. To switch to another account:

1. Touch the icon. The Mail application opens and your emails appear.
2. Touch **Mailboxes** at the top of the screen while viewing a list of messages in a folder. A list of all active inboxes and accounts appears, as shown in **Figure 5**.
3. Touch an account. The Inbox associated with the selected account appears.

You can also touch **All Inboxes** to view all emails from the accounts attached to your phone in a single joint folder.

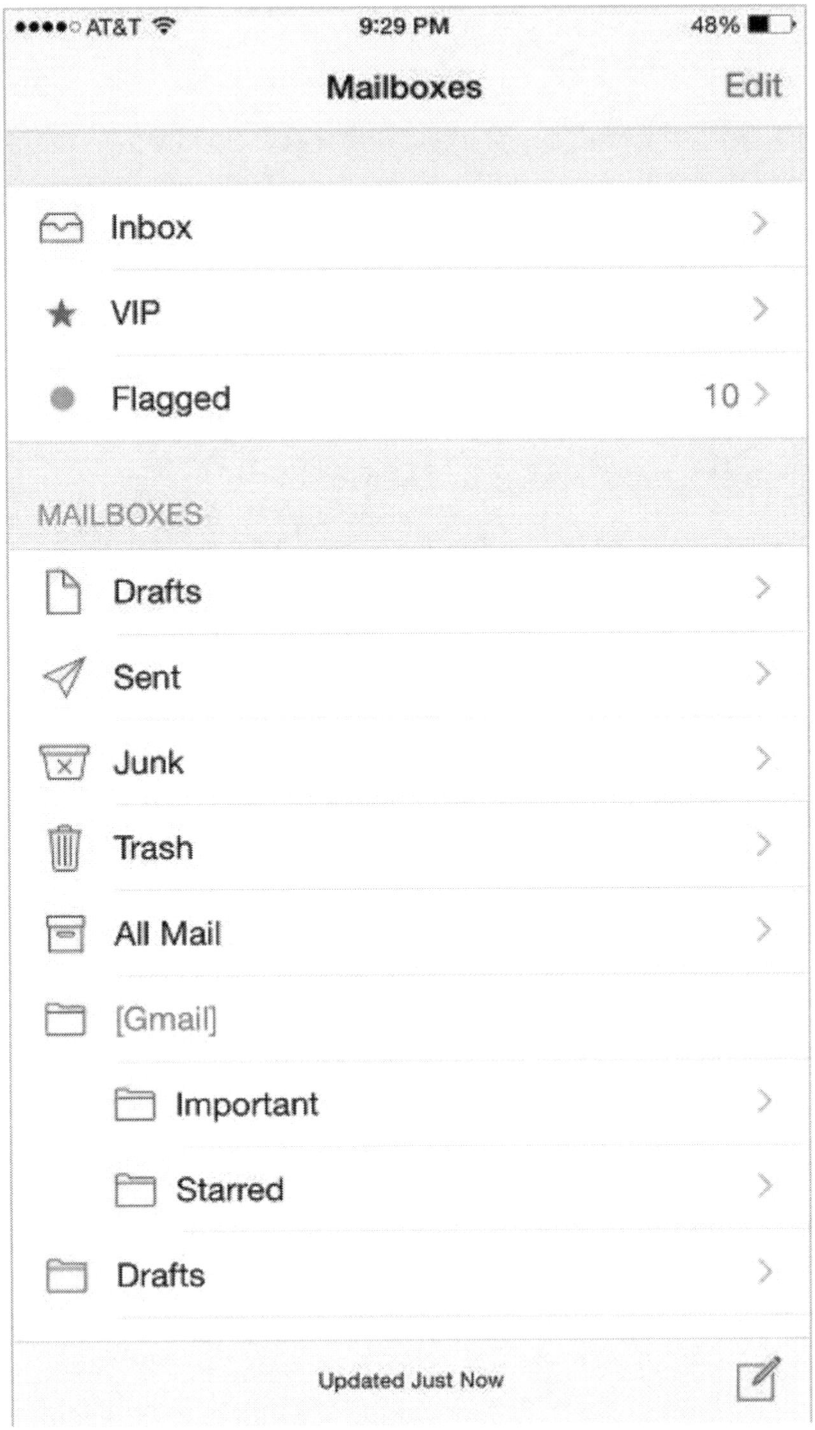

Figure 5: List of Active Inboxes and Accounts

4. Writing an Email

Compose email directly from the phone using the Mail application. To write an email while using the Mail application:

1. Touch the button. The New Email screen appears, as shown in **Figure 6**.
2. Start entering the name of a contact. A list of matching contacts appears as you type.
3. Touch the name of the contact that you wish to email. The contact's email address is added to the addressee list. Alternatively, enter an email address from scratch. Enter as many additional addressees as desired.
4. Touch the **return** key on the keyboard. The cursor jumps to the subject of the email. Enter a topic for the message.
5. Touch the **return** key on the keyboard. The cursor jumps to the body of the email. Enter the content of the email, and touch **Send** at the top of the screen. The email is sent.

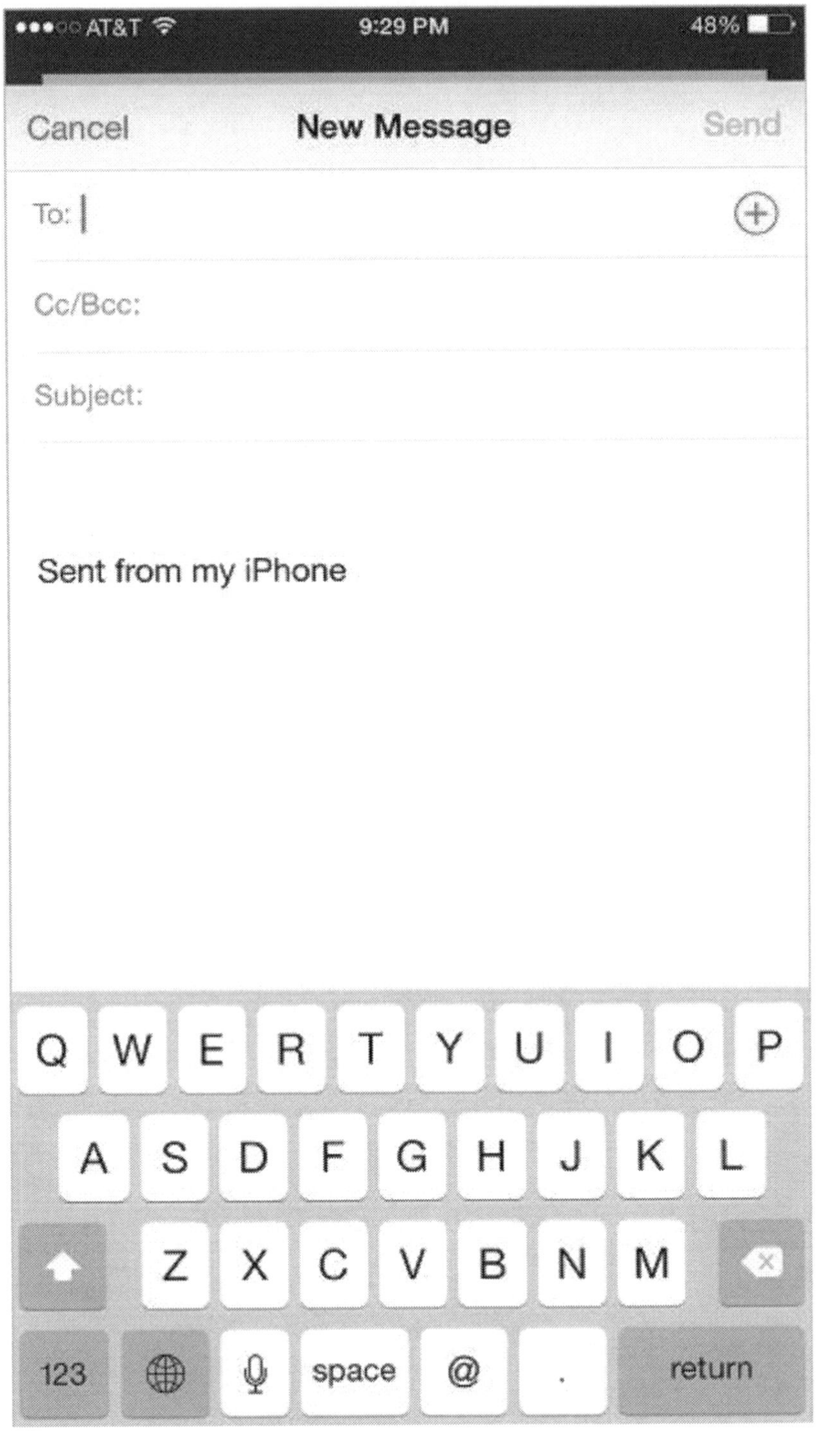

Figure 6: New Email Screen

5. Referring to Another Email when Composing a New Message

While composing an email, you may wish to refer to another message for reference. To do so, touch and hold **New Message** at the top of the screen, and drag your finger to the bottom of the screen. The New Message screen is hidden, and you may use the Mail application normally. To continue writing your email where you left off, touch **New Message** at the bottom of the screen. If you have already entered a subject, 'New Message' will be replaced by the subject.

6. Formatting Text

When writing an email on your phone, you can format the text to add bold, italics, underline, or increase the quote level.

To add bold, italics, or underline text while writing an email:

- Touch and hold the text in the email that you wish to format. The Select menu appears above the text, as shown in **Figure 7**.
- Touch **Select All**. All of the text is selected. To select a single word, touch **Select**. Blue dots appear around the word or phrase.
- Touch and hold one of the blue dots and drag it in any direction. The text between the dots is highlighted and a Text menu appears, as shown in **Figure 8**.
- Touch the [B*I*U] button. 'Bold', 'Italics', and 'Underline' appear. If you do not

  see [B*I*U] button, touch the [▶] button in the Text menu.
- Touch one of the formatting options. The associated formatting is applied to the selected text.

You can also increase the left margin, or quote level, in an email. To increase the quote level:

1. Touch and hold any location in your email. The text cursor flashes in the selected location.
2. Touch the [▶] button in the Text menu. The Text Format menu appears.
3. Touch **Quote Level**. The Quote Level options appear.
4. Touch **Decrease** or **Increase** to adjust the Quote Level accordingly. The new Quote Level is set and applied to the paragraph where the text cursor is currently flashing.

Figure 7: Select Menu

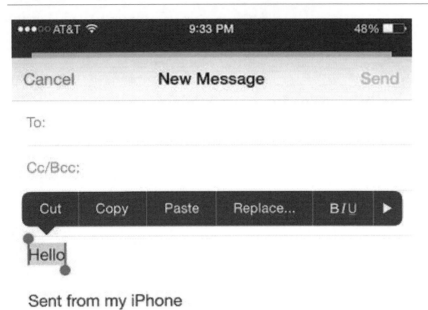

Figure 8: Text Menu

7. Replying to and Forwarding Emails

After receiving an email, you can reply to the sender or forward the email to a new recipient. To reply to, or forward, an email message:

1. Touch the icon. The Mail application opens.
2. Touch an email. The email appears.
3. Touch the button. The Reply menu appears, as shown in **Figure 9**.
4. Touch **Reply** to reply to the message, or touch **Forward** to forward the message. The New Message screen appears. The subject at the top is preceded by 'Re:' if replying or 'Fwd:' if forwarding. The original email is copied in the body. If replying, the addressee field is filled in.
5. Touch the text field next to 'To:', and enter an addressee, if necessary. The addressee is entered. The address of the sender is automatically entered when replying to an email.
6. Touch the text field to the right of 'Subject' to enter a different subject for your message, if desired. The subject is entered.
7. Touch the text field below 'Subject' and enter a message, if desired. The message is entered.
8. Touch **Send** at the top of the screen. The email is sent.

Note: When forwarding an email, the attachment menu will appear if the original message has an attachment. Touch **Include** *if you wish to include the attachment when you forward the email. Otherwise, touch* **Don't Include***.*

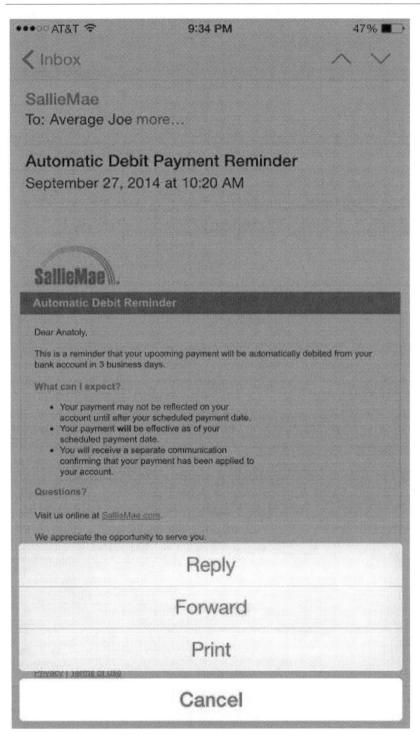

Figure 9: Reply Menu

8. Attaching a Picture or Video to an Email

While composing an email, you may wish to attach a picture or video to send to the recipient. To attach a picture or video to an email:

1. Touch and hold anywhere in the content of the email. The Select menu appears above the text.
2. Touch **Insert Photo or Video**. A list of photo albums stored on your phone appears, as shown in **Figure 10**.
3. Touch the photo album that contains the photo that you wish to attach. The photo album opens and a list of photo thumbnails appears, as shown in **Figure 11**.
4. Touch the photo that you wish to attach. A preview of the photo appears.
5. Touch **Choose**. The selected photo is attached. Alternatively, touch **Cancel** to return to the list of photos.

Note: You may move or delete the photo in the same way that you would delete text.

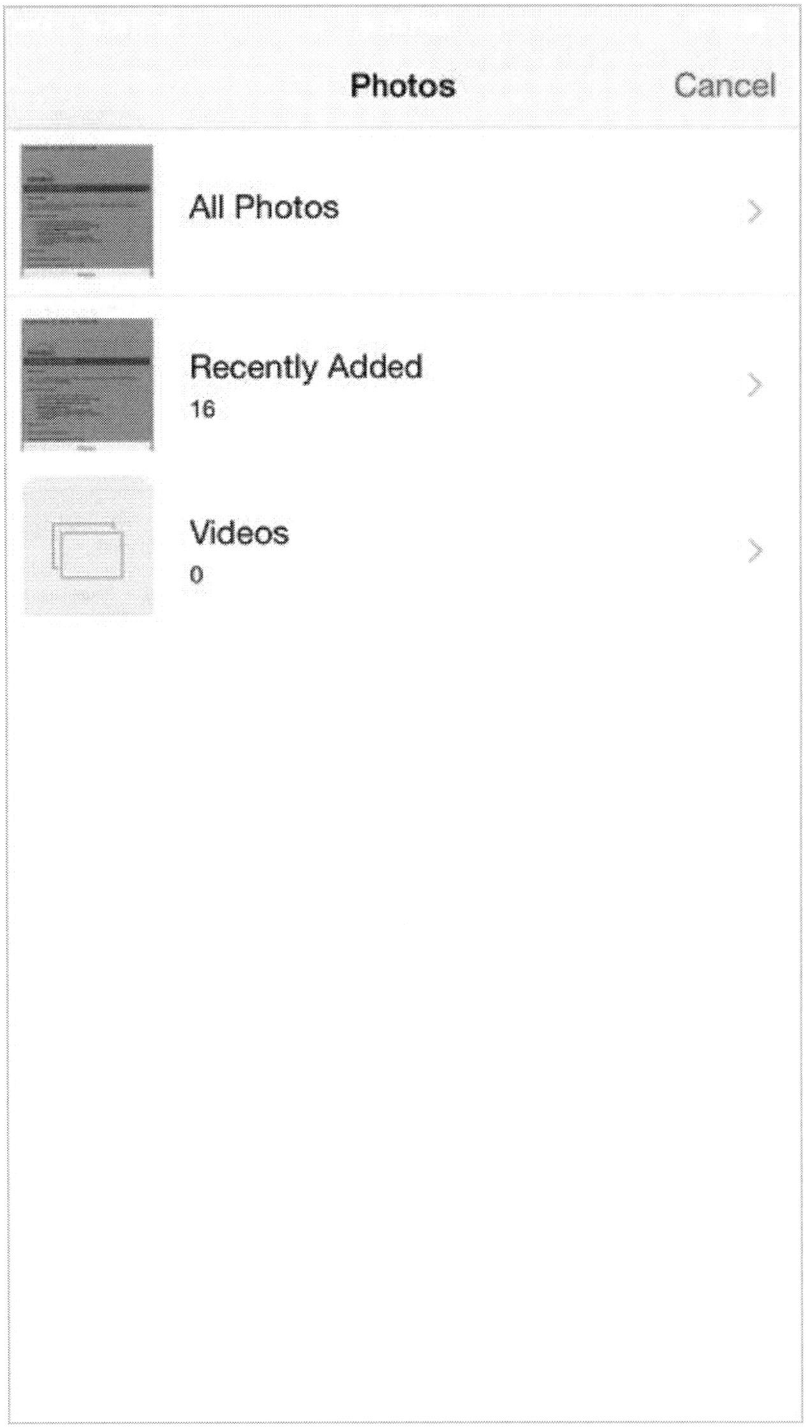

Figure 10: List of Photo Albums

Figure 11: List of Photo Thumbnails

9. Moving an Email in the Inbox to Another Folder

You may wish to organize emails into folders so that you can find them more easily. To move an email in the Inbox to another folder:

1. Touch an email in the Inbox. The email opens.
2. Touch the ⬜ button. A list of available folders appears, as shown in **Figure 12**.
3. Touch the name of a folder. The selected email is moved to the selected folder. To view a list of your folders, touch **Mailboxes** at the top of the screen while viewing the Inbox.

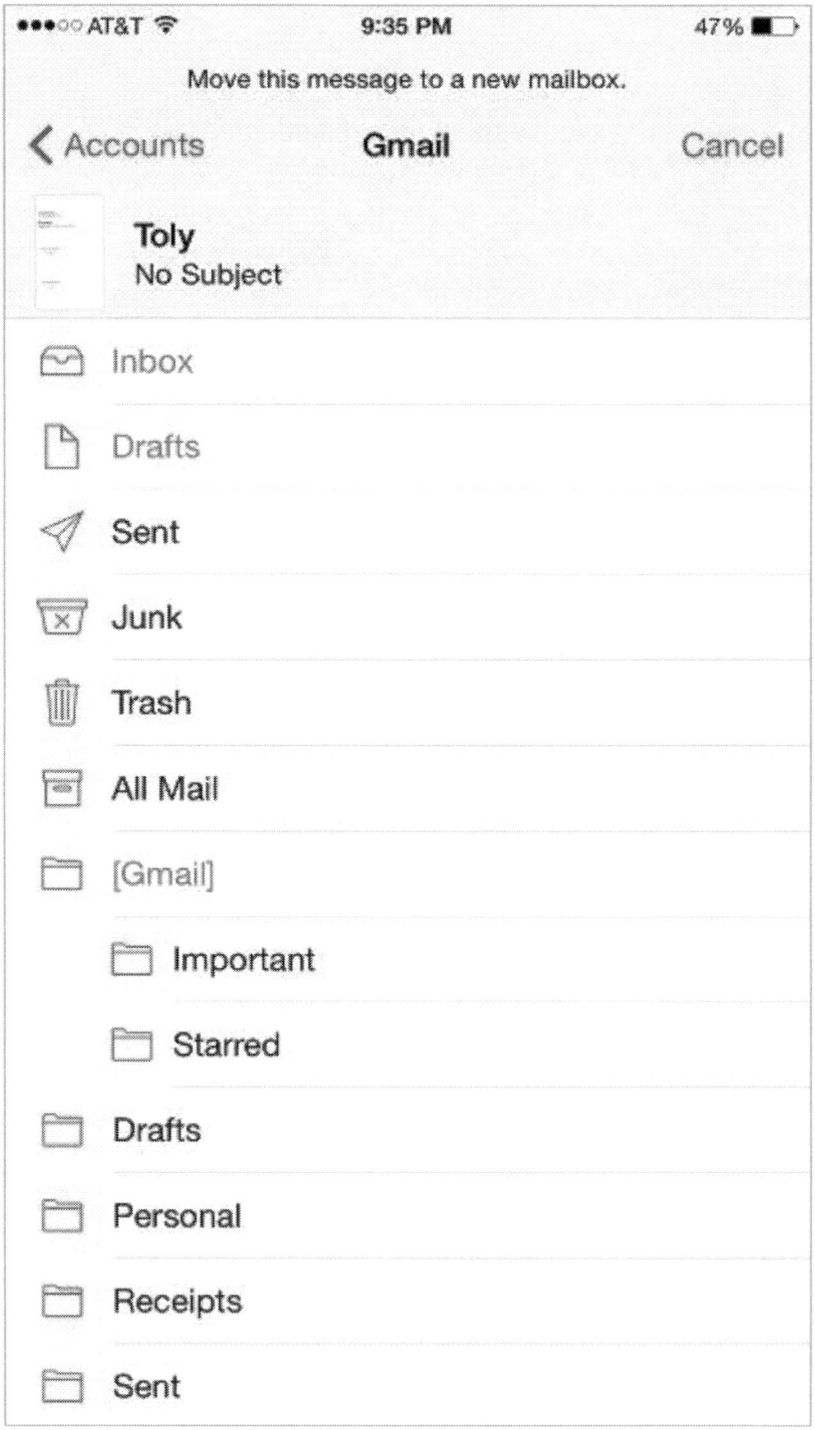

Figure 12: List of Available Folders

10. Flagging an Important Email

You may flag emails that are of the greatest importance in order to find them more quickly. This feature is especially useful if you do not have the time to read the email immediately, and wish to return to it in the near future. To flag an important email:

1. Touch an email in the Inbox. The email opens.

2. Touch the ⚑ button. The Flagging menu appears, as shown in **Figure 13**.

3. Touch **Flag**. The email is flagged as 'Important'. You may also touch **Mark as Unread** to flag the email so that you remember to read it later.

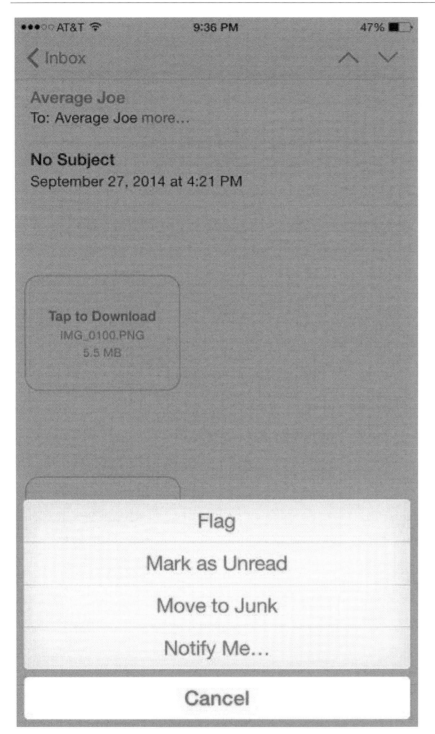

Figure 13: Flagging Menu

11. Archiving Emails

You may archive emails from your Inbox to free up space and improve organization. Archiving emails moves them to a folder that does not take up space on your phone. Therefore, you never need to delete an email, and can always recover it if you did not mean to delete it. You may archive as many emails as you like. To archive an email:

1. Touch the icon. The email application opens.
2. Touch and hold an email in the list and drag your finger to the left until the email disappears. The email is sent to the 'All Mail' folder, and disappears from the Inbox. You can also archive an email by touching the ⬚ icon while viewing an open email.
3. Touch **Mailboxes** at the top of the screen, and then touch **All Mail** to view all emails, including those that have been archived.

12. Changing the Default Signature

The phone can set a default signature that will be attached to the end of each email that is sent from the phone. To set or change this signature:

1. Touch the ⚙ icon. The Settings screen appears.
2. Touch **Mail, Contacts, Calendars**. The Mail, Contacts, Calendars screen appears.
3. Scroll down and touch **Signature**. The Signature screen appears, as shown in **Figure 14**.
4. Enter a signature, and then touch **Mail, Contacts...** at the top of the screen. The new signature is saved.

Figure 14: Signature Screen

13. Changing How You Receive Email

There are two options for receiving email on the phone. The phone can check for new email only when you refresh the Inbox, or it can constantly check for email and display an alert when a new email arrives. To set the phone to either check for email at regular intervals or only when you refresh the Inbox:

1. Touch the ⊚ icon. The Settings screen appears.
2. Touch **Mail, Contacts, Calendars** at the bottom of the screen. The Mail, Contacts, Calendars screen appears.
3. Touch **Fetch New Data**. The Fetch New Data screen appears, as shown in **Figure 15**.
4. Touch the ⬭ switch next to 'Push'. Push is turned on, and the Mail application will constantly check for new email and alert you when a new one arrives.
5. Touch the ⬬ switch next to 'Push'. Push is turned off, and the Mail application will only check for new email when you touch the top of the Inbox and slide your finger down to refresh it.

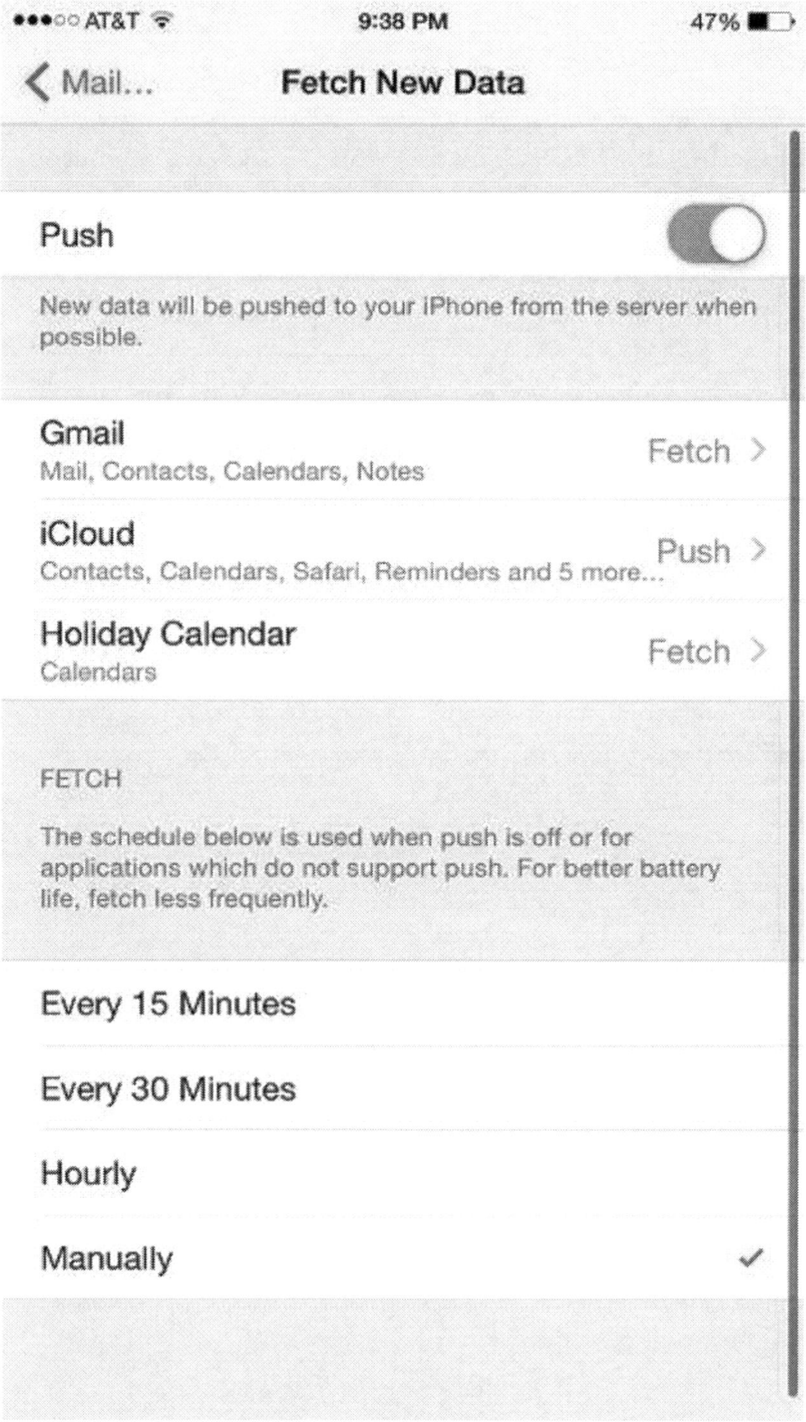

●●●○○ AT&T 📶   9:38 PM   47% 🔋

‹ Mail...   **Fetch New Data**

Push   🔘

New data will be pushed to your iPhone from the server when possible.

Gmail   Fetch ›
Mail, Contacts, Calendars, Notes

iCloud   Push ›
Contacts, Calendars, Safari, Reminders and 5 more...

Holiday Calendar   Fetch ›
Calendars

FETCH

The schedule below is used when push is off or for applications which do not support push. For better battery life, fetch less frequently.

Every 15 Minutes

Every 30 Minutes

Hourly

Manually   ✓

Figure 15: Fetch New Data Screen

14. Changing Email Options

There are various options that change the way your Mail application works. Touch the ⊚ icon, and then touch **Mail, Contacts, Calendars** to change one of the following options:

- **Preview** - Choose the number of lines of an email message to preview in the Inbox.
- **Show To/Cc Label** - Choose whether to hide the 'To' and 'Cc' labels and show only addresses.
- **Swipe Options** - Changes the swipe action used to flag an email, or mark an email as 'Unread'.
- **Flag Style** - Choose the type of shape to use (color or shape) when flagging an email.
- **Ask Before Deleting** - Choose whether to display a confirmation before deleting an email.
- **Load Remote Images** - Choose whether to load images in an email automatically.
- **Organize by Thread** - Choose whether to group all emails with the same contact as a conversation.
- **Always Bcc Myself** - Choose whether the email application sends a copy of each email to your own email address for your records.
- **Increase Quote Level** - Choose whether to increase the left margin when replying to or forwarding an email.

15. Viewing the Inbox in Landscape

The iPhone 6 and 6 Plus have the ability to display the email Inbox in landscape view. This view allows you to view the list of emails on the left, and the content of the currently selected email on the right. To view the Email screen in landscape view, you must first set the Display Zoom to 'Standard'. If your phone is already is in 'Standard' zoom, just hold your phone horizontally while it is upright. The Landscape Inbox appears, as shown in **Figure 16**. Otherwise, refer to *"Setting the Display Zoom"* on page 308 to learn how.

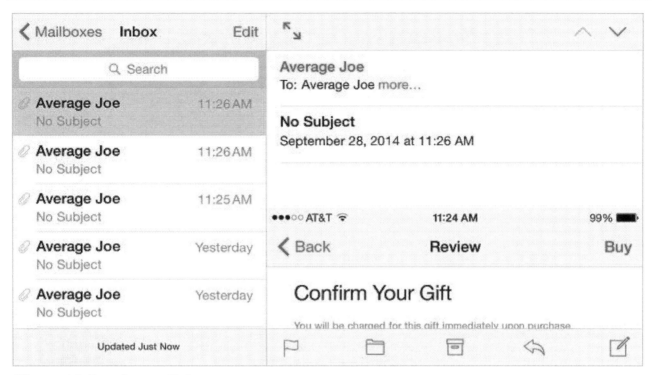

Figure 16: Landscape Inbox

Managing Applications

Table of Contents

1. Signing In to an iTunes Account

In order to buy applications, you will need to have an iTunes account. To set up a new iTunes account:

1. Touch the ⚙ icon. The Settings screen appears, as shown in **Figure 1**.
2. Scroll down and touch **iTunes & App Store**. The iTunes & App Store Settings screen appears, as shown in **Figure 2**.
3. If you already have an Apple ID, enter your Apple ID and password, and touch **Sign In**. Otherwise, navigate to **https://appleid.apple.com/account** using your computer's Web browser to register for an Apple ID.

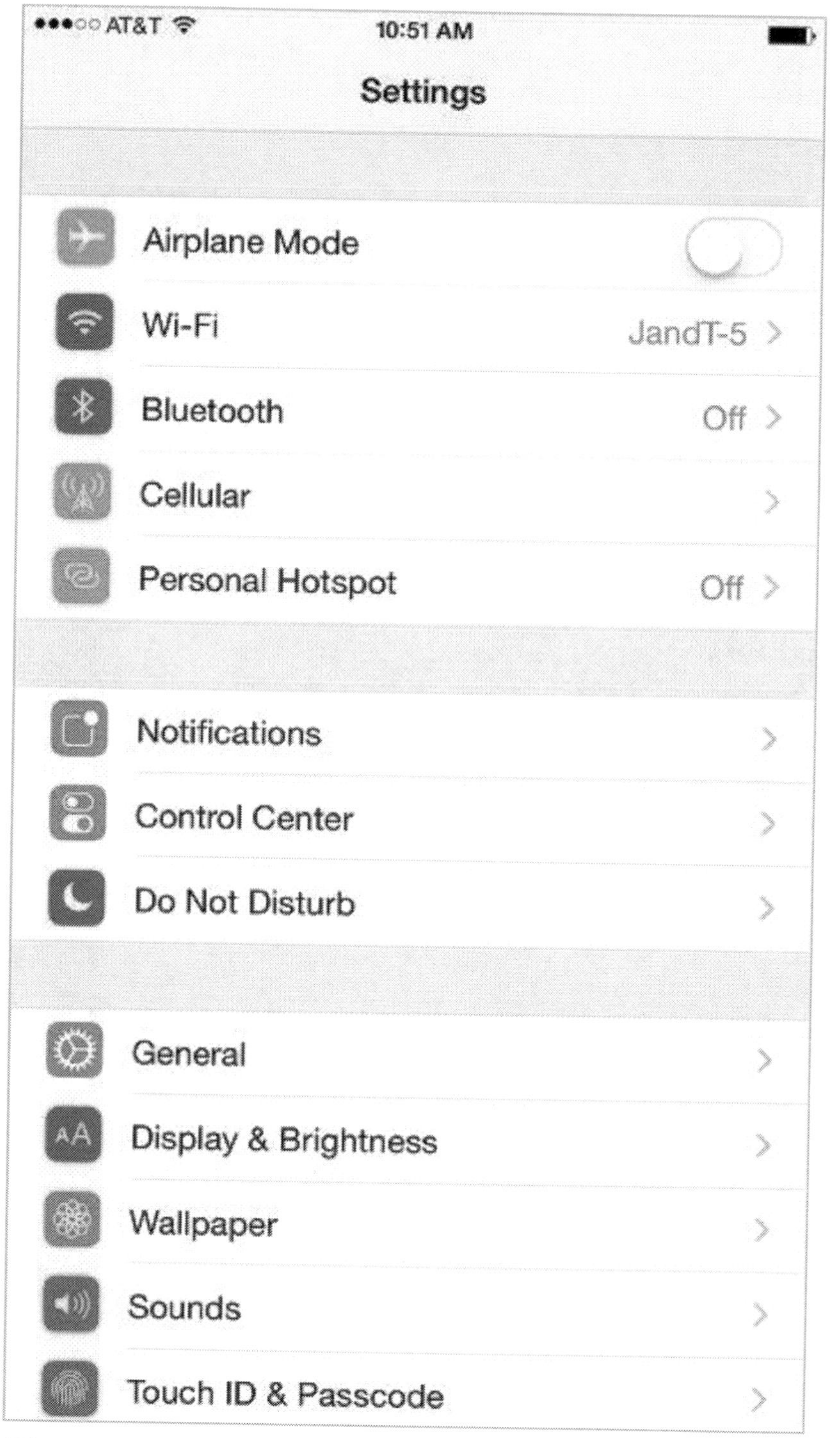

Figure 1: Settings Screen

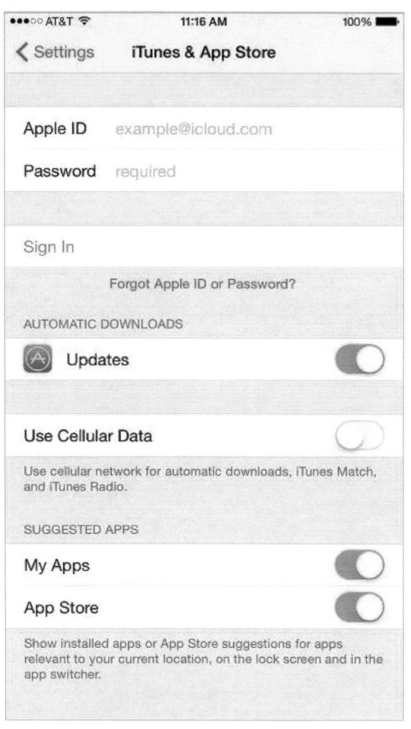

Figure 2: Store Settings Screen

2. Signing In to a Different iTunes Account

If more than one person uses your phone, you may wish to sign in with an alternate Apple ID. Only one Apple ID may be signed in at a time. To sign out and sign in to a different iTunes account:

1. Touch the icon. The Settings screen appears.
2. Scroll down and touch **iTunes & App Store**. The iTunes & App Store Settings screen appears. If someone is signed in to their iTunes account on the phone, their email appears at the top of the screen.
3. Touch the email address at the top of the screen. The Apple ID window appears, as shown in **Figure 3**.
4. Touch **Sign Out**. The account is signed out.
5. Touch **Apple ID**. The virtual keyboard appears.
6. Enter your registered email address and password.
7. Touch **Sign In**. The account is signed in, and the owner's email is shown at the top of the iTunes & App Store screen.

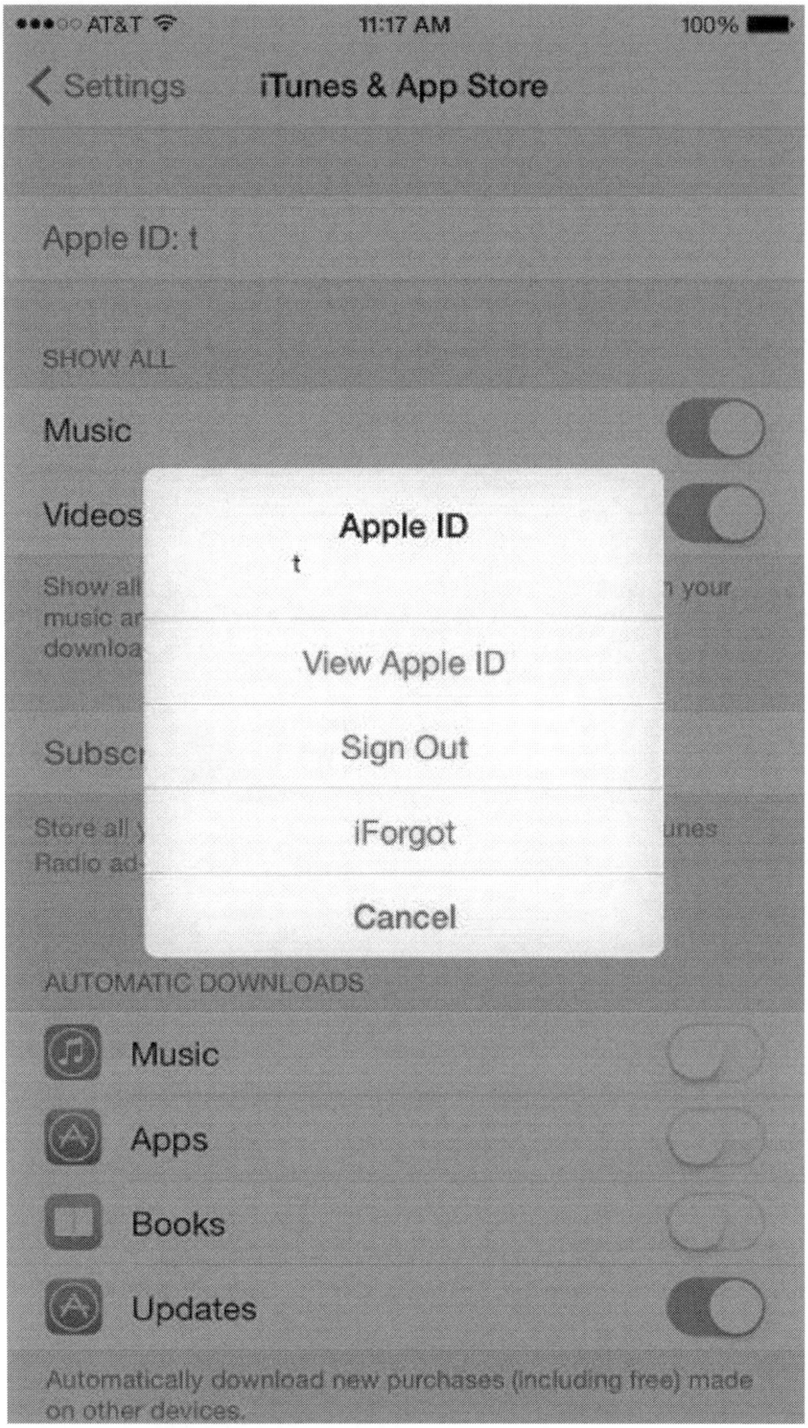

Figure 3: Apple ID Window

3. Editing iTunes Account Information

You must keep your account information up to date in order to purchase applications from the iTunes Application Store. For instance, when your billing address changes or your credit card expires, you must change your information. To edit iTunes account information:

1. Touch the ⬤ icon. The Settings screen appears.
2. Scroll down and touch **iTunes & App Store**. The iTunes & App Store Settings screen appears. If someone is signed in to their iTunes account on the phone, their email appears at the top of the screen.
3. If you are not already signed in, enter your registered email and password, and touch **Done**. You are signed in.
4. Touch your email at the top of the screen. The Apple ID window appears.
5. Touch **View Apple ID**. The Account Screen appears with your personal account information.
6. Touch a field to edit it, and then touch **Done**. The new information is saved.

4. Searching for an Application to Purchase

Use the Application Store to search for applications. There are three ways to search for applications:

Manual Search

To search for an application manually:

1. Touch the ⬤ icon. The Application Store opens, as shown in **Figure 4**.
2. Touch the 🔍 button at the bottom of the screen. The Search screen appears, as shown in **Figure 5**.
3. Touch **Search** at the top of the screen. The virtual keyboard appears at the bottom of the screen.
4. Enter the name of an application and touch **Search** at the bottom of the screen. A list of matching results appears.

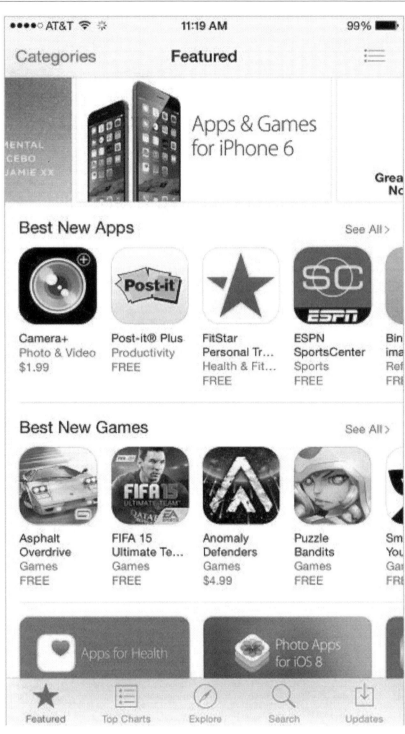

Figure 4: Application Store

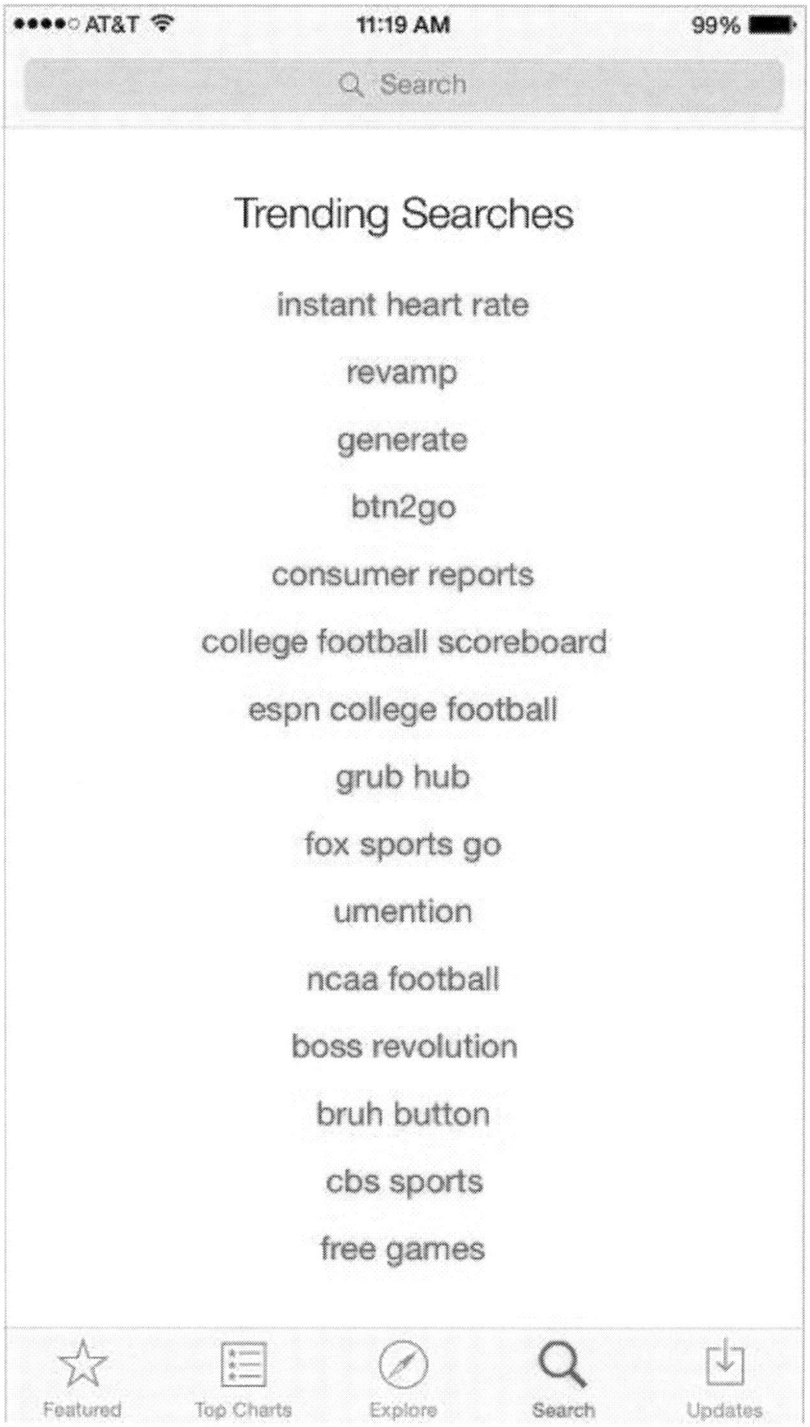

Figure 5: Search Screen

Browse by Category

To browse applications by category:

1. Touch the icon. The Application Store opens.
2. Touch Categories at the top of the screen. The Categories screen appears, as shown in **Figure 6**. Touch the screen and move your finger up or down to scroll through the categories.
3. Touch a category to browse it. Some categories have sub-categories. Repeat step 2 to find the sub-category that you need.

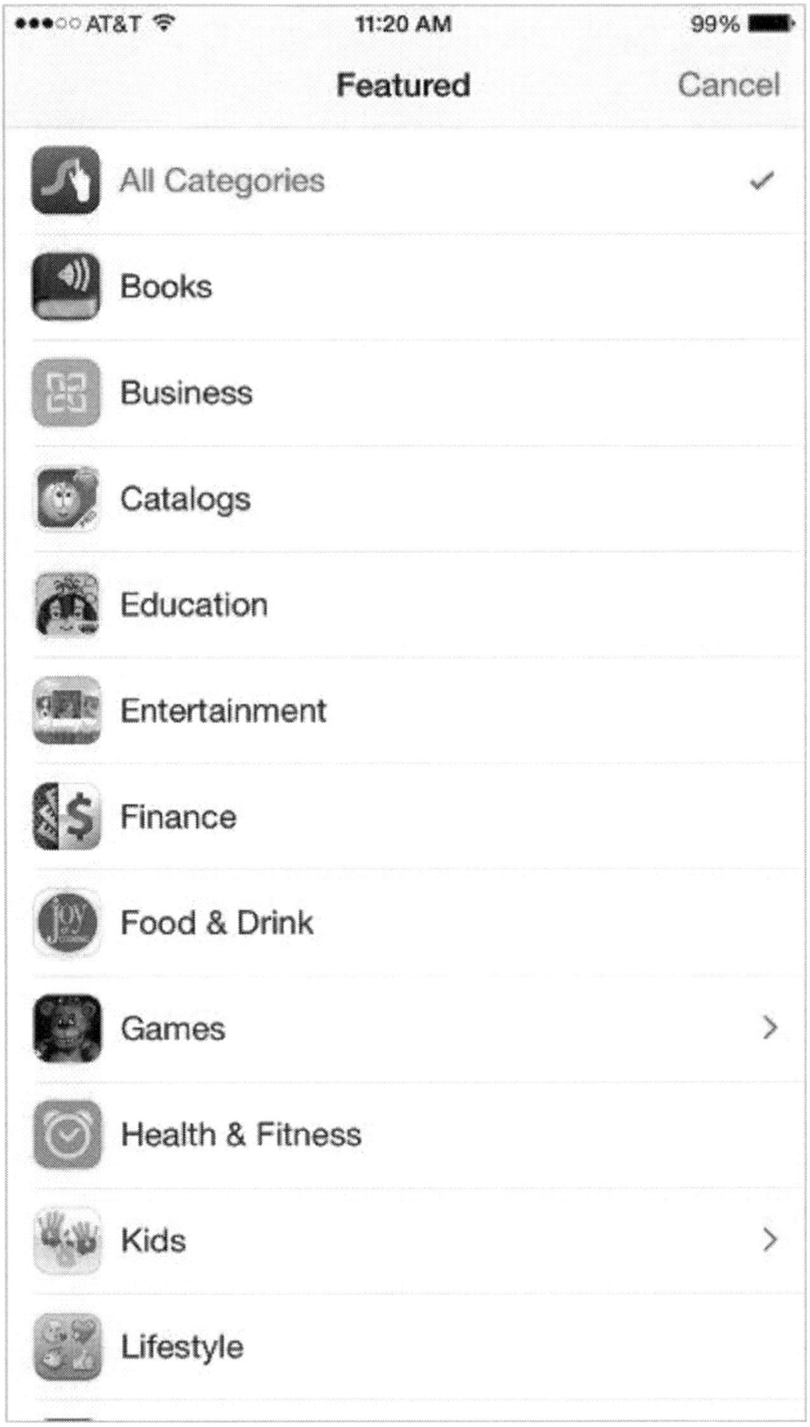

●●●○○ AT&T 📶	11:20 AM	99% 🔋

Featured   Cancel

All Categories   ✓

Books

Business

Catalogs

Education

Entertainment

Finance

Food & Drink

Games   >

Health & Fitness

Kids   >

Lifestyle

Figure 6: Categories Screen

Browse by Popularity

To browse applications by popularity:

1. Touch the [icon] icon. The Application Store opens.
2. Touch the [icon] icon at the bottom of the screen. The Top Charts screen appears, as shown in **Figure 7**.
3. Touch one of the following to browse applications:

   - **Paid** - View the most popular paid applications.
   - **Free** - View the most popular free applications.
   - **Top Grossing** - View the most popular applications that have earned their creators the most money. Some Top Grossing apps are free, but in-app purchases are considered when calculating the top grossing applications.

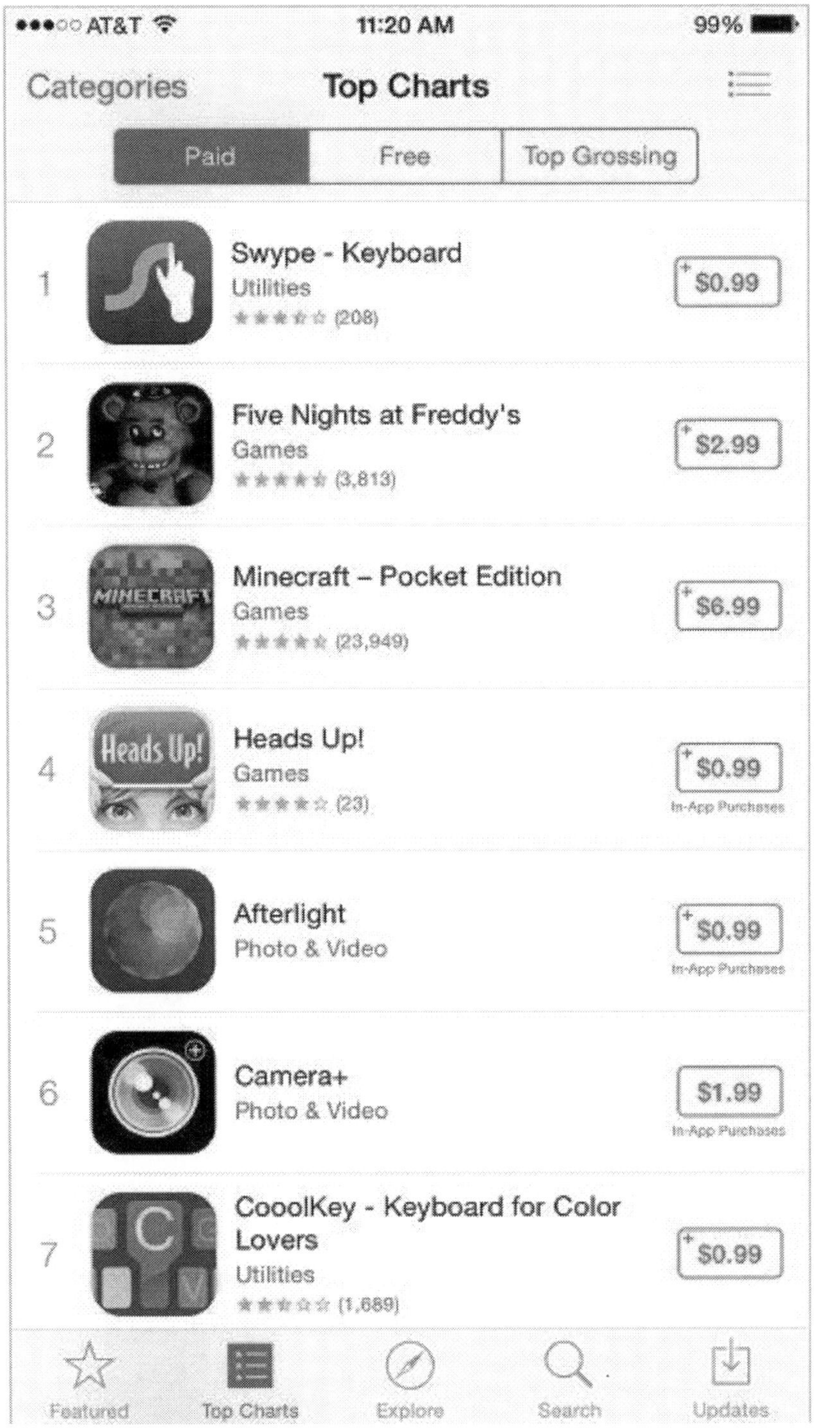

Figure 7: Top Charts Screen

5. Buying an Application

You may purchase applications directly from your phone. To buy an application:

1. Touch the ![icon] icon. The Application Store opens.
2. Find an application. Refer to *"Searching for an Application to Purchase"* on page 213 to learn how.
3. Touch an application in the list. The Application description appears, as shown in **Figure 8**.
4. Touch the price of the application, or touch the word **FREE**, next to the name of the application. 'BUY' appears if the application is paid or 'INSTALL' if the application is free. If the application is already downloaded to your phone, 'INSTALLED' appears. Touch **BUY** or**INSTALL**. The password prompt appears.
5. Enter your iTunes password and touch **OK**. The phone returns to the Home screen, and the application is downloaded and installed.

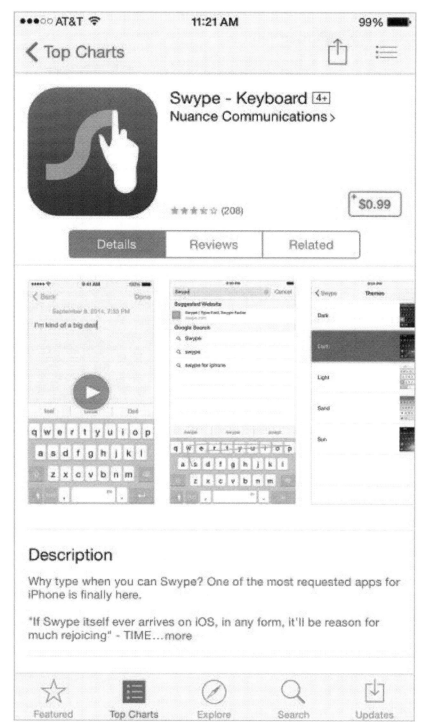

Figure 8: Application Description

6. Using Wi-Fi to Download an Application

Applications that are over 10MB in size require the phone to be connected to a Wi-Fi network to download. These applications will display the following message: "Application over 10MB. Connect to a Wi-Fi network or use iTunes on your computer to download >APP NAME<'"', where APP NAME refers to the name of the application you are trying to download. Refer to *"Using Wi-Fi"* on page 29 to learn how to turn on Wi-Fi.

7. Switching Between Applications

The phone allows you to switch between running applications without having to exit any of them. For instance, you can listen to Pandora radio and read an eBook at the same time. To switch between applications:

1. Touch an application icon on one of your Home screens. The application opens.
2. Press the **Home** button. The Home screen appears.
3. Open another application.
4. Press the **Home** button twice quickly. All of the open applications are displayed, as shown in **Figure 9**.
5. Touch an application icon. The phone switches to the selected application.

Note: When switching to another application, the first application is never automatically closed. The application is simply running in the background. Refer to "Closing an Application Running in the Background" on page 224 *to learn how to close an application.*

Figure 9: Open Applications

8. Closing an Application Running in the Background

After pressing the Home button to exit an application, it is not closed, but is left running in the background instead. It is good to have the application running, because you can always switch to it quickly. However, if an application stops responding or if your battery is dying too quickly, you may wish to close it. To close an application running in the background, press the **Home** button twice quickly. All of the open applications are displayed. Touch and hold an application icon and slide your finger up. The application is closed. You can also close multiple applications at the same time by touching two or more applications and sliding your fingers up.

9. Organizing Applications into Folders

To learn how to organize applications into folders, refer to *"Creating an Icon Folder"* on page 27.

10. Reading User Reviews

In order to make a more informed decision when purchasing an application, you can read the reviews written by other users. However, be aware that people who have not used the application can also post reviews, which are uninformed. To read user reviews for an application:

1. Touch the icon. The Application Store opens.
2. Find an application. Refer to *"Searching for an Application to Purchase"* on page 213 to learn how.
3. Touch an application icon. The Application description appears.
4. Touch **Reviews** below the name of the application. The reviews for the application appear.

11. Changing Application Settings

Some applications have settings that can be changed from the Settings screen. To change the Application settings, touch the icon. The Settings screen appears. Touch an application below 'Game Center' at the bottom of the screen. The Application Settings screen appears. The settings on this screen depend on the particular application.

12. Deleting an Application

You may delete most applications from your phone to free up space on your memory card or Home screen. To delete an unwanted application:

1. Touch and hold an application icon. All of the applications on the Home screen begin to shake. Applications that can be erased have an ⊗ button in their top left corner.

2. Touch the ⊗ button next to an application icon. A confirmation dialog appears.

3. Touch **Delete**. The application is deleted.

4. Press the **Home** button. The application icons stop shaking and the ⊗ buttons disappear.

Note: If you delete a paid application, you can download it again free of charge at any time. Refer to "Buying an Application" on page 220, and follow the instructions for buying the application to re-download it.

13. Sending an Application as a Gift

On the phone, applications can be sent as gifts. The recipient receives an email notification, and can then download the gifted application from the Application Store. To send an application as a gift:

1. Touch the icon. The Application Store opens.
2. Find the application that you want to give as a gift. Refer to *"Searching for an Application to Purchase"* on page 213 to learn how.
3. Touch the application icon. The application description appears.
4. Touch the ⬆ icon in the upper right-hand corner of the screen. The Application options appear at the bottom of the screen, as shown in **Figure 10**.
5. Touch **Gift**. The Send Gift screen appears, as shown in **Figure 11**.
6. Touch **To:** and enter the email address of the recipient of the gift. Enter an optional message.
7. Touch **Today** to select when the gift should be shared, if the date is other than the current day.
8. Touch **Next** at the top of the screen. The Theme Selection screen appears.

9. Select a theme and touch **Next** at the top of the screen. The Gift Confirmation screen appears, as shown in **Figure 12**.

10. Touch **Buy** at the top of the screen. 'BUY NOW' appears as a confirmation.

11. Touch **BUY NOW**. The password prompt appears.

12. Enter your iTunes password and touch **OK**. The gift is purchased and sent.

Note: You are charged for the gifted application as soon as you purchase it.

Figure 10: Application Options

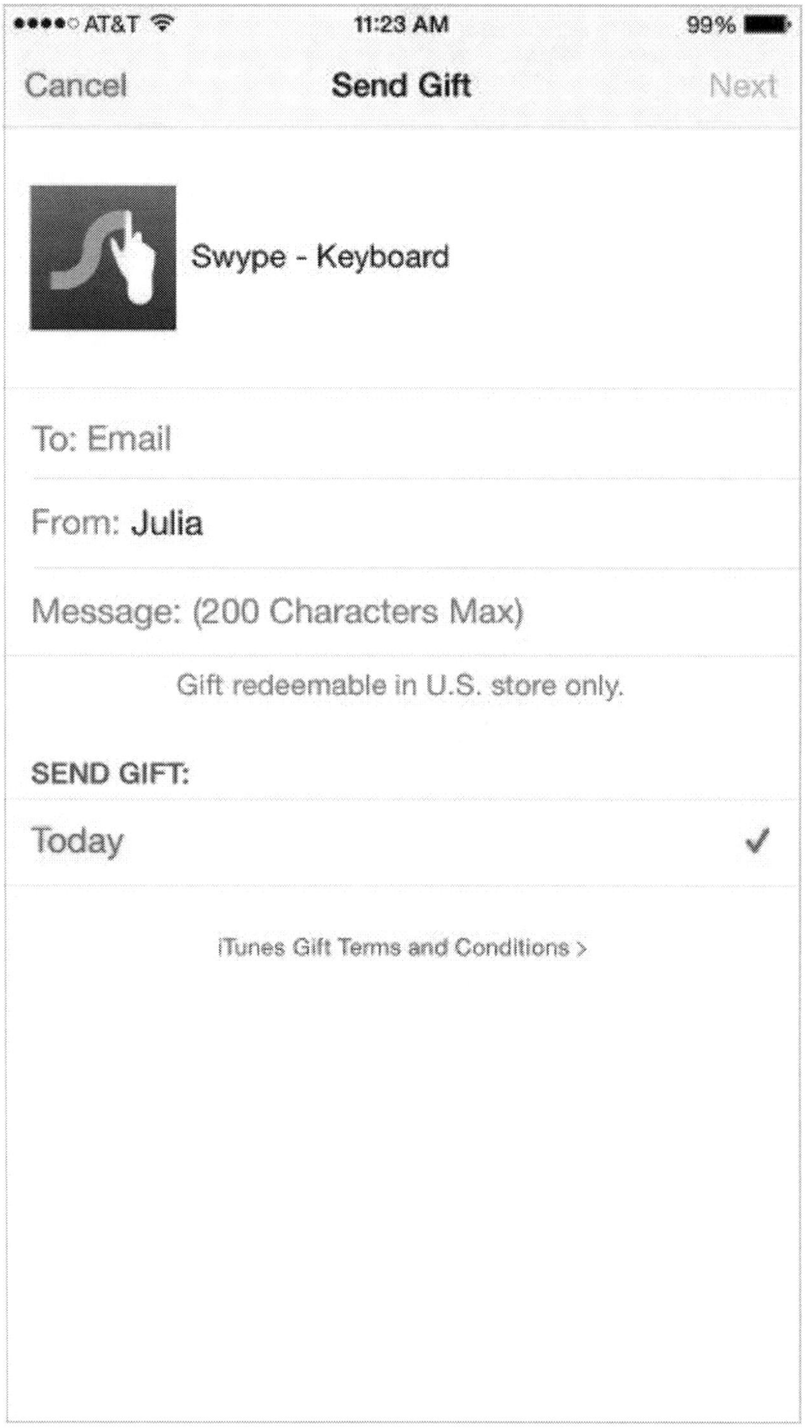

●●●●○ AT&T 📶   11:23 AM   99% ▬▶

| Cancel | **Send Gift** | Next |

Swype - Keyboard

To: Email

From: **Julia**

Message: (200 Characters Max)

Gift redeemable in U.S. store only.

SEND GIFT:

Today   ✓

iTunes Gift Terms and Conditions >

Figure 11: Send Gift Screen

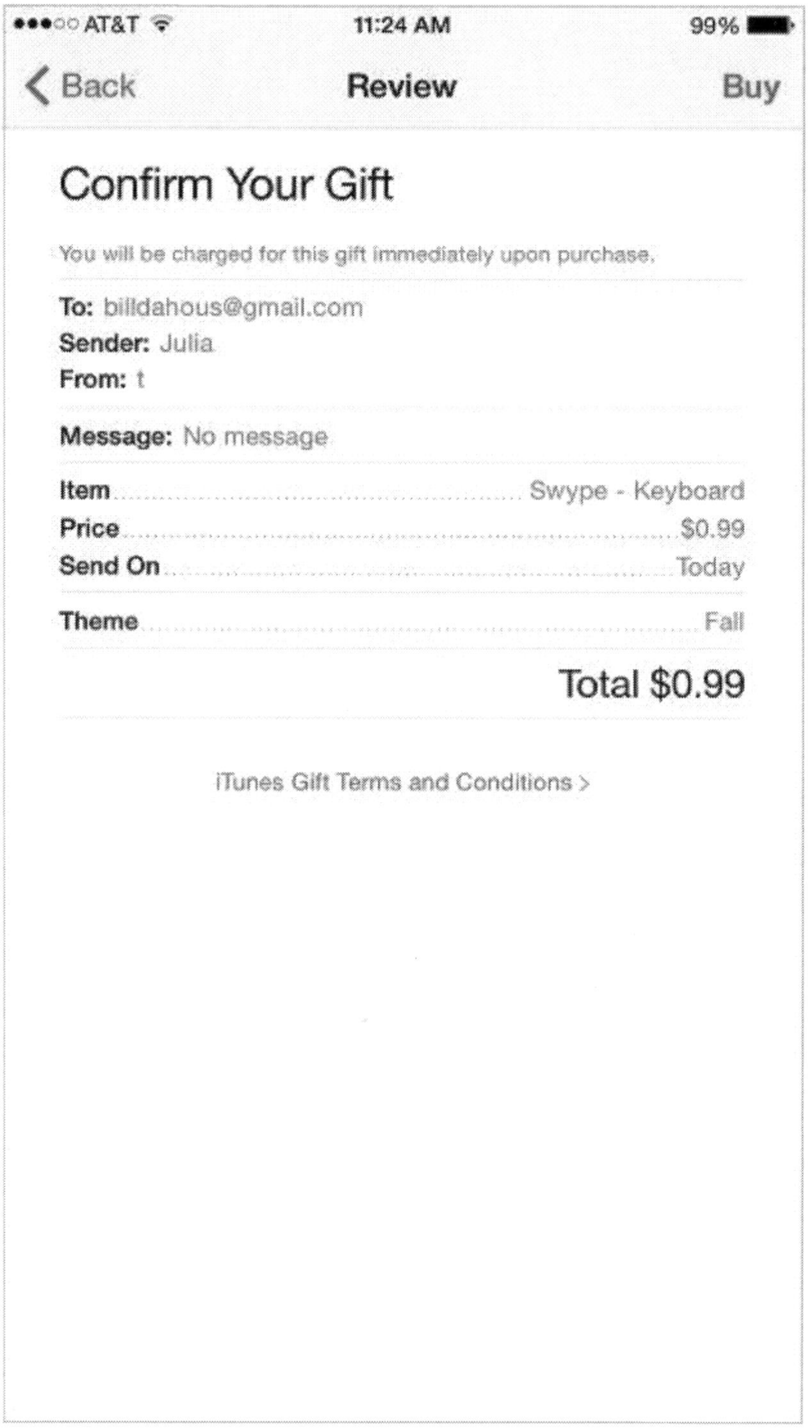
AT&T
11:24 AM
99%
Back
Review
Buy
Confirm Your Gift
You will be charged for this gift immediately upon purchase.
To: billdahous@gmail.com
Sender: Julia
From: t
Message: No message
Item ... Swype - Keyboard
Price ... $0.99
Send On ... Today
Theme ... Fall
Total $0.99
iTunes Gift Terms and Conditions >

Figure 12: Gift Confirmation Screen

14. Redeeming a Gifted Application

When receiving an application as a gift, you must redeem it in order to download it. To redeem a gift and download the application using your phone:

1. Touch the icon. The email application opens.
2. Touch the email with the subject **'NAME sent you an iTunes Gift'**, where NAME represents the name of the sender. The email opens. Refer to *"Reading Email"* on page 184 to learn how to find an email.
3. Touch the **Redeem Now** button in the email. The Application Store opens.
4. Touch **Redeem** at the top of the screen. The gifted application is downloaded and installed. If the application is over 10MB, you must first turn on Wi-Fi. Refer to *"Using Wi-Fi"* on page 29 to learn how to turn Wi-Fi on. If this is your first time downloading an application from the iTunes store, you will need to touch **Agree** several times to accept several pages of terms and conditions.

15. Turning Automatic Application Updates On or Off

The phone can automatically download updates for applications when new versions are released. To turn automatic application updates on or off:

1. Touch the icon. The Settings screen appears.
2. Scroll down and touch **iTunes & App Store**. The iTunes & App Store Settings screen appears.
3. Touch the switch next to 'Updates' under 'Automatic Downloads'. The switch appears Automatic application updates are turned off.
4. Touch the switch next to 'Updates' under 'Automatic Downloads'. The switch appears Automatic application updates are turned on.

Using Siri

Siri is a voice assistant that comes with every iPhone 6. Follow the tips in this chapter to use Siri to its full potential.

Table of Contents

1. Making a Call (Siri)

To make a call using Siri, press and hold the **Home** button or hold the phone up to your ear and wait for Siri to speak. Say one of the following phrases:

- **Call John** (use any name)
- **Call Suzy Mobile**
- **Call Dexter on his work phone**
- **Call 123 555 1345**
- **Call home**
- **FaceTime Jacob**

Note: These phrases are only suggestions. Siri is flexible, and you can use many synonymous phrases.

2. Sending and Receiving Text Messages (Siri)

To send, read, or reply to a text message using Siri, press and hold the **Home** button or hold the phone up to your ear and wait for Siri to speak. Say one of the following phrases:

- **Tell Anne See you soon**
- **Send a message to Rob Burr**
- **Send a message to Larry saying What's your address?**
- **Send a message to Julie on her mobile saying I got an iPhone 6 6!**
- **Send a message to 999 555 2222**
- **Text Jude and Prudence What are you guys up to today?**
- **Read my new messages**
- **Read it again**
- **Reply that's great news**
- **Tell him ETA is 20 minutes**
- **Call her**

Note: These phrases are only suggestions. Siri is flexible, and you can use many synonymous phrases.

3. Managing the Address Book (Siri)

To manage the address book using Siri, press and hold the **Home** button or hold the phone up to your ear and wait for Siri to speak. Say one of the following phrases:

- **What's Joe's address?**
- **What is Susan Park's phone number?**
- **When is my grandfather's birthday?**
- **Show Bobby's email address**
- **Show Pete Abred**
- **Find people named Apple**
- **My brother is Trudy Ages** (assigns a relationship to the name)
- **Who is Colin Card?** (indicates Colin Card's relationship to you)
- **Call my brother at home** (calls the number assigned to the relationship)

Note: These phrases are only suggestions. Siri is flexible, and you can use many synonymous phrases.

4. Setting Up and Managing Meetings (Siri)

To set up and manage meetings using Siri, press and hold the **Home** button or hold the phone up to your ear and wait for Siri to speak. Say one of the following phrases:

- Set up a meeting at 10
- Set up a meeting with Zoe at 9
- Meet with Nikki at noon
- New appointment with Dan Delion Tuesday at 4
- Schedule a focus group meeting at 3:30 today in the boardroom
- Move my 2pm meeting to 3:30
- Add Wendy to my meeting with Waldo
- Cancel the focus group meeting
- What does the rest of my day look like?
- What's on my calendar for Monday?
- When is my next appointment?
- Where is my next meeting?

Note: These phrases are only suggestions. Siri is flexible, and you can use many synonymous phrases.

5. Checking the Time and Setting Alarms (Siri)

To check the time and set alarms using Siri, press and hold the **Home** button or hold the phone up to your ear and wait for Siri to speak. Say one of the following phrases:

- **Wake me up tomorrow at 6am**
- **Set an alarm for 6:30am**
- **Wake me up in 8 hours**
- **Change my 5:30 alarm to 6:30**
- **Turn off my 4:30 alarm**
- **What time is it?**
- **What time is it in Moscow?**
- **What is today's date?**
- **What's the date this Friday?**
- **Set the timer for 30 minutes**
- **Show the timer**
- **Pause the timer**
- **Resume**

- **Reset the timer**
- **Stop it**

Note: These phrases are only suggestions. Siri is flexible, and you can use many synonymous phrases.

6. Sending and Receiving Email (Siri)

To send and receive email using Siri, press and hold the **Home** button or hold the phone up to your ear and wait for Siri to speak. Say one of the following phrases:

- **Email Dave about the trip**
- **Email New email to John Diss**
- **Mail Dad about dinner**
- **Email Dr. Spaulding and say Got your message**
- **Mail Jack and Jill about the party and say It was awesome**
- **Check email**
- **Any new email from Mom today?**
- **Show new mail about the apartment**
- **Show the email from Roger yesterday**
- **Reply Dear Mark I'm sorry for your loss**

Note: These phrases are only suggestions. Siri is flexible, and you can use many synonymous phrases.

7. Getting Directions and Finding Businesses (Siri)

To get directions and find businesses using Siri, press and hold the **Home** button or hold the phone up to your ear and wait for Siri to speak. Say one of the following phrases:

- **How do I get home?**
- **Show 10 Park Ave. Boston Massachusetts**
- **Directions to my parents' home**
- **Find coffee near me**
- **Where is the closest Starbucks?**
- **Find a Mexican restaurant in New Mexico**
- **Find a gas station within walking distance**

Note: These phrases are only suggestions. Siri is flexible, and you can use many synonymous phrases.

8. Playing Music (Siri)

To play music using Siri, press and hold the **Home** button or hold the phone up to your ear and wait for Siri to speak. Say one of the following phrases:

- **Play Hotel California**
- **Play Coldplay shuffled**
- **Play Dave Matthews Band**
- **Play some folk**
- **Play my roadtrip playlist**
- **Shuffle my party playlist**
- **Play**
- **Pause**
- **Skip**

Note: These phrases are only suggestions. Siri is flexible, and you can use many synonymous phrases.

9. Searching the Web and Asking Questions (Siri)

To search the web using Siri, press and hold the **Home** button or hold the phone up to your ear and wait for Siri to speak. Say one of the following phrases:

- **Search the web for Apple News**
- **Search for chili recipes**
- **Google the humane society**
- **Search Wikipedia for Duckbilled Platypus**
- **Bing Secondhand Serenade**
- **How many calories in a doughnut?**
- **What is an 18% tip on $180.45 for six people?**
- **How long do cats live?**
- **What's 25 squared?**
- **How many dollars is 60 euros?**
- **How many days until Christmas?**
- **When is the next solar eclipse?**

- **Show me the Ursula Major constellation**
- **What is the meaning of life?**
- **What's the price of gasoline in Boston?**

Note: These phrases are only suggestions. Siri is flexible, and you can use many synonymous phrases.

10. Looking Up Words in the Dictionary (Siri)

To look up words using Siri, press and hold the **Home** button or hold the phone up to your ear and wait for Siri to speak. Say one of the following phrases:

- **What is the meaning of meticulous?**
- **Define albeit**
- **Look up the word jargon**

Note: These phrases are only suggestions. Siri is flexible, and you can use many phrases synonymous with these suggestions.

Adjusting Wireless Settings

Table of Contents

1. Turning Airplane Mode On or Off

Most airplanes do not allow wireless communications while in flight. Continue using the phone by enabling Airplane mode before take-off. You may not place or receive calls, send or receive text messages or emails, or surf the Web while in Airplane mode. Airplane Mode is also useful when traveling outside of your area of service to avoid any roaming charges and to preserve battery life. To turn Airplane Mode on or off:

1. Touch the ⊚ icon. The Settings screen appears, as shown in **Figure 1**.

2. Touch the ⬭ switch next to 'Airplane Mode'. The ⬤ switch appears and Airplane mode is turned on.

3. Touch the ⬤ switch next to 'Airplane Mode'. The ⬭ switch appears and Airplane mode is turned off.

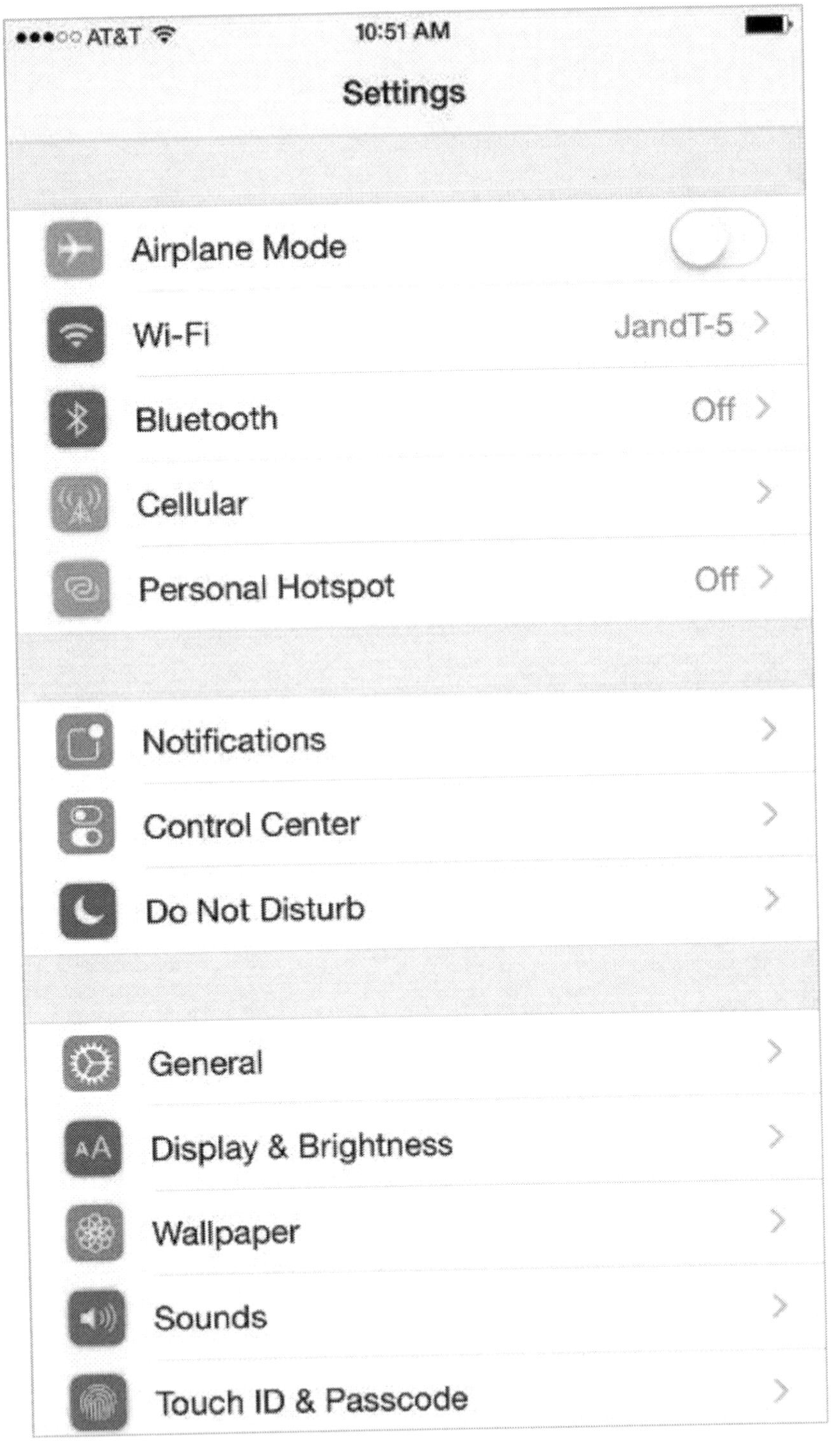

Figure 1: Settings Screen

2. Turning Location Services On or Off

Some applications, such as Maps, require the Location Services feature to be turned on, which determines your current location. To turn Location Services on or off:

1. Touch the ⊚ icon. The Settings screen appears.
2. Scroll down and touch **Privacy**. The Privacy Settings screen appears, as shown in **Figure 2**.
3. Touch **Location Services**. The Location Services screen appears, as shown in **Figure 3**.
4. Touch the ⬭ switch next to 'Location Services'. The ⬤ switch appears and Location Services are turned on.
5. Touch the ⬤ switch next to 'Location Services'. The ⬭ switch appears and Location Services are turned off.

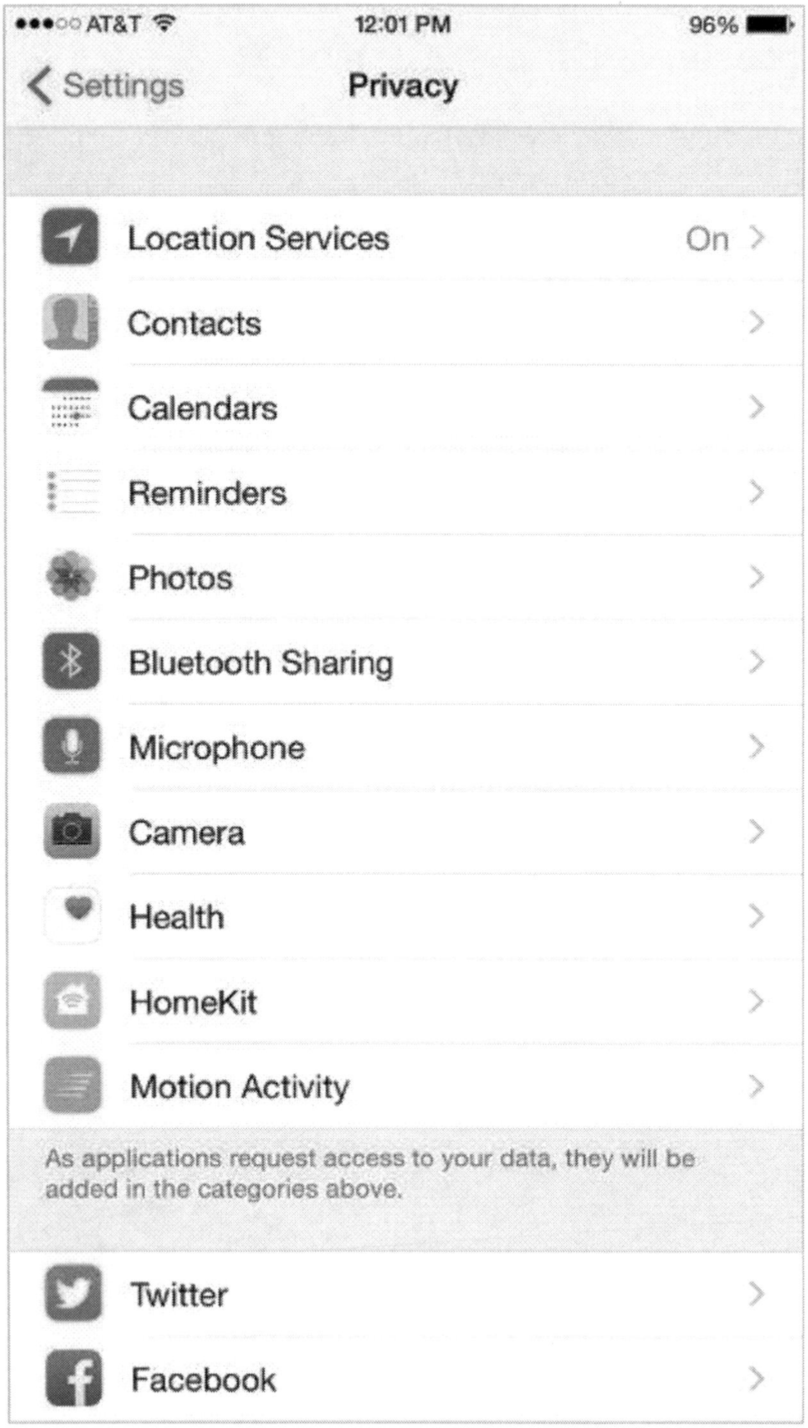

●●●○○ AT&T 📶	12:01 PM	96% 🔋

< Settings **Privacy**

📍	Location Services	On >
👤	Contacts	>
📅	Calendars	>
☰	Reminders	>
❁	Photos	>
✳	Bluetooth Sharing	>
🎤	Microphone	>
📷	Camera	>
♥	Health	>
⌂	HomeKit	>
▤	Motion Activity	>

As applications request access to your data, they will be added in the categories above.

🐦	Twitter	>
f	Facebook	>

Figure 2: Privacy Settings Screen

●●●○○ AT&T 🛜   12:02 PM   96% ▬

< Privacy   **Location Services**

Location Services   🔵⚪

Location Services uses GPS, Bluetooth, and crowd-sourced Wi-Fi hotspot and cell tower locations to determine your approximate location. About Location Services & Privacy...

Share My Location   >

📷 Camera	➤ While Using	>
◎ Chrome	While Using	>
◻ Messages	Never	>
🌸 Photos	➤ While Using	>
🎙 Siri	While Using	>
▦ SmartPay	Always	>
☁ Weather	Never	>
System Services		>

➤ A purple location services icon will appear next to an item that has recently used your location.

Figure 3: Location Services Screen

3. Customizing Cellular Data Usage

To surf the internet and download applications when not connected to Wi-Fi, you need to turn on cellular data. However, you can turn off cellular data if you wish to conserve battery life in an area with little or no 4G service. To turn cellular data on or off:

1. Touch the ⚙ icon. The Settings screen appears.
2. Touch **Cellular**. The Cellular Settings screen appears, as shown in **Figure 4**.
3. Touch the ⬜ switch next to 'Cellular Data'. The 🔘 switch appears and cellular data is turned on.
4. Touch the 🔘 switch next to 'Cellular Data'. The ⬜ switch appears and cellular data is turned off.

You may also manage the cellular data usage from the Cellular Settings screen. To manage cellular data usage:

1. Touch the 🔘 switch next to 'Mail', 'Passbook', or another application. Cellular data is turned off for the corresponding application.
2. Touch the ⬜ switch next to the name of an application. Cellular data is turned on for the corresponding application.
3. Touch **System Services** to view the amount of data used by each service on your phone.

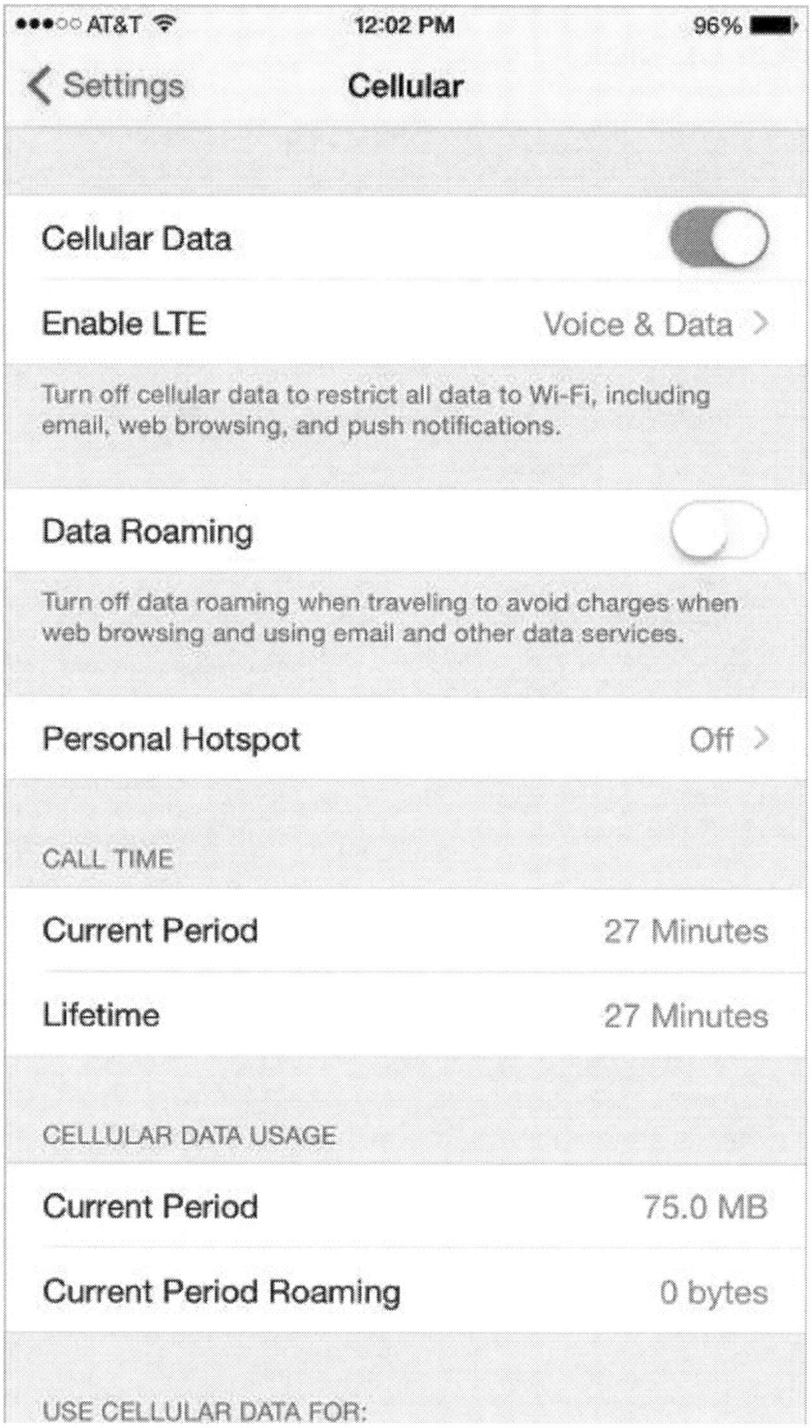

●●●○○ AT&T 🛜   12:02 PM   96% ▬▬▶

❮ Settings   Cellular

Cellular Data	⬤
Enable LTE	Voice & Data ❯

Turn off cellular data to restrict all data to Wi-Fi, including email, web browsing, and push notifications.

Data Roaming	⬯

Turn off data roaming when traveling to avoid charges when web browsing and using email and other data services.

Personal Hotspot	Off ❯

CALL TIME

Current Period	27 Minutes
Lifetime	27 Minutes

CELLULAR DATA USAGE

Current Period	75.0 MB
Current Period Roaming	0 bytes

USE CELLULAR DATA FOR:

Figure 4: Cellular Settings Screen

4. Turning Data Roaming On or Off

When you are in an area with no 4G coverage, the phone can use the Data Roaming feature to acquire signal from other networks. Be aware that Data Roaming can be extremely costly. Contact your network provider for details. To turn Data Roaming on or off:

1. Touch the icon. The Settings screen appears.
2. Touch **Cellular**. The Cellular Settings screen appears.
3. Touch the ⬯ switch next to 'Data Roaming'. The ⬮ switch appears and Data Roaming is turned on.
4. Touch the ⬮ switch next to 'Data Roaming'. The ⬯ switch appears and Data Roaming is turned off.

5. Setting Up a Virtual Private Network (VPN)

You can use your phone to connect to an external network, such as a corporate one. To set up a VPN:

1. Touch the icon. The Settings screen appears.
2. Touch **General**. The General Settings screen appears, as shown in **Figure 5**.
3. Scroll down and touch **VPN**. The VPN screen appears, as shown in **Figure 6**.
4. Touch **Add VPN Configuration**. The Add Configuration screen appears, as shown in **Figure 7**.
5. Touch each field and enter the required information. Touch **Save** at the top of the screen when you are finished. The VPN is set up.

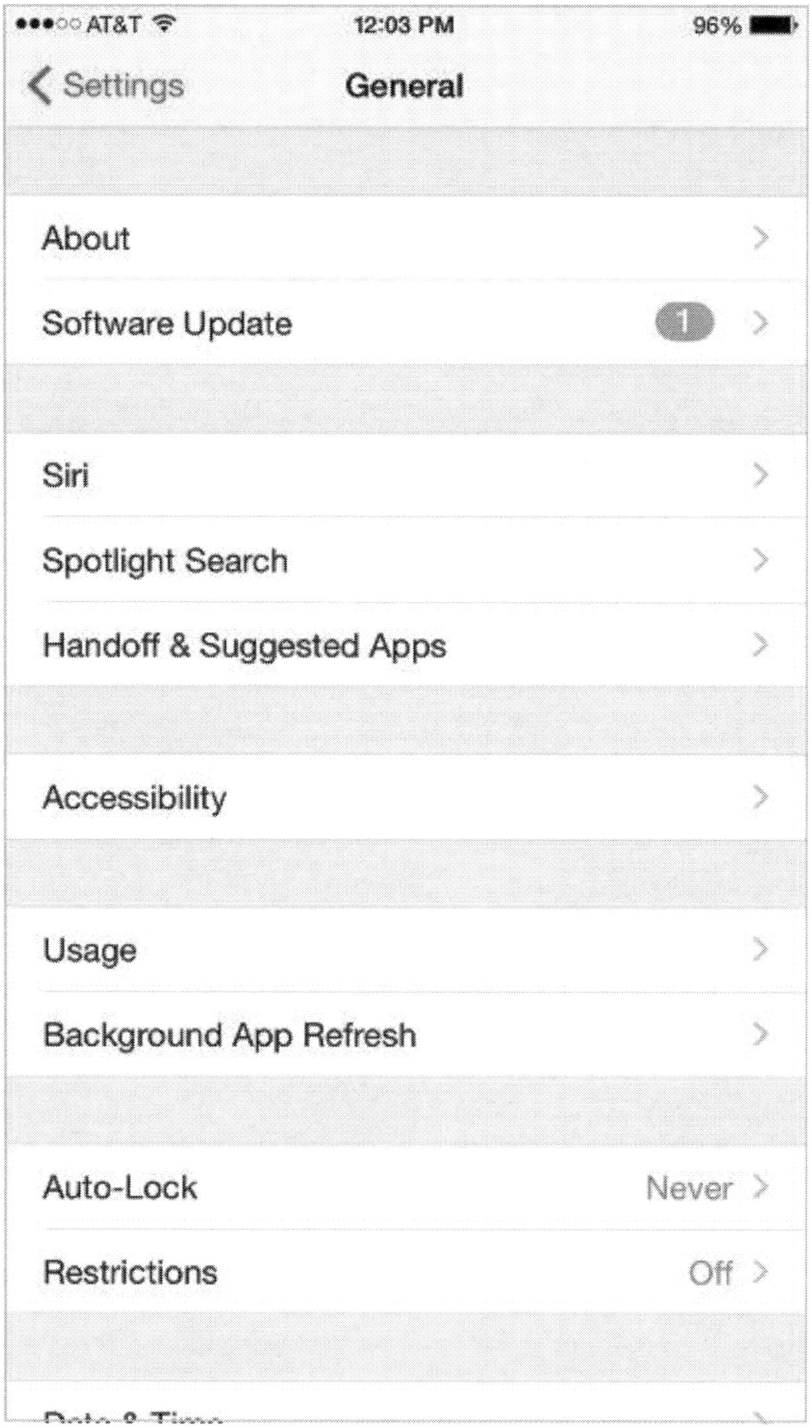

●●●○○ AT&T 🛜　　　　12:03 PM　　　　96% ▬▬▬▷

❮ Settings　　　**General**

About　　　　　　　　　　　　　　　　>

Software Update　　　　　　　**1**　>

Siri　　　　　　　　　　　　　　　　>

Spotlight Search　　　　　　　　　　>

Handoff & Suggested Apps　　　　　>

Accessibility　　　　　　　　　　　　>

Usage　　　　　　　　　　　　　　　>

Background App Refresh　　　　　　　>

Auto-Lock　　　　　　　　　Never　>

Restrictions　　　　　　　　　Off　>

Figure 5: General Settings Screen

Figure 6: VPN Screen

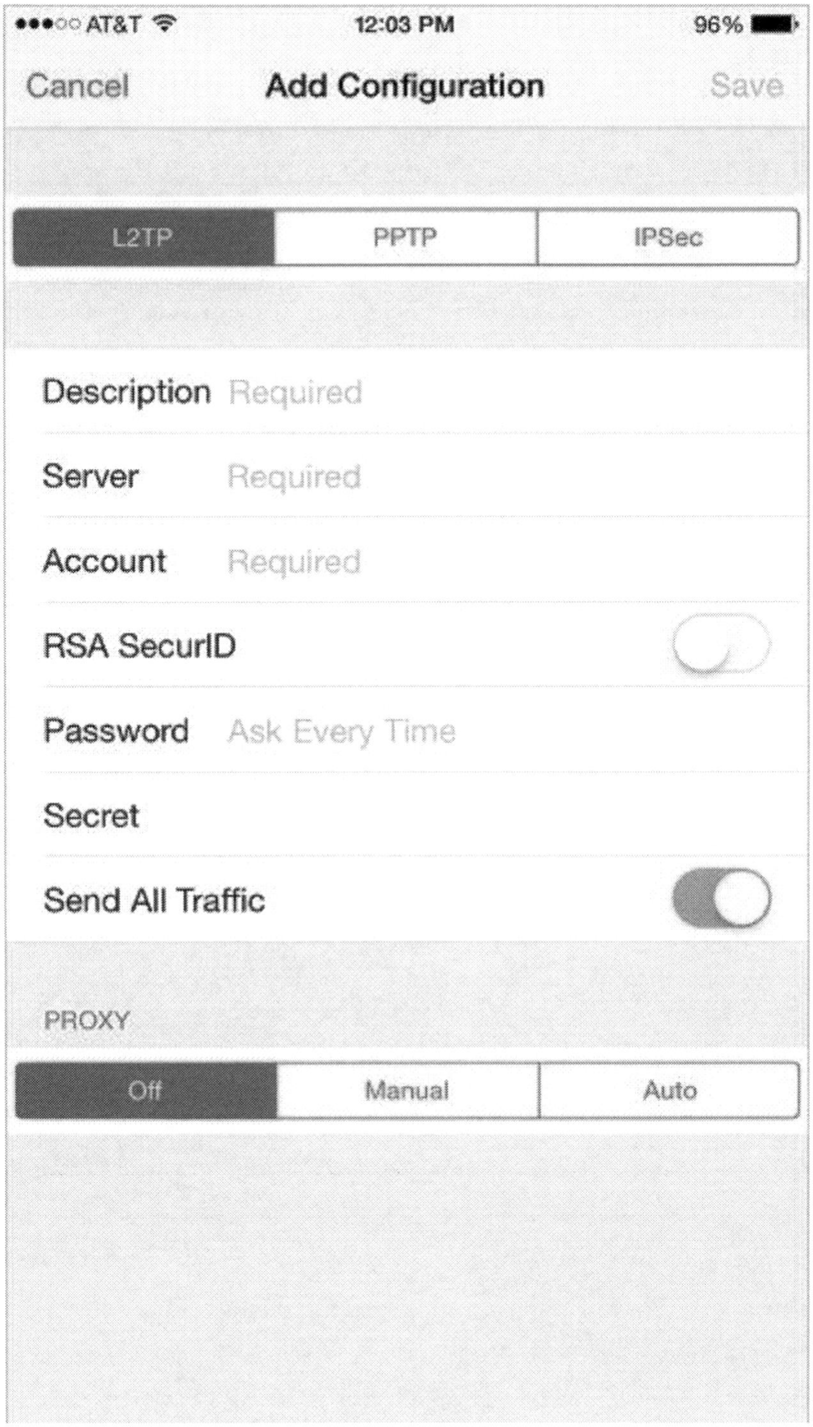

●●●○○ AT&T 📶   12:03 PM   96% ▬▶

Cancel   **Add Configuration**   Save

| L2TP | PPTP | IPSec |

Description   Required

Server   Required

Account   Required

RSA SecurID

Password   Ask Every Time

Secret

Send All Traffic

PROXY

| Off | Manual | Auto |

Figure 7: Add Configuration Screen

6. Turning Bluetooth On or Off

A wireless Bluetooth headset can be used with the phone. Be aware that leaving Bluetooth turned on while the headset is not in use eats up a lot of battery life. To turn Bluetooth on or off:

1. Touch the ⚙ icon. The Settings screen appears.
2. Touch **Bluetooth**. The Bluetooth Settings screen appears, as shown in **Figure 8**.
3. Touch the ⬭ switch next to 'Bluetooth'. Bluetooth is turned on and a list of devices appears. If there are no Bluetooth devices near the phone, the list will be empty.
4. Touch the ⬭ switch next to 'Bluetooth'. Bluetooth is turned off.

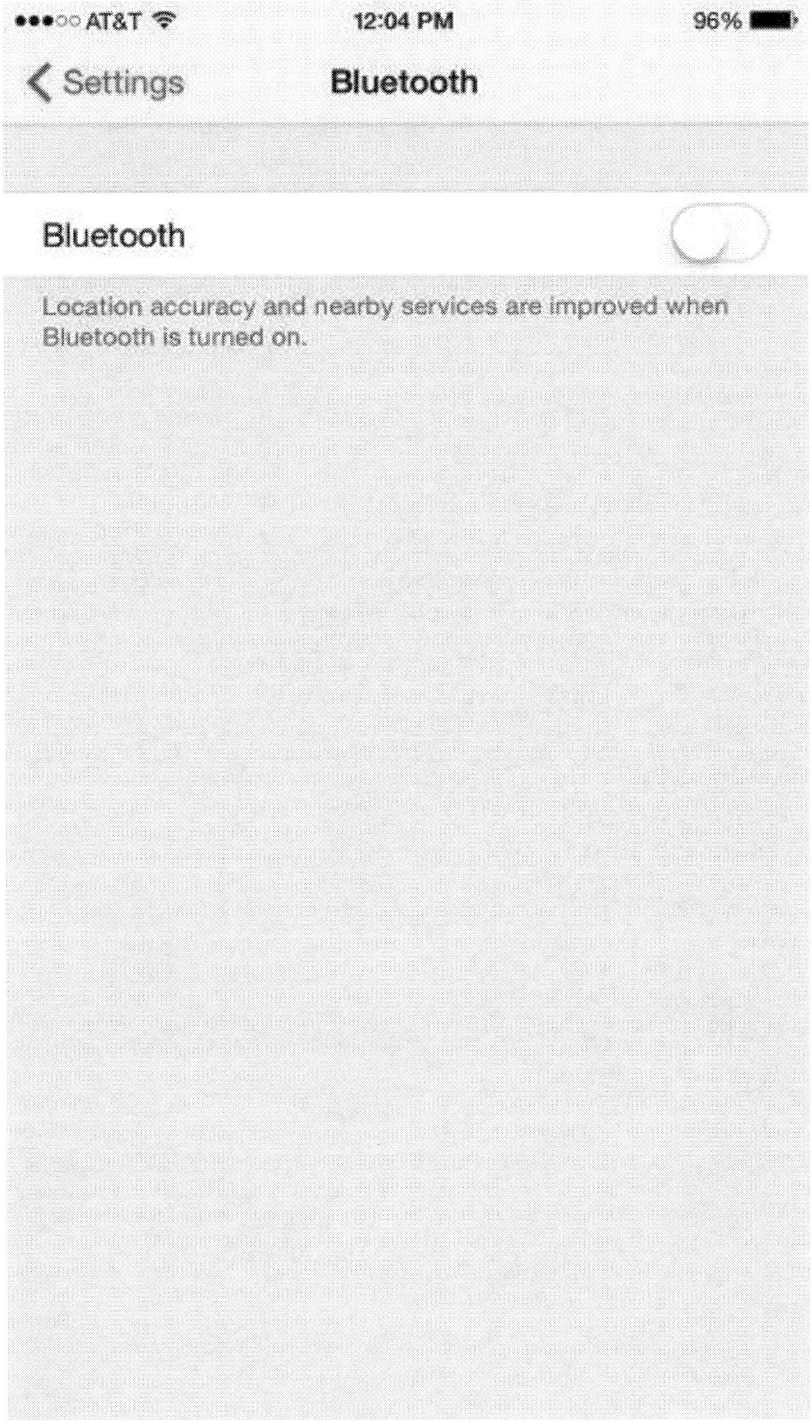

Figure 8: Bluetooth Settings Screen

7. Using Wi-Fi to Sync Your Phone with Your Computer

Syncing your phone with your computer allows you save your media library on your computer in case you have to erase your phone, or if you buy a new phone. Instead of connecting your phone to your computer to sync music, applications, and other media, you may sync wirelessly using Wi-Fi. Before you can use this feature, you must turn it on using iTunes on your computer. Refer to **https://www.apple.com/support/itunes/** if you need help using iTunes. To use Wi-Fi to sync your phone with your computer:

Note: You may only use Wi-Fi syncing when your phone is plugged in to an outlet, and Wi-Fi is turned on.

1. Connect your phone to your computer using the cable that was provided when you purchased it. On some computers, iTunes opens automatically. If it does not, open iTunes.
2. Click the name of the phone at the top or left side of the screen, depending on the version of iTunes. The iPhone information screen appears, as shown in **Figure 9**. You may need to first click **Continue**, and then click **Get Started** before this screen appears.
3. Click **Sync with this iPhone over Wi-Fi**. A check mark appears next to 'Sync with this iPhone over Wi-Fi'.
4. Click **Apply**. The Wi-Fi Sync feature is turned on.
5. Disconnect your phone from your computer, and plug it into an outlet, as if you are charging it. Your phone should automatically Sync with your computer. If it does not sync, follow steps 6-9 below.

6. Touch the icon. The Settings screen appears.
7. Touch **General**. The General Settings screen appears.
8. Scroll down and touch **iTunes Wi-Fi Sync**. The iTunes Wi-Fi Sync screen appears.
9. Touch **Sync Now**. Your phone syncs with your computer.

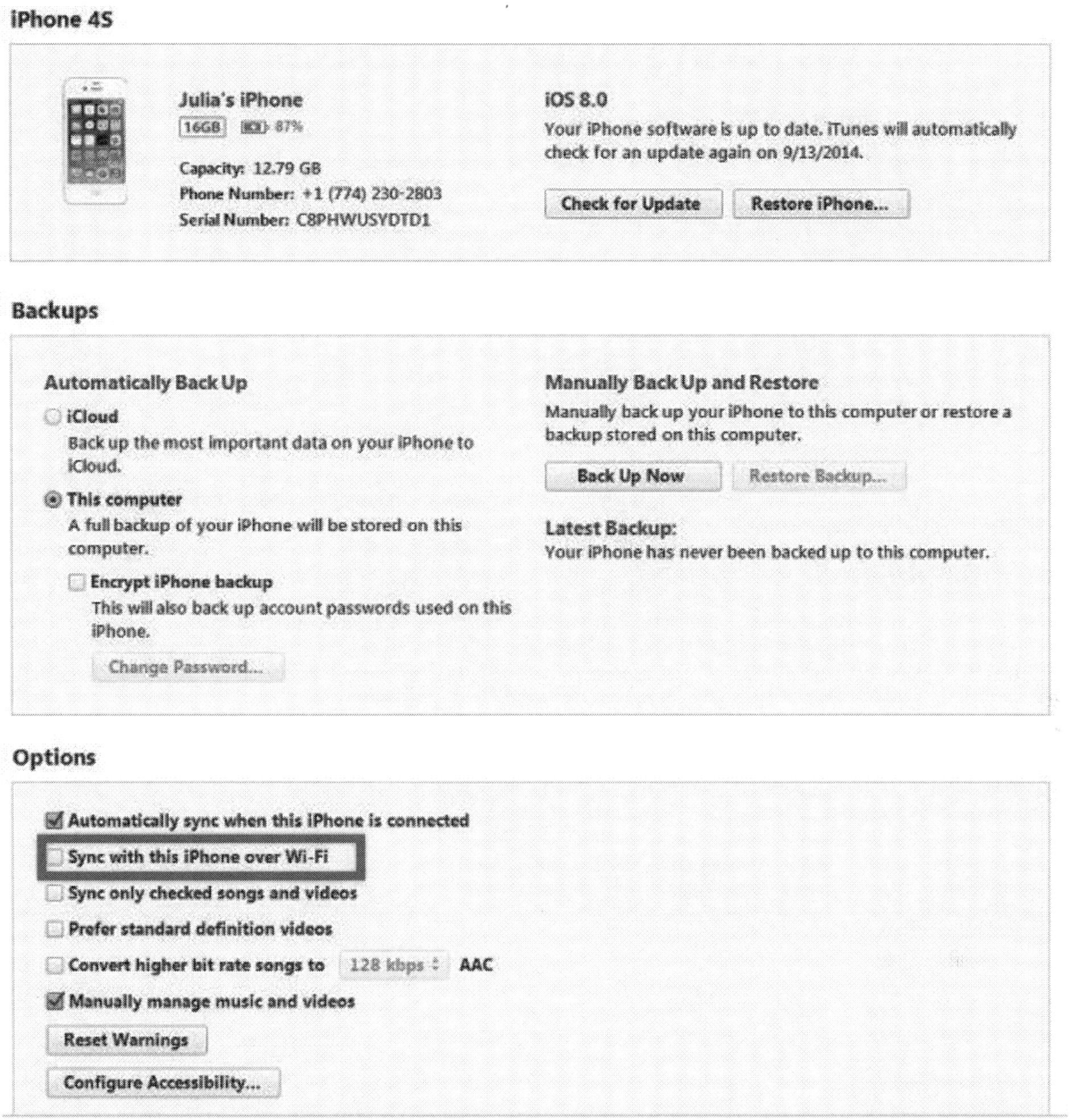

iPhone 4S

Julia's iPhone
[16GB] [XX] 87%

Capacity: 12.79 GB
Phone Number: +1 (774) 230-2803
Serial Number: C8PHWUSYDTD1

iOS 8.0

Your iPhone software is up to date. iTunes will automatically check for an update again on 9/13/2014.

[Check for Update] [Restore iPhone...]

Backups

Automatically Back Up

○ iCloud
Back up the most important data on your iPhone to iCloud.

◉ This computer
A full backup of your iPhone will be stored on this computer.

☐ Encrypt iPhone backup
This will also back up account passwords used on this iPhone.

[Change Password...]

Manually Back Up and Restore

Manually back up your iPhone to this computer or restore a backup stored on this computer.

[Back Up Now] [Restore Backup...]

Latest Backup:
Your iPhone has never been backed up to this computer.

Options

☑ Automatically sync when this iPhone is connected
☐ Sync with this iPhone over Wi-Fi
☐ Sync only checked songs and videos
☐ Prefer standard definition videos
☐ Convert higher bit rate songs to [128 kbps ÷] AAC
☑ Manually manage music and videos

[Reset Warnings]

[Configure Accessibility...]

Figure 9: iPhone Information Screen

Adjusting Sound Settings

Table of Contents

1. Turning Vibration On or Off

The phone can be set to vibrate every time it rings, or only while it is in Silent Mode.
To turn Ringer Vibration on or off:

1. Touch the ⊚ icon. The Settings screen appears, as shown in **Figure 1**.
2. Touch **Sounds**. The Sound Settings screen appears, as shown in **Figure 2**.

3. Touch the ⬭ switch next to 'Vibrate on Ring' under the 'Vibrate' section. The ⬭ switch appears and Ringer Vibration is turned on. The phone will vibrate whenever there is an incoming call.

4. Touch the ⬭ switch. Ringer Vibration is turned off and the phone will not vibrate for incoming calls.

To turn Silent Mode vibration on or off:

1. Touch the ⊚ icon. The Settings screen appears.
2. Touch **Sounds**. The Sound Settings screen appears.

3. Touch the ⬭ switch next to 'Vibrate on Silent' under the 'Vibrate' section.

   The ⬭ switch appears and Silent Mode vibration is turned on. The phone will vibrate whenever a call or message is received in Silent Mode.

4. Touch the switch. Silent Mode Vibration is turned off. The phone will not vibrate when it is in Silent Mode.

Note: To turn on Silent Mode on the phone, put the vibration switch in the down position so that a red dot appears beneath the switch. Silent mode is turned on and the *icon appears on the screen. Refer to "Button Layout" on page 10 to view the location of the Vibration switch.*

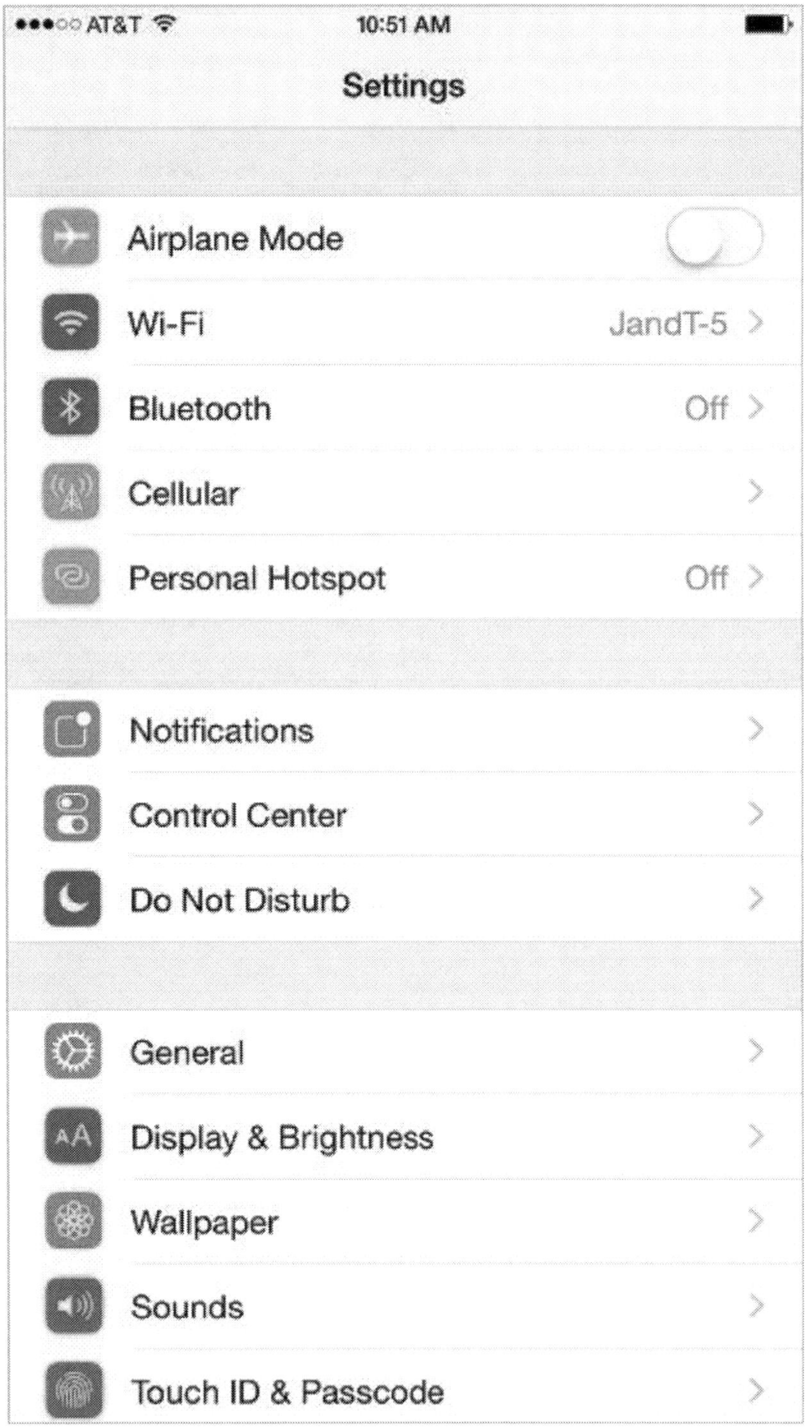

Figure 1: Settings Screen

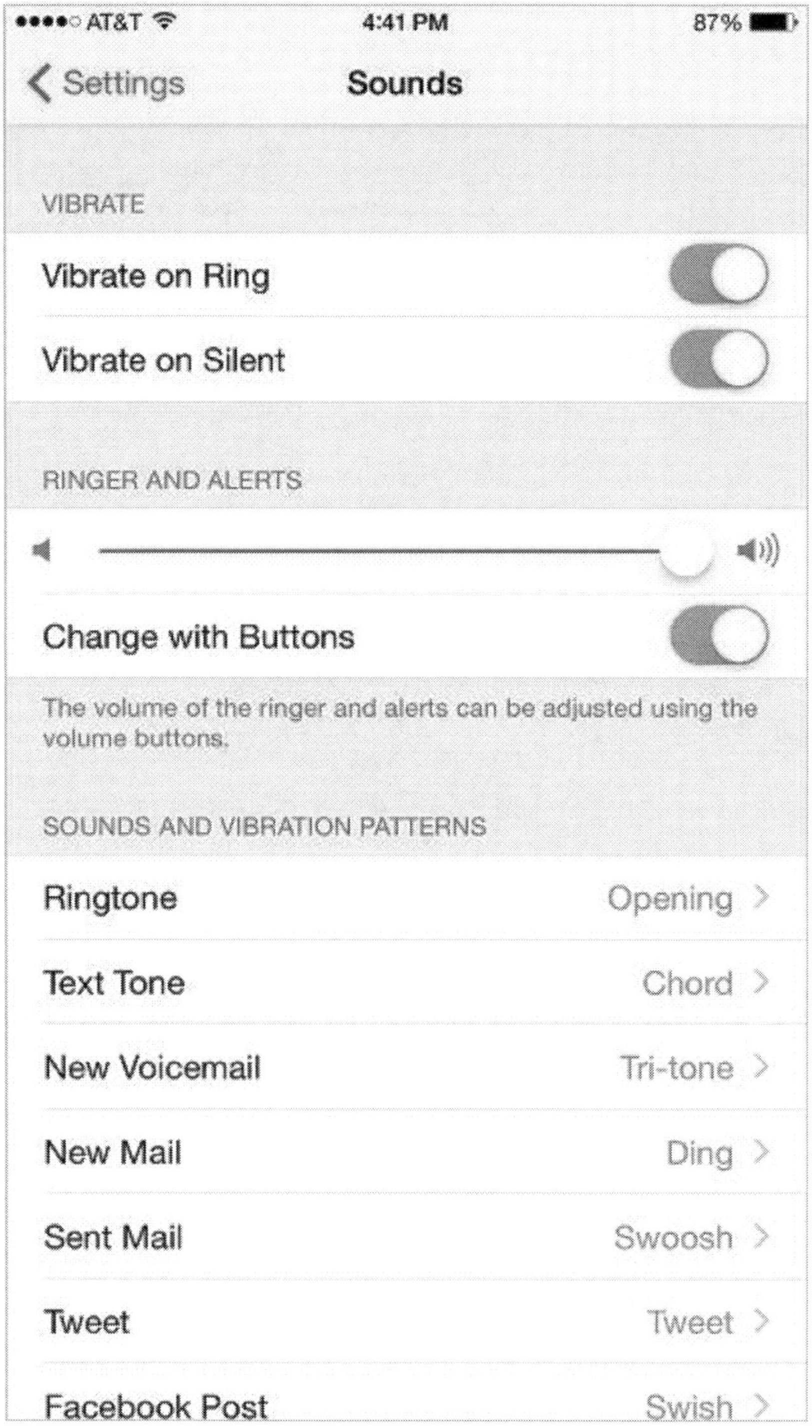

Figure 2: Sound Settings Screen

2. Turning Volume Button Functionality On or Off

The volume buttons can be used to adjust the volume of the media, alerts, and the ringer. When the volume button functionality is disabled, they no longer work. To turn the volume button functionality on or off:

1. Touch the [icon] icon. The Settings screen appears.
2. Scroll down and touch **Sounds**. The Sound Settings screen appears.
3. Touch the [switch] switch next to 'Change with Buttons' under the 'Ringer and Alerts' section. The [switch] switch appears and volume button functionality is turned off.
4. Touch the [switch] switch next to 'Change with Buttons'. The [switch] switch appears and the volume button functionality is turned on.

3. Setting the Default Ringtone

You may change the ringtone that sounds every time somebody calls you. To set a default ringtone:

1. Touch the [icon] icon. The Settings screen appears.
2. Touch **Sounds**. The Sound Settings screen appears.
3. Touch **Ringtone** under the 'Sounds and Vibration Patterns' section. A list of ringtones appears, as shown in **Figure 3**
4. Touch a ringtone. The new default ringtone is selected and a preview plays.
5. Touch **Sounds** at the top of the screen. The new ringtone is set as the default.

*Note: You can also touch **Store** at the top of the screen to purchase more ringtones.*

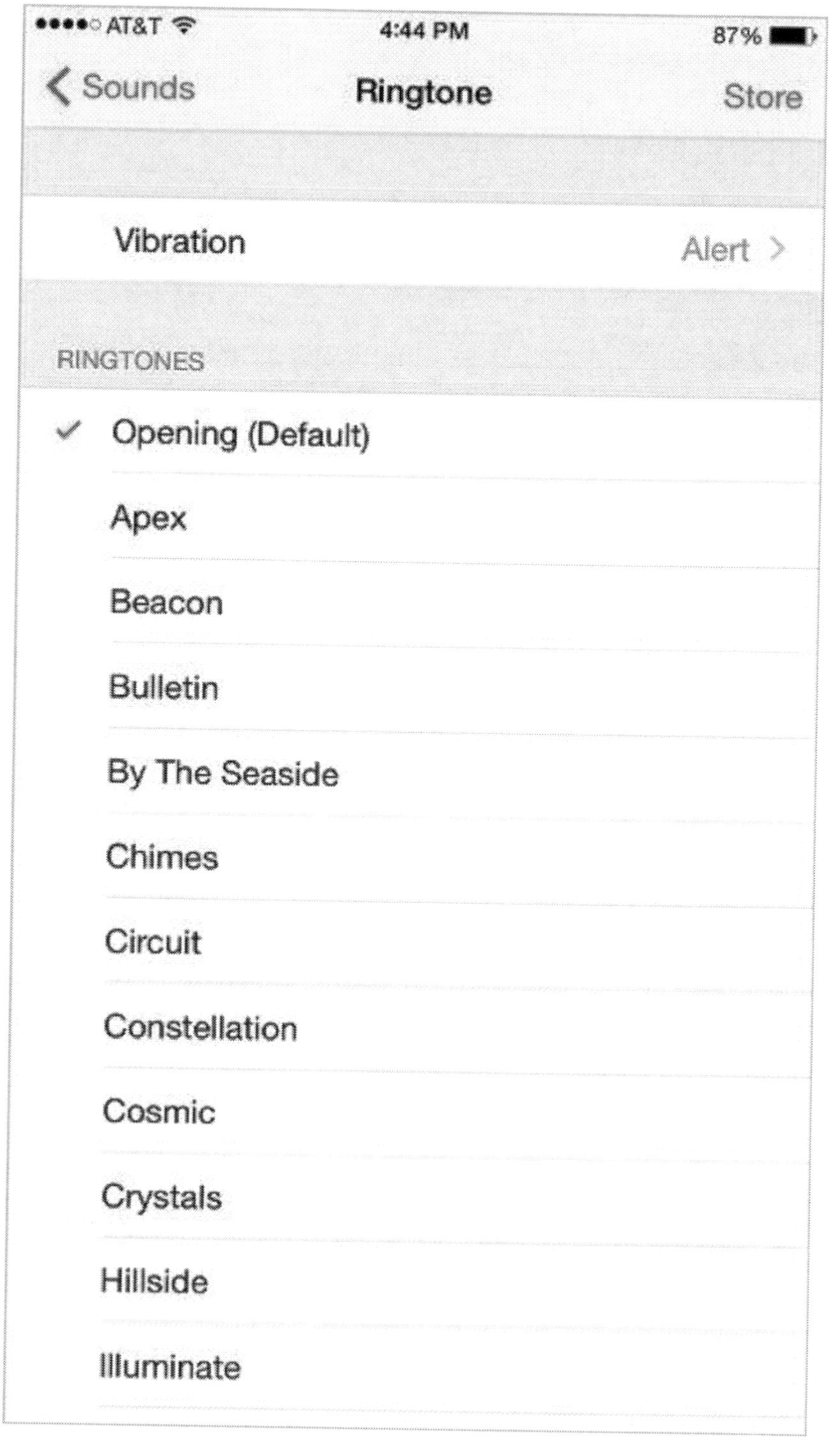

Figure 3: List of Ringtones

4. Customizing Notification and Alert Sounds

There are several notification and alert sounds that can be changed on the phone. To customize notification and alert sounds:

1. Touch the icon. The Settings screen appears.
2. Touch **Sounds**. The Sound Settings screen appears.
3. Touch one of the following options under the 'Sounds and Vibration Patterns' section to change the corresponding sound:

   - **Text Tone** - Plays when a new text message arrives.
   - **New Voicemail** - Plays when a new voicemail arrives .
   - **New Mail** - Plays when a new email arrives.
   - **Sent Mail** - Plays when an email is sent from the phone.
   - **Tweet** - Plays when a new Tweet arrives.
   - **Facebook Post** - Plays when one of your Facebook friends creates a new post.
   - **Calendar Alerts** - Plays as a reminder for a calendar event.
   - **Reminder Alerts** - Plays as a notification of a previously set reminder.

5. Turning Lock Sounds On or Off

The phone can make a sound every time it is locked or unlocked. By default, this sound is turned on. To turn Lock Sounds on or off:

1. Touch the icon. The Settings screen appears.
2. Touch **Sounds**. The Sound Settings screen appears.
3. Scroll down and touch the switch next to 'Lock Sounds'. The switch appears and lock sounds are turned off.
4. Touch the switch next to 'Lock Sounds'. The switch appears and lock sounds are turned on.

6. Turning Keyboard Clicks On or Off

The phone can make a sound every time a key is touched on the virtual keyboard. By default, keyboard clicks are turned on. To turn Keyboard Clicks on or off:

1. Touch the icon. The Settings screen appears.
2. Touch **Sounds**. The Sound Settings screen appears.
3. Touch the switch next to 'Keyboard Clicks'. The switch appears and Keyboard Clicks are turned off.
4. Touch the switch next to 'Keyboard Clicks'. The switch appears and Keyboard Clicks are turned on.

Adjusting Language and Keyboard Settings

Table of Contents

1. Customizing Spelling and Grammar Settings

Customize the Spelling and Grammar settings on your phone to improve typing accuracy when composing text messages or emails. To customize the Spelling and Grammar settings:

1. Touch the icon. The Settings screen appears, as shown in **Figure 1**.
2. Touch **General**. The General Settings screen appears, as shown in **Figure 2**.
3. Scroll down and touch **Keyboard**. The Keyboard Settings screen appears, as shown in **Figure 3**.
4. Touch one of the switches on the right side of the screen to turn the corresponding setting on or off:

- **Auto-Capitalization** - Capitalizes the first word of every sentence automatically.
- **Auto-Correction** - Suggests and makes spelling corrections while you type.
- **Check Spelling** - Underlines all misspelled words.

- **Enable Caps Lock** - Allows you to turn Caps Lock on by quickly touching the key twice on the virtual keyboard. While Caps Lock is turned on, all capital letters are typed without the need to use the key.
- **Predictive** - The Predictive Text feature offers suggestions for the next word in a sentence as you type, which is intelligently based on the words that you have already typed.
- **."" Shortcut** - Allows a period and an extra space to be inserted when you quickly touch the space bar twice.

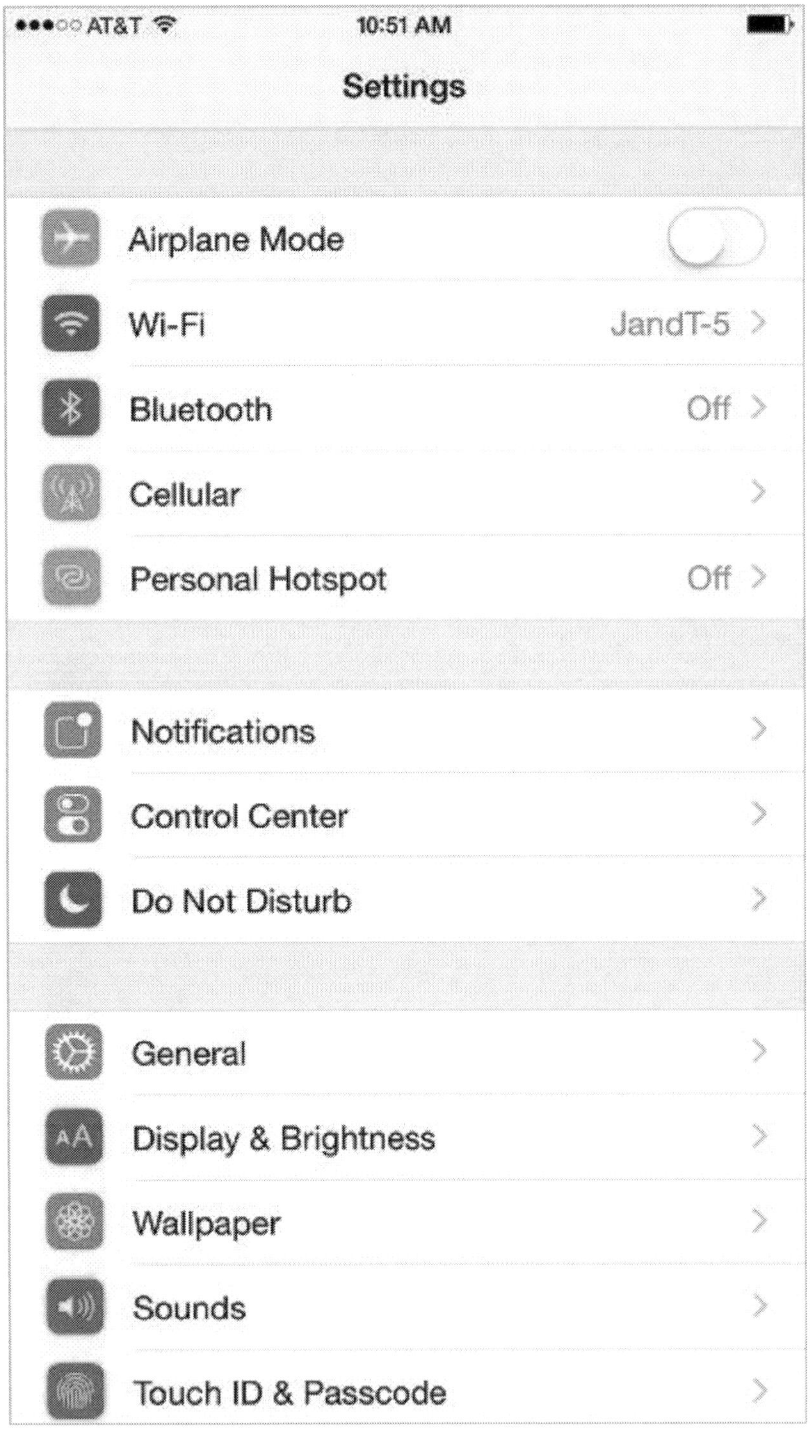

Figure 1: Settings Screen

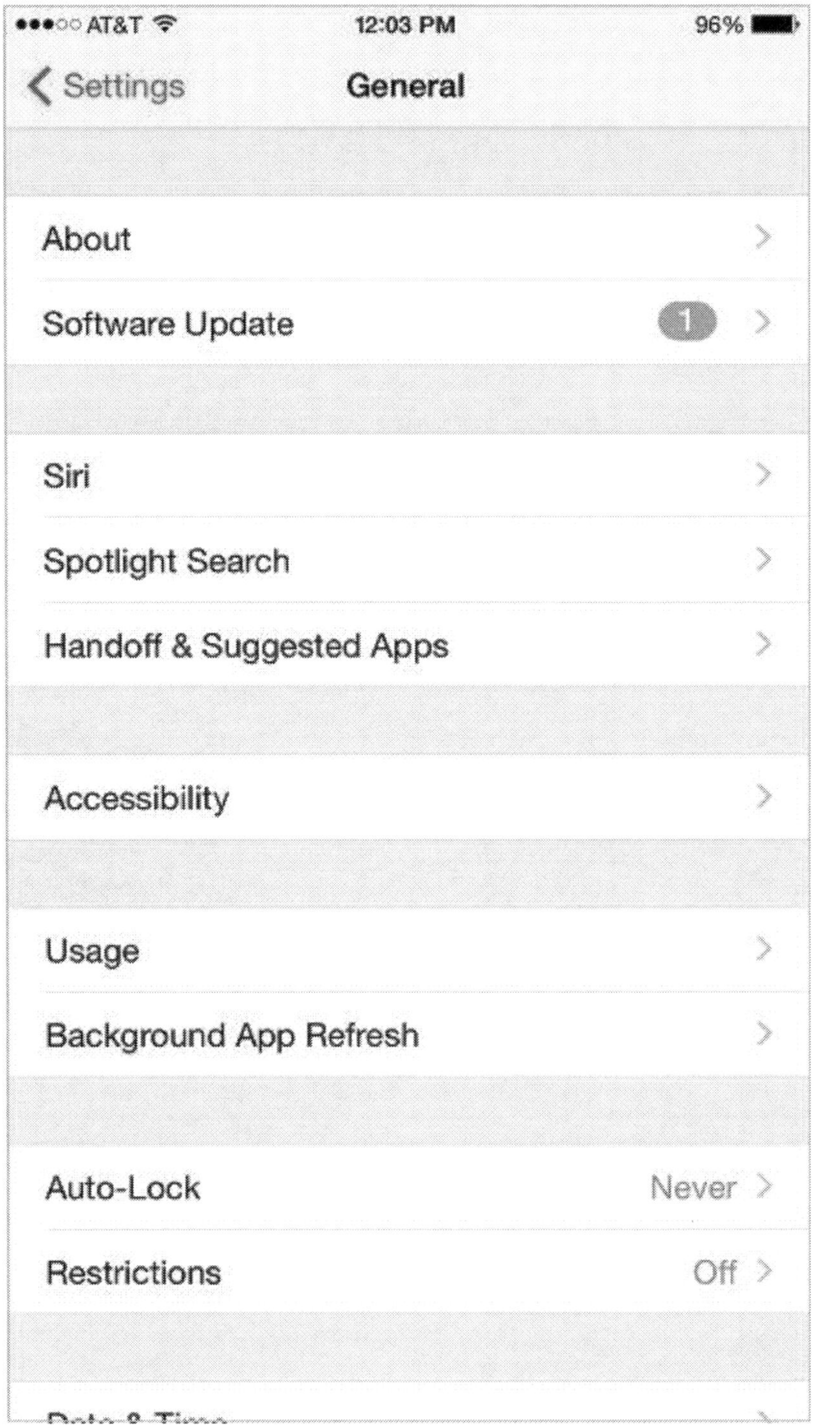

●●●○○ AT&T 📶   12:03 PM   96% 🔋

‹ Settings   General

About   ›

Software Update   ❶ ›

Siri   ›

Spotlight Search   ›

Handoff & Suggested Apps   ›

Accessibility   ›

Usage   ›

Background App Refresh   ›

Auto-Lock   Never ›

Restrictions   Off ›

Date & Time   ›

Figure 2: General Settings Screen

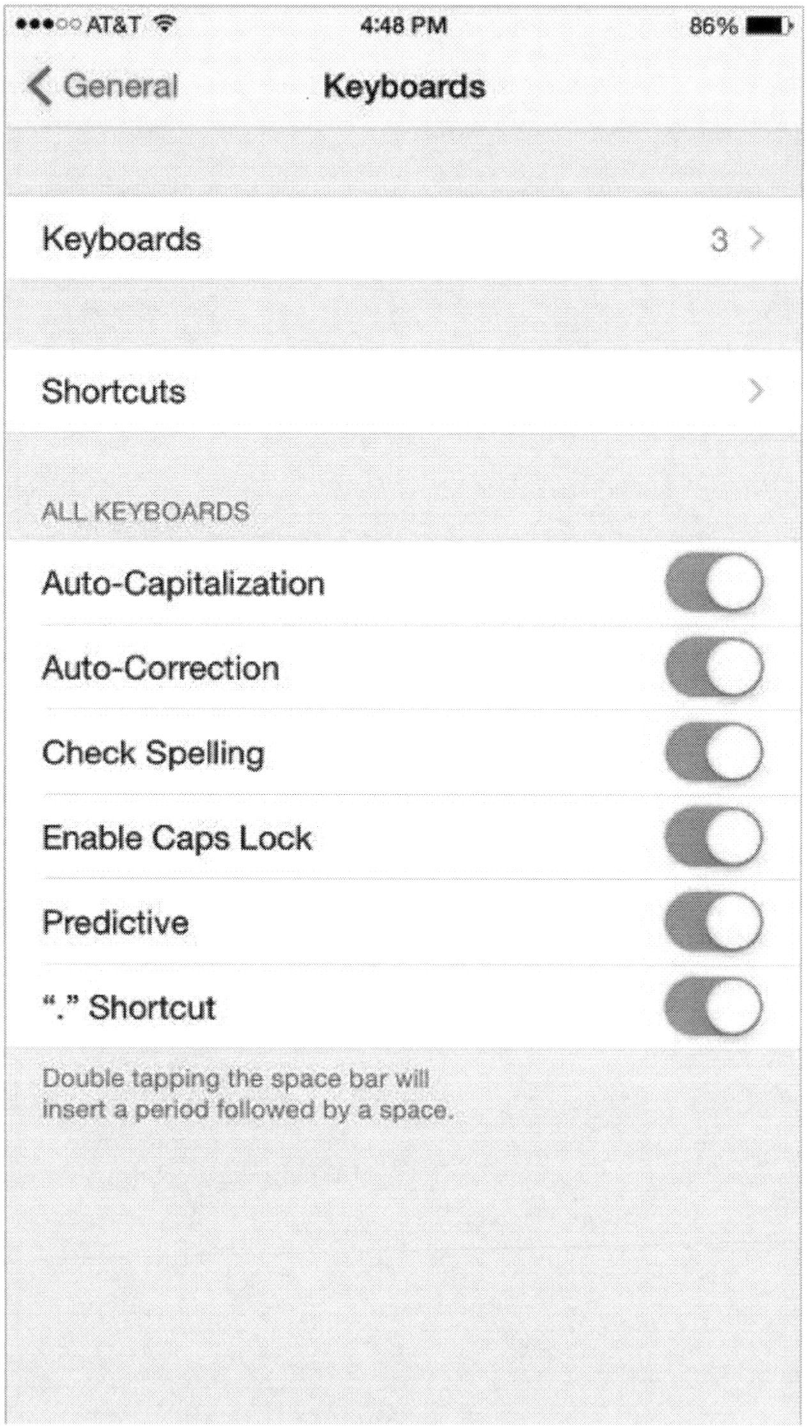

●●●○○ AT&T 📶   4:48 PM   86% ■■▶

< General   **Keyboards**

Keyboards   3 >

Shortcuts   >

ALL KEYBOARDS

Auto-Capitalization

Auto-Correction

Check Spelling

Enable Caps Lock

Predictive

"." Shortcut

Double tapping the space bar will insert a period followed by a space.

Figure 3: Keyboard Settings Screen

2. Adding an International Keyboard

The phone allows you to use international keyboards when entering text on the virtual keyboard. To add an international keyboard:

1. Touch the icon. The Settings screen appears.
2. Touch **General**. The General Settings screen appears.
3. Scroll down and touch **Keyboard**. The Keyboard Settings screen appears.
4. Touch **Keyboards**. The Keyboards screen appears, as shown in **Figure 4**.
5. Touch **Add New Keyboard**. A list of international keyboards appears, as shown in **Figure 5**.
6. Touch a keyboard. The keyboard is added. While typing, touch the ⊕ key at the bottom of the virtual keyboard to switch to an international one.
7. You may remove a keyboard from the list by touching and holding it, and then sliding your finger to the left until 'Delete' appears. Touch **Delete** to remove the keyboard.

Note: If you only add the Emoji keyboard (emoticons) in addition to the English keyboard, the ☺

key appears instead of the ⊕ *key.*

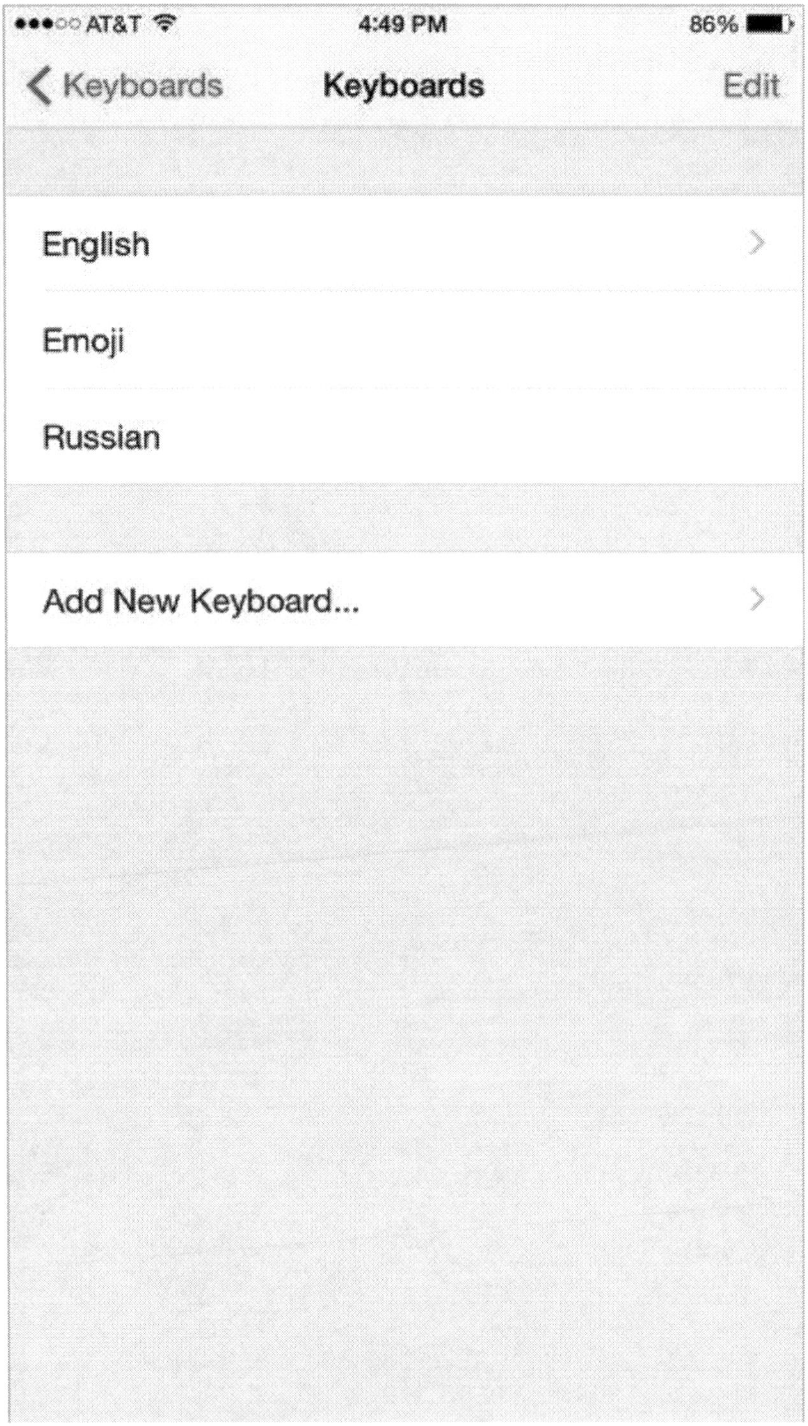

●●●○○ AT&T 🔆   4:49 PM   86% ▬▭▷

❮ Keyboards   **Keyboards**   Edit

English   ❯

Emoji

Russian

Add New Keyboard...   ❯

Figure 4: Keyboards Screen

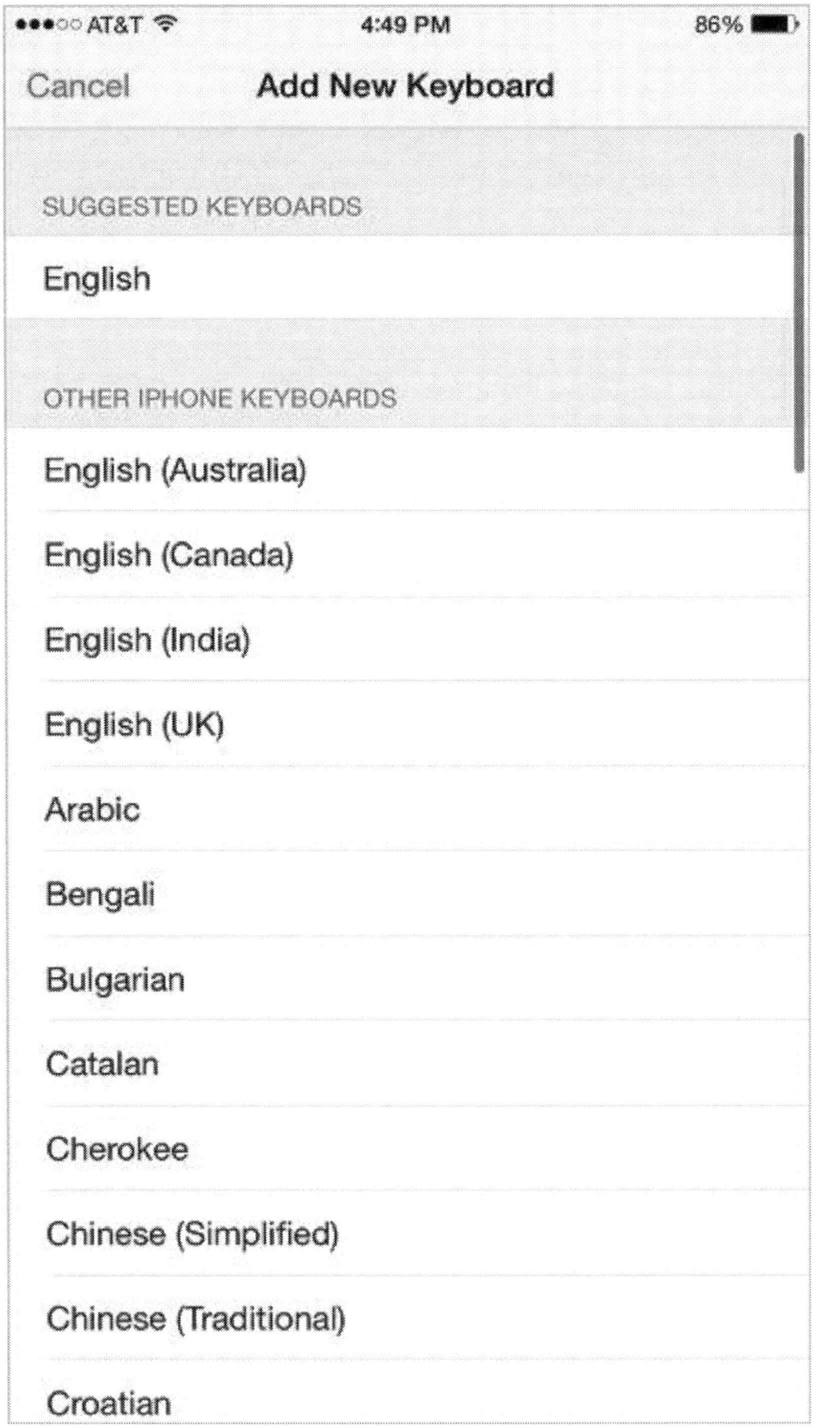

●●●○○ AT&T 🛜   4:49 PM   86% 🔋

Cancel   **Add New Keyboard**

SUGGESTED KEYBOARDS

English

OTHER IPHONE KEYBOARDS

English (Australia)

English (Canada)

English (India)

English (UK)

Arabic

Bengali

Bulgarian

Catalan

Cherokee

Chinese (Simplified)

Chinese (Traditional)

Croatian

Figure 5: List of International Keyboards

3. Adding a Keyboard Shortcut

The phone allows you to add custom Keyboard shortcuts. For example, "ur" for "your" or "ttyl" for "talk to you later" are substituted when the corresponding abbreviation is typed. To add a Keyboard shortcut:

1. Touch the ⊚ icon. The Settings screen appears.
2. Touch **General**. The General Settings screen appears.
3. Scroll down and touch **Keyboard**. The Keyboard Settings screen appears.
4. Touch **Shortcuts**. A list of existing shortcuts appears, as shown in **Figure 6**.
5. Touch the ✛ button in the upper right-hand corner of the screen. The Add Shortcut screen appears, as shown in **Figure 7**.
6. Enter the desired phrase to be substituted for the shortcut. Touch **return**.
7. Enter the desired shortcut and touch **Save** at the top of the screen. The keyboard shortcut is added. To use the shortcut, type it and touch the space bar.

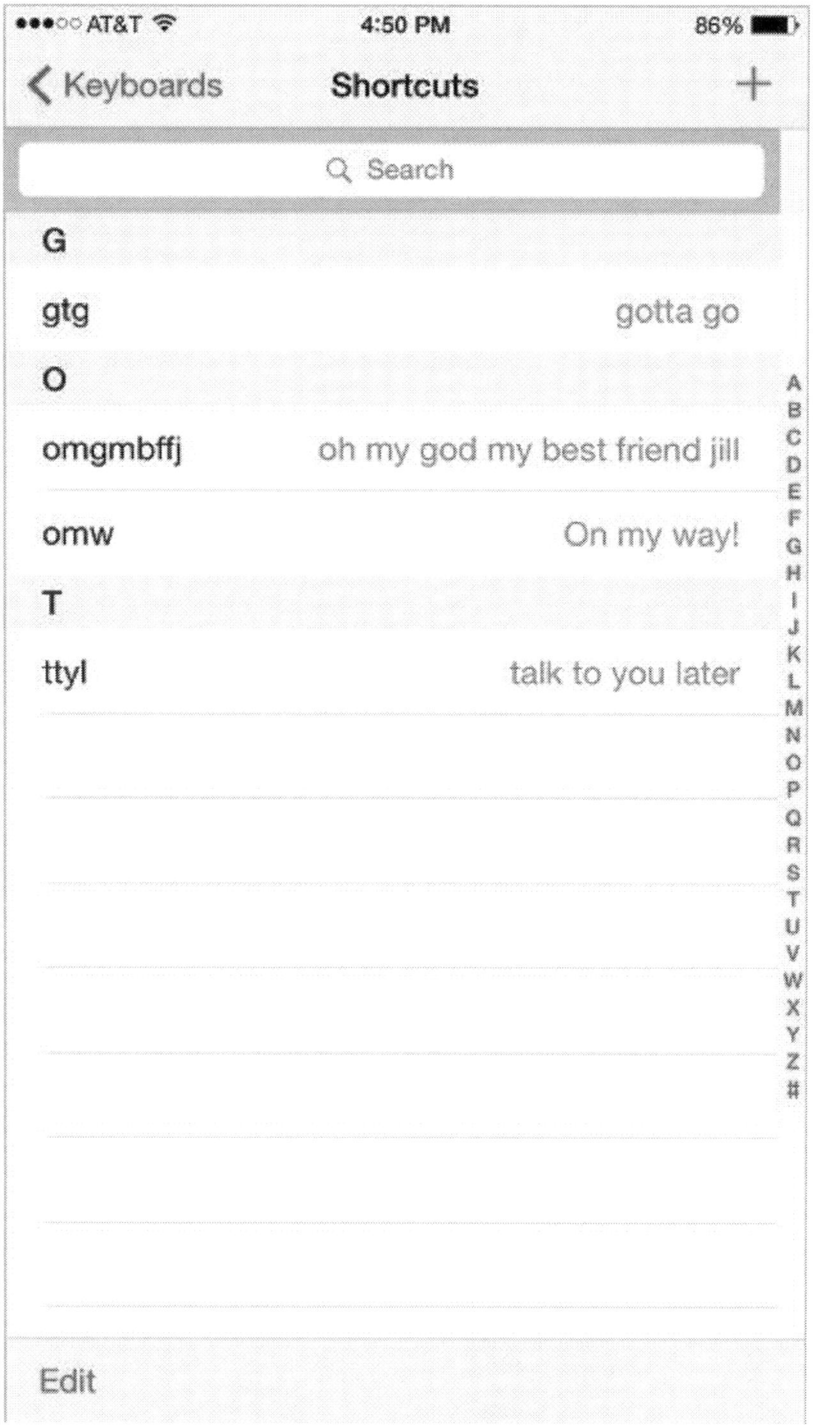

Figure 6: List of Existing Shortcuts

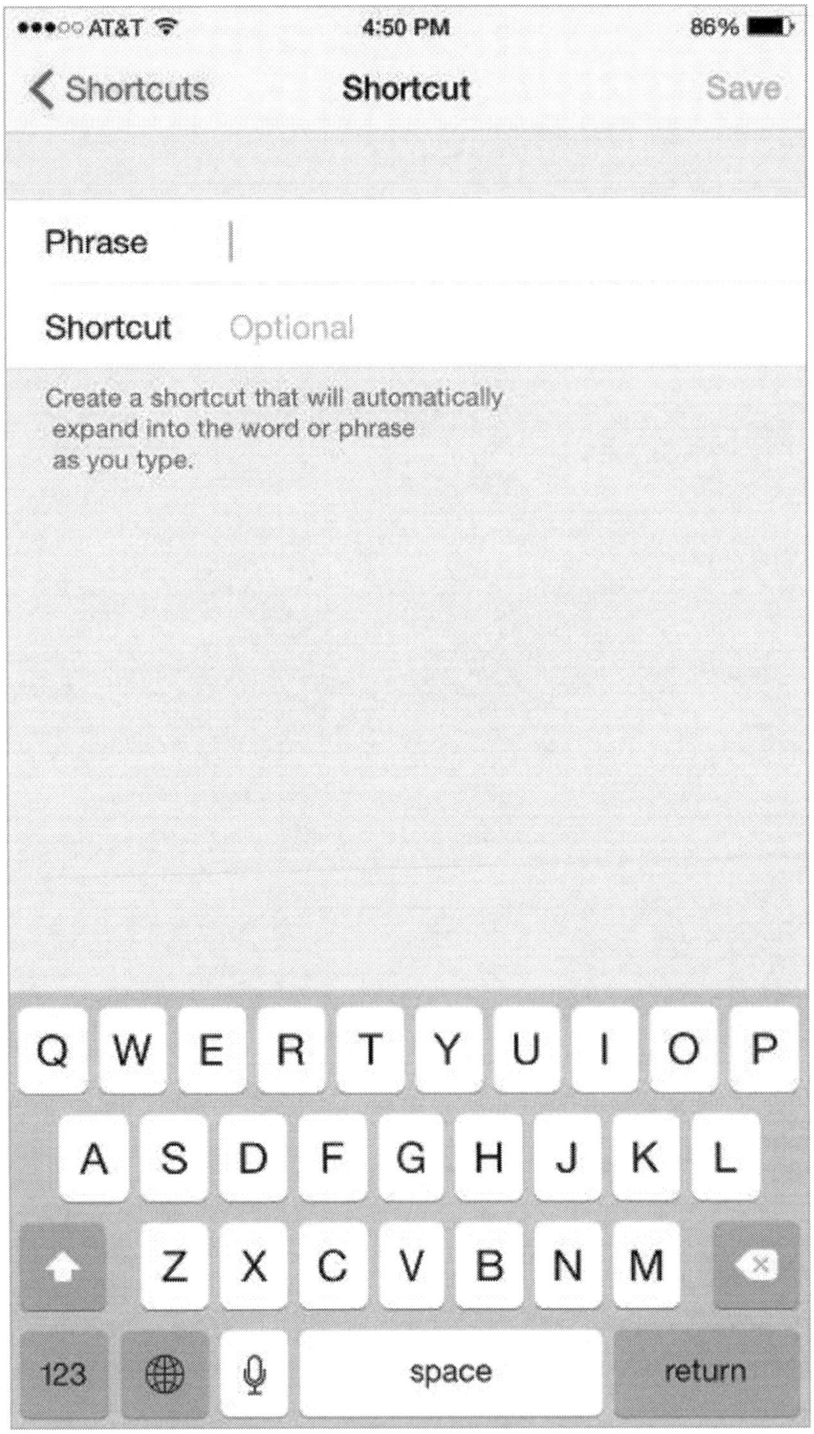

●●●○○ AT&T 🛜   4:50 PM   86% ▇▇▸

‹ Shortcuts   **Shortcut**   Save

Phrase |

Shortcut   Optional

Create a shortcut that will automatically
expand into the word or phrase
as you type.

| Q | W | E | R | T | Y | U | I | O | P |

| A | S | D | F | G | H | J | K | L |

⬆   Z   X   C   V   B   N   M   ⌫

123   🌐   🎤   space   return

Figure 7: Add Shortcut Screen

4. Changing the Operating System Language

The phone can display all menus and options in a language other than English. To change the Operating System Language:

1. Touch the ⊚ icon. The Settings screen appears.
2. Touch **General**. The General Settings screen appears.
3. Scroll down and touch **Language & Region**. The Language & Region screen appears, as shown in **Figure 8**.
4. Touch **iPhone Language**. A list of available languages appears, as shown in **Figure 9**.
5. Touch a language, and then touch **Done** at the top of the screen. A confirmation dialog appears at the bottom of the screen.
6. Touch **Change to LANGUAGE**, where LANGUAGE is the language that you selected in step 5. The selected language is applied and all menus and options reflect the change.

Note: It may take some time to install the language. This delay is normal.

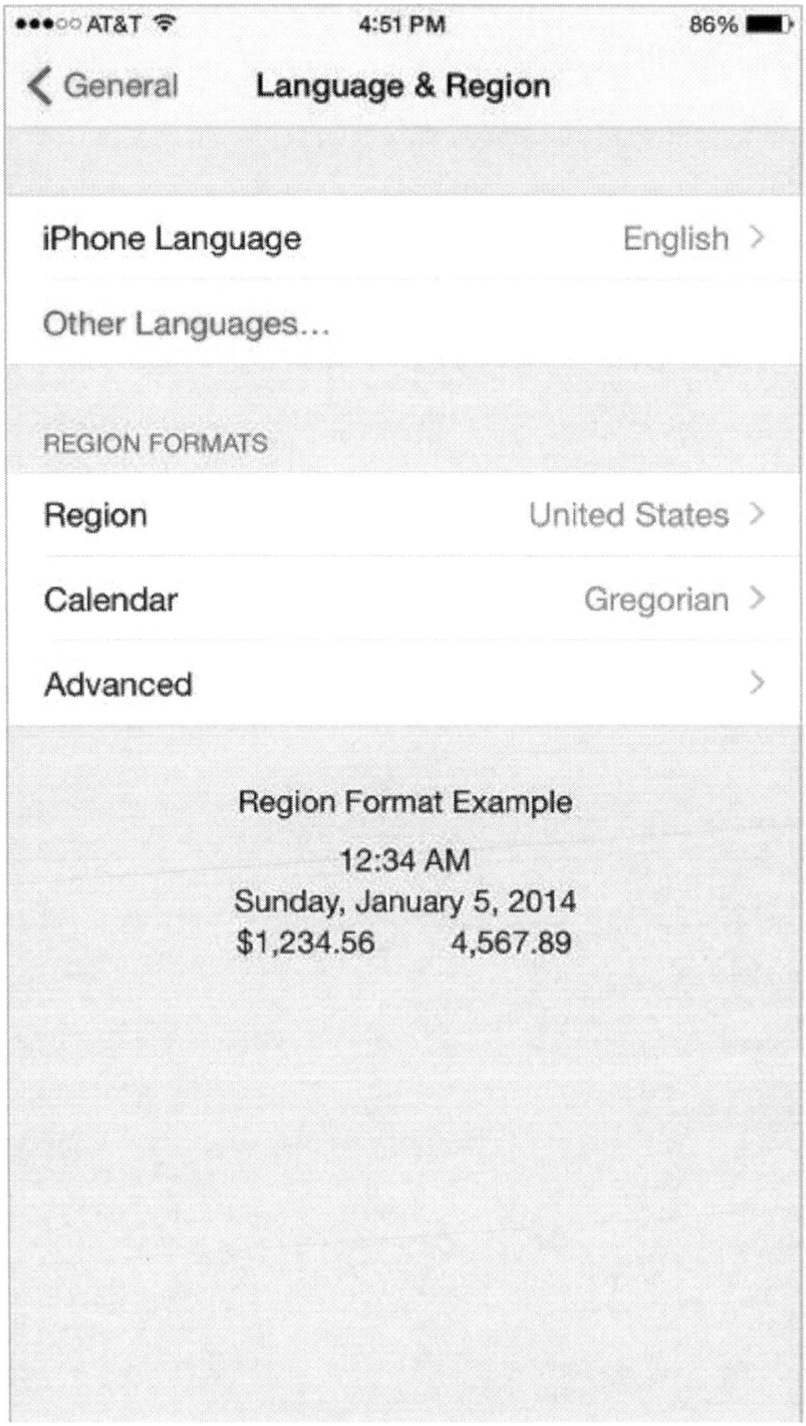

●●●○○ AT&T 📶   4:51 PM   86% 🔋

< General   **Language & Region**

iPhone Language   English >

Other Languages...

REGION FORMATS

Region   United States >

Calendar   Gregorian >

Advanced   >

Region Format Example

12:34 AM
Sunday, January 5, 2014
$1,234.56   4,567.89

Figure 8: Language & Region Screen

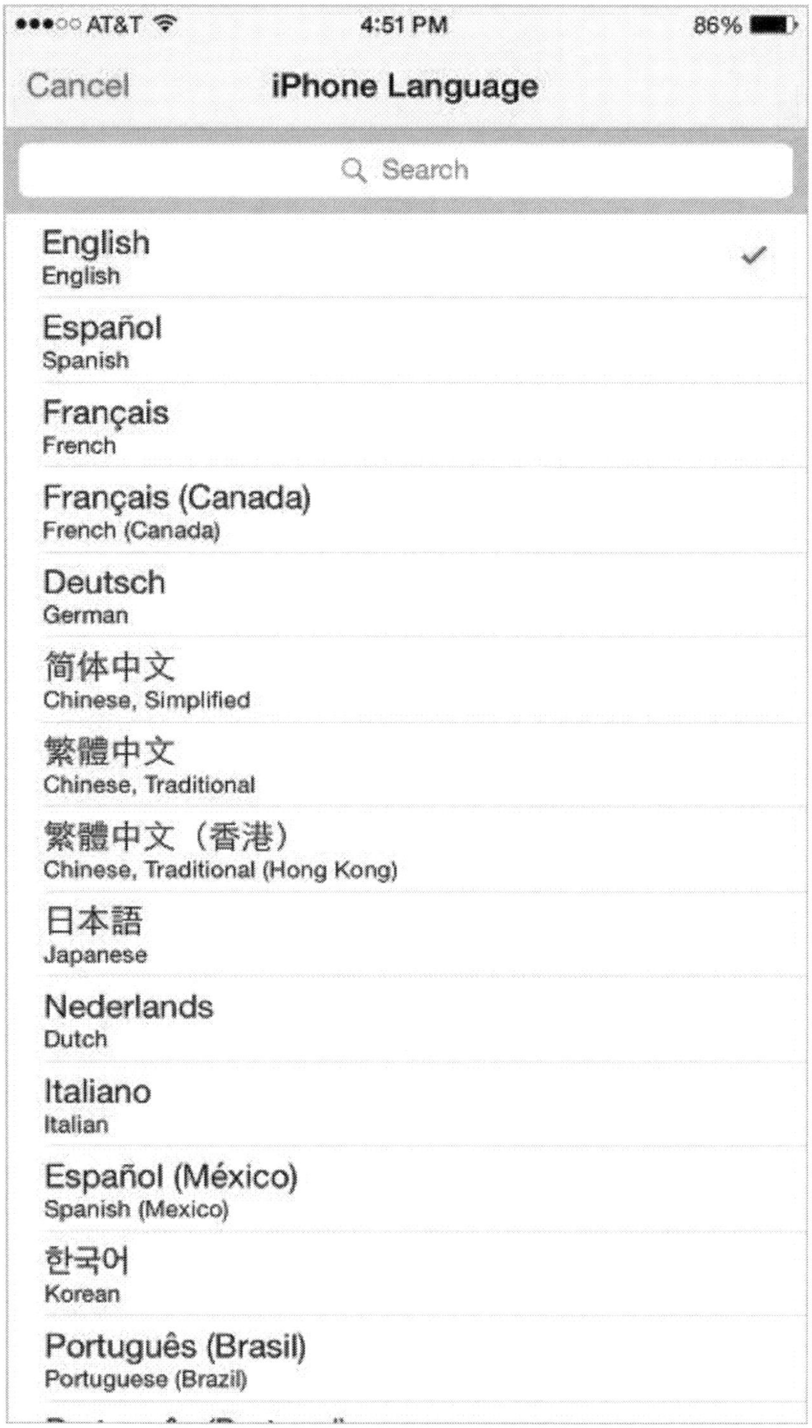

●●●○○ AT&T 📶	4:51 PM	86% 🔋

Cancel   **iPhone Language**

🔍 Search

English
English ✓

Español
Spanish

Français
French

Français (Canada)
French (Canada)

Deutsch
German

简体中文
Chinese, Simplified

繁體中文
Chinese, Traditional

繁體中文（香港）
Chinese, Traditional (Hong Kong)

日本語
Japanese

Nederlands
Dutch

Italiano
Italian

Español (México)
Spanish (Mexico)

한국어
Korean

Português (Brasil)
Portuguese (Brazil)

Figure 9: List of Available Languages

5. Changing the Siri Language

You can change the input language that Siri recognizes, as well as the language that the assistant uses to speak. To change the Siri language:

1. Touch the ⚙ icon. The Settings screen appears.
2. Touch **General**. The General Settings screen appears.
3. Touch **Siri**. The Siri Settings screen appears, as shown in **Figure 10**.
4. Touch **Language**. A list of languages appears.
5. Touch a language. The selected language will be used for Siri.

Note: Press and hold the **Home** *button to activate Siri.*

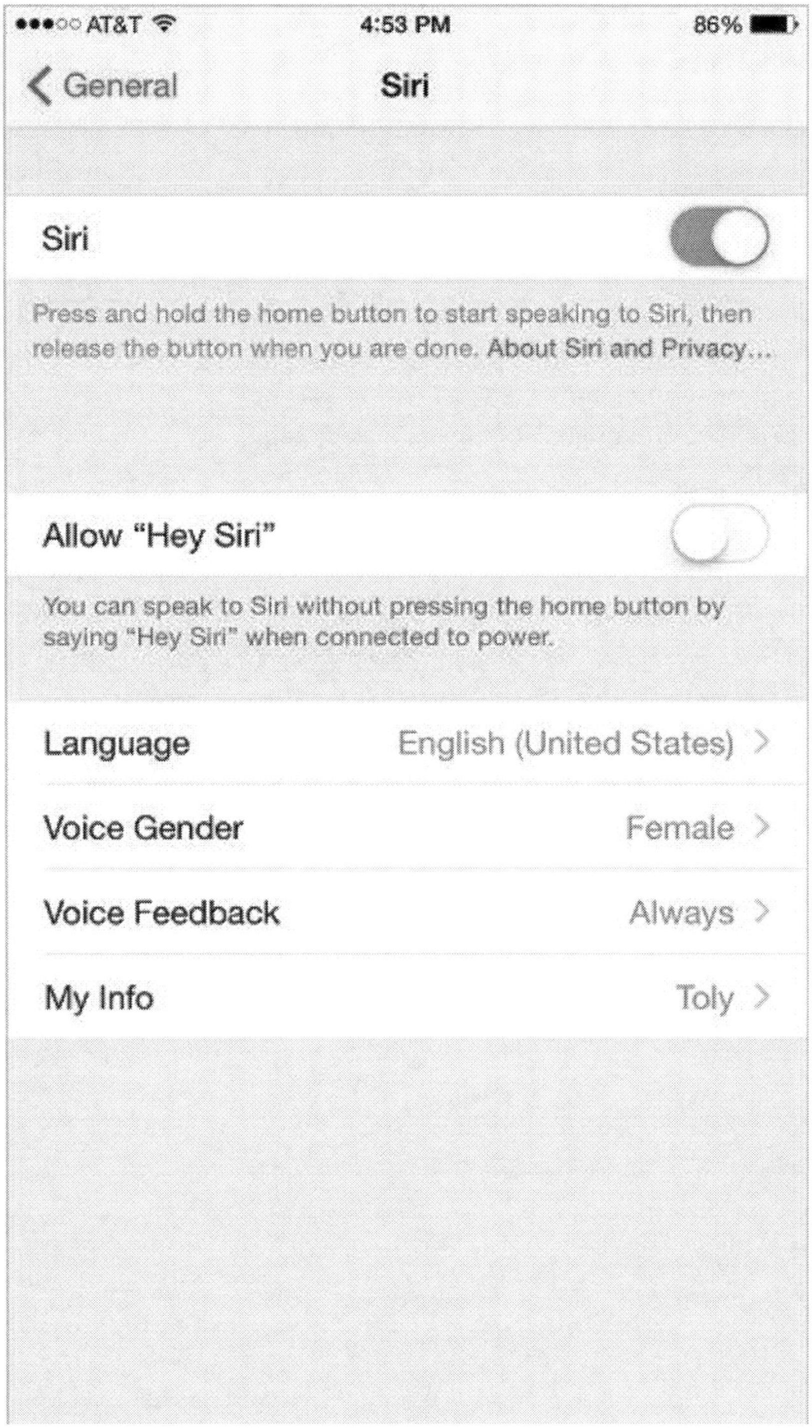

Figure 10: Siri Settings Screen

6. Changing the Keyboard Layout

The layout of the keyboard in most languages can be changed according to personal preference. For instance, the English keyboard can be set display in default QWERTY, as shown in **Figure 11**, AZERTY, as shown in **Figure 12**, or QWERTZ as shown in **Figure 13**. To change the Keyboard Layout:

1. Touch the ⚙ icon. The Settings screen appears.
2. Touch **General**. The General Settings screen appears.
3. Scroll down and touch **Keyboard**. The Keyboard Settings screen appears.
4. Touch **Keyboards**. The Keyboards screen appears.
5. Touch the language of the keyboard that you wish to change. The Keyboard Layout screen appears.
6. Touch the desired layout. The new Keyboard Layout is set.

Note: The English keyboard layouts are shown below only as an example. The keyboard layouts vary based on the language that you select. Refer to "Adding an International Keyboard" on page 265 to learn how to add a keyboard.

Figure 11: QWERTY Keyboard

Figure 12: AZERTY Keyboard

Figure 13: QWERTZ Keyboard

7. Changing the Region Format

The region format on the phone determines how dates, times, and phone numbers are universally displayed. For instance, a European country may display the 30th day of the first month in the year 2011 as 30/01/2011, whereas the U.S. would display the same date as 01/30/2011. To change the region format:

1. Touch the icon. The Settings screen appears.
2. Touch **General**. The General Settings screen appears.
3. Touch **Language & Region**. The Language & Region screen appears.
4. Touch **Region**. A list of regions appears, as shown in **Figure 14**.
5. Touch the desired region. The new region format is set.

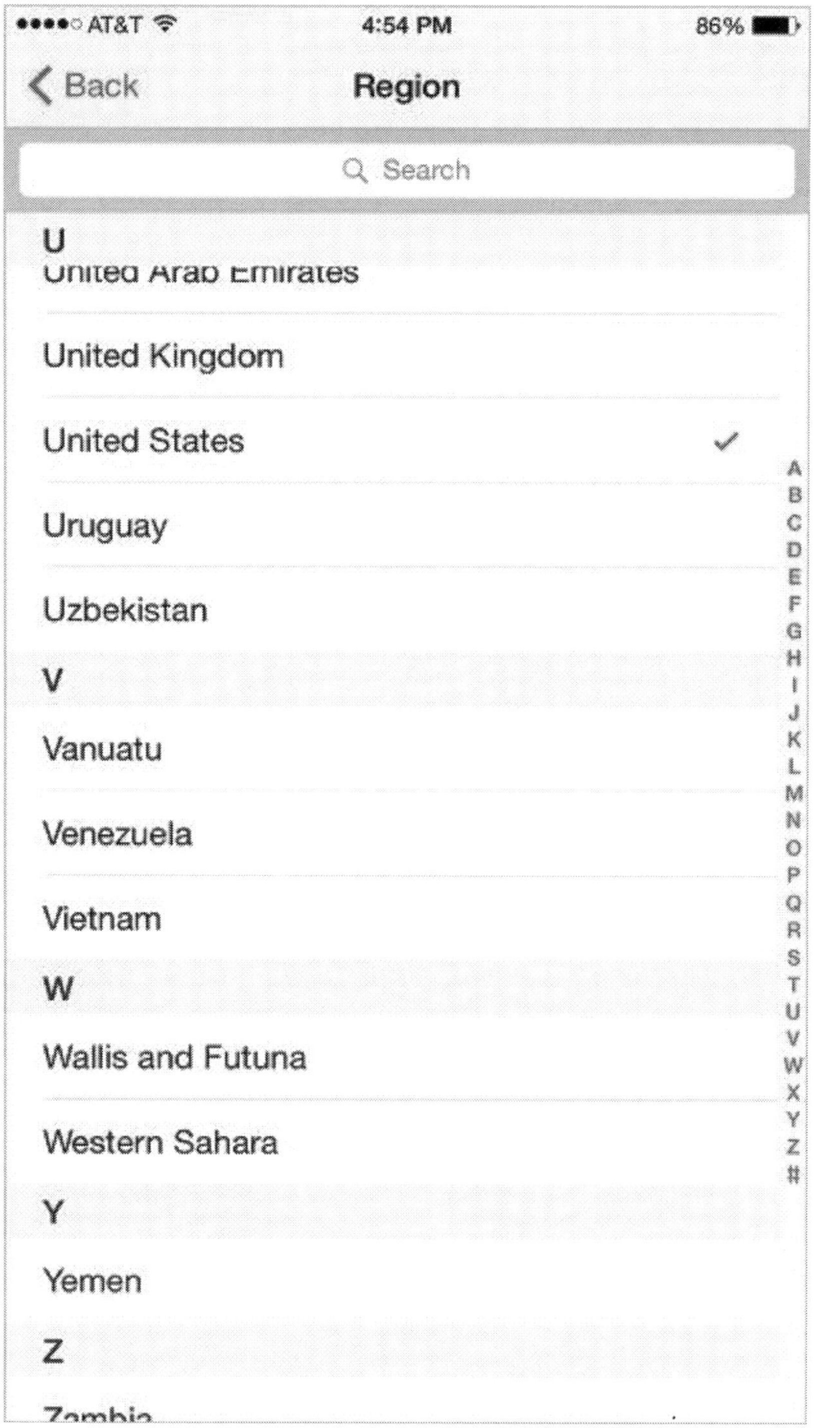

< Back   Region

Q Search

U

~~United Arab Emirates~~

United Kingdom

United States   ✓

Uruguay

Uzbekistan

V

Vanuatu

Venezuela

Vietnam

W

Wallis and Futuna

Western Sahara

Y

Yemen

Z

~~Zambia~~

A
B
C
D
E
F
G
H
I
J
K
L
M
N
O
P
Q
R
S
T
U
V
W
X
Y
Z
#

Figure 14: List of Regions

Adjusting General Settings

Table of Contents

1. Changing Auto-Lock Settings

The phone can lock itself when it is idle in order to save battery life, and to avoid unintentionally pressing buttons. When it is locked, the phone can still receive calls and text messages. By default, the phone is set to automatically lock after one minute. To change the length of time that will pass before the phone locks itself:

1. Touch the icon. The Settings screen appears, as shown in **Figure 1**.
2. Touch **General**. The General Settings screen appears, as shown in **Figure 2**.
3. Scroll down and touch **Auto-Lock**. The Auto-Lock Settings screen appears, as shown in **Figure 3**.
4. Touch an amount of time, or touch **Never** if you do not want the phone to automatically lock itself. The change is applied and the phone will wait the selected amount of time before automatically locking itself.

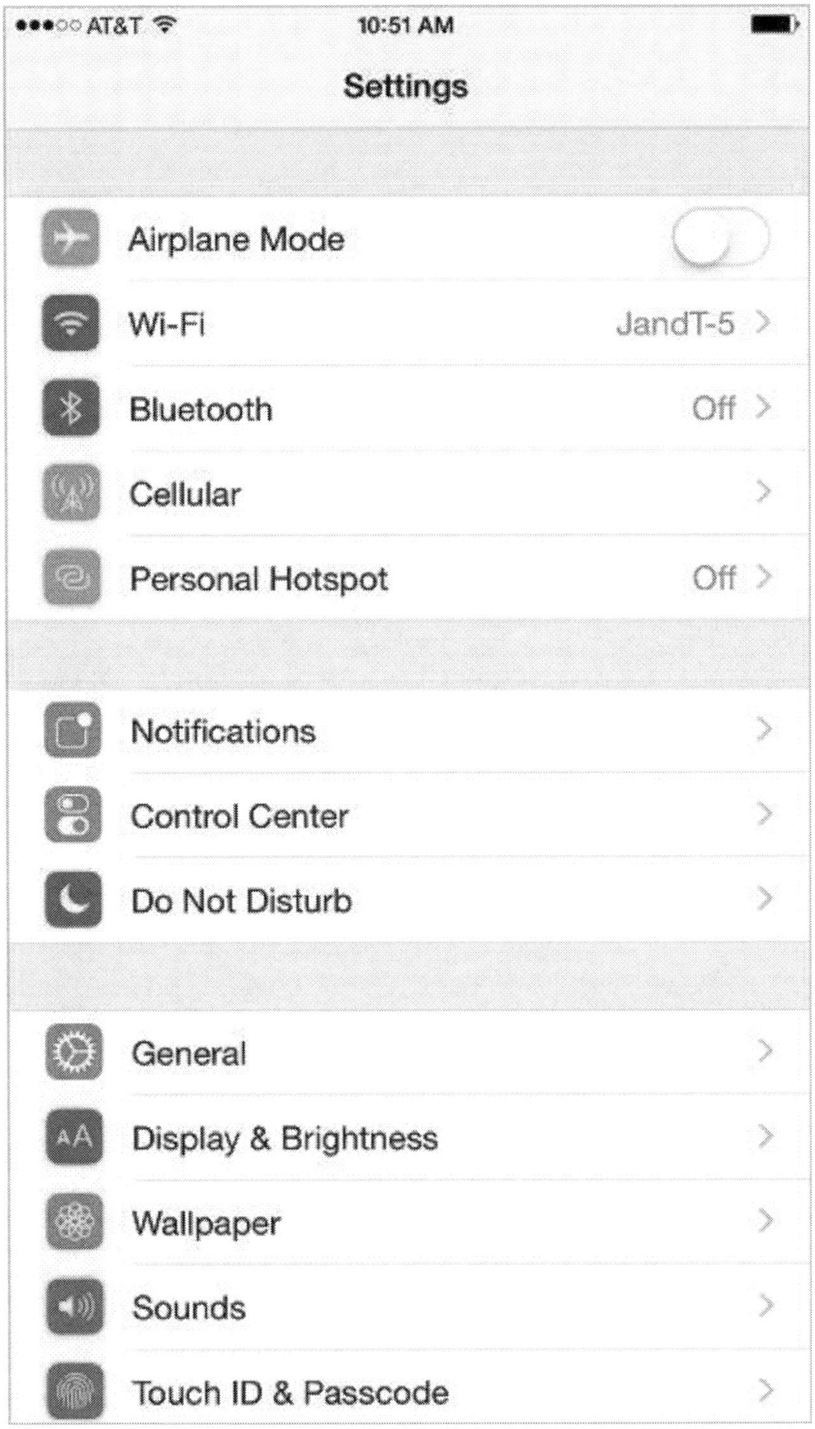

Figure 1: Settings Screen

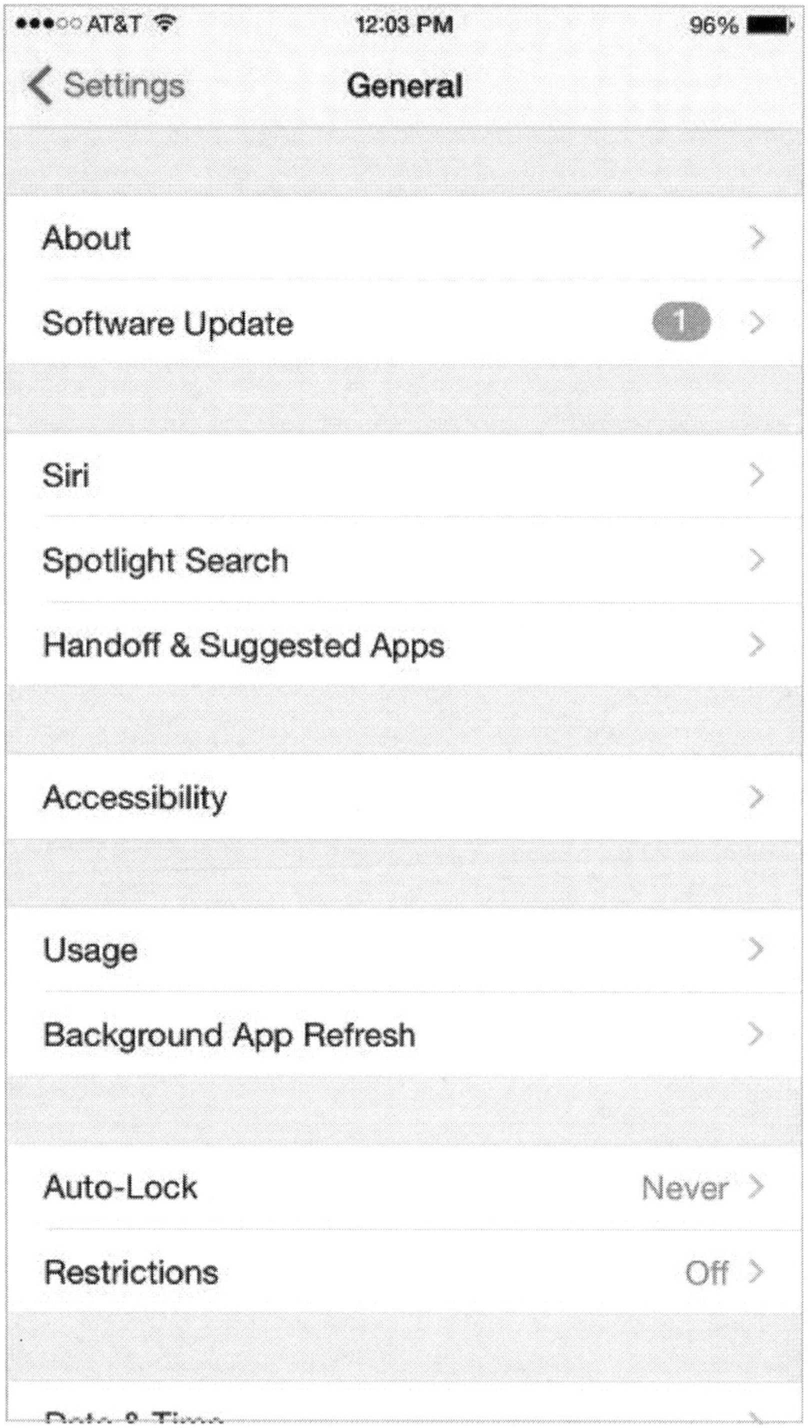

●●●○○ AT&T 📶   12:03 PM   96% ▬▬▶

❮ Settings   **General**

About	❯
Software Update	**1** ❯

Siri	❯
Spotlight Search	❯
Handoff & Suggested Apps	❯

Accessibility	❯

Usage	❯
Background App Refresh	❯

Auto-Lock	Never ❯
Restrictions	Off ❯

Data & Time ❯

Figure 2: General Settings Screen

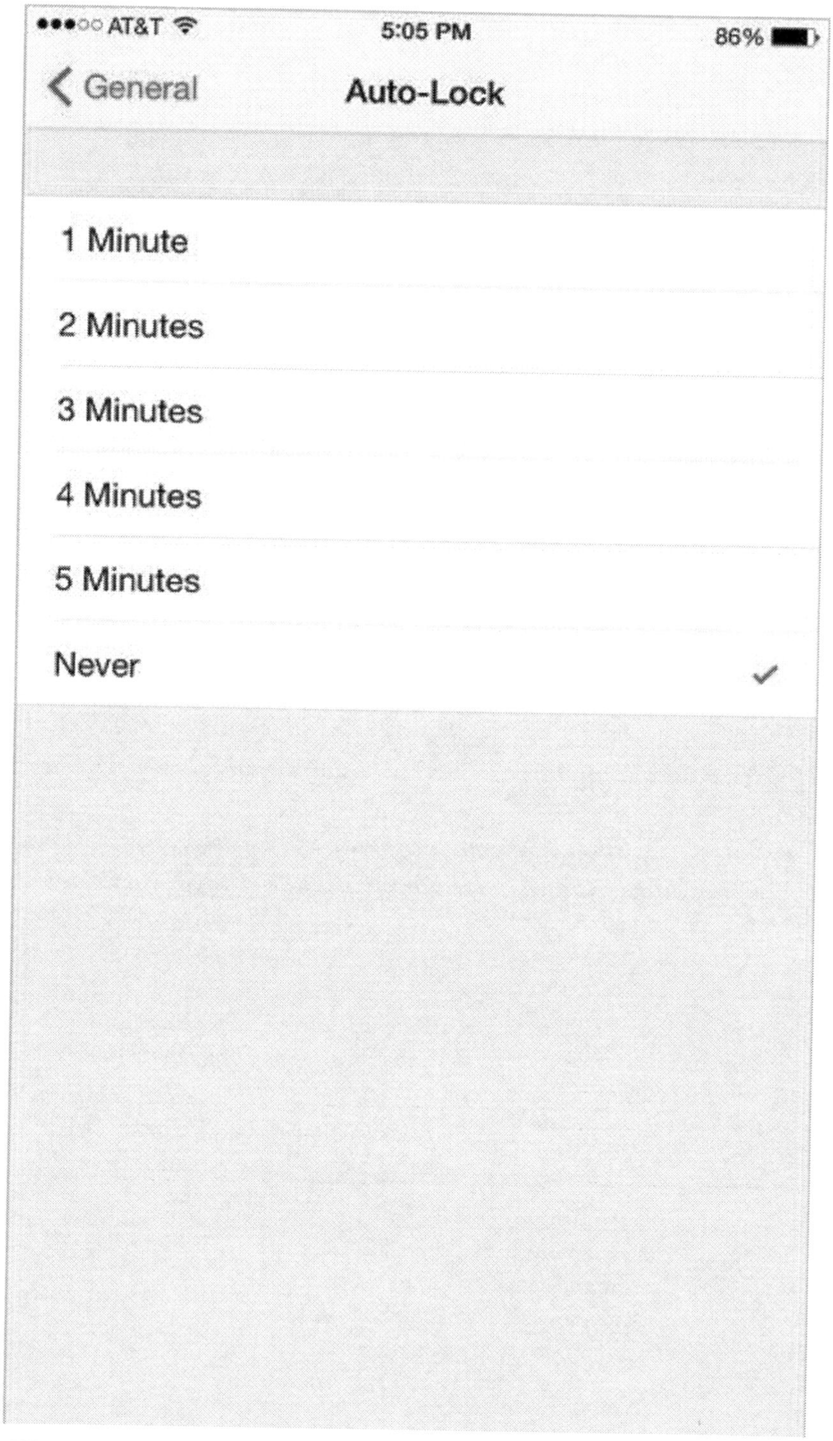

●●●○○ AT&T 🛜   5:05 PM   86% ▬▬

❮ General   **Auto-Lock**

1 Minute

2 Minutes

3 Minutes

4 Minutes

5 Minutes

Never   ✓

Figure 3: Auto-Lock Settings Screen

2. Adjusting the Brightness

You may wish to increase the brightness of the screen on your phone when you are in a sunny area. On the other hand, you may wish to decrease the brightness in a dark area to conserve battery life. You can also turn Auto-Brightness on or off, which will determine whether or not the phone automatically sets the brightness based on the lighting conditions. To adjust the brightness:

1. Touch the ⚙ icon. The Settings screen appears.
2. Touch **Display & Brightness**. The Display & Brightness Settings screen appears, as shown in **Figure 4**.
3. Touch the ⬤ switch next to 'Auto-Brightness' to disable Auto-Brightness. You may manually adjust the brightness when Auto-Brightness is turned off, as shown in step 4 below. Touch the ◯ switch to enable Auto-Brightness again.
4. Touch the ⬤ on the ▬▬▬◯ bar and drag it towards the small ☀ icon to decrease the brightness, or drag it towards the large ☀ icon to increase it.

Note: While Auto-Brightness is enabled, you can still temporarily adjust the brightness of the screen. However, as soon as the lighting conditions change, the phone will automatically change the brightness.

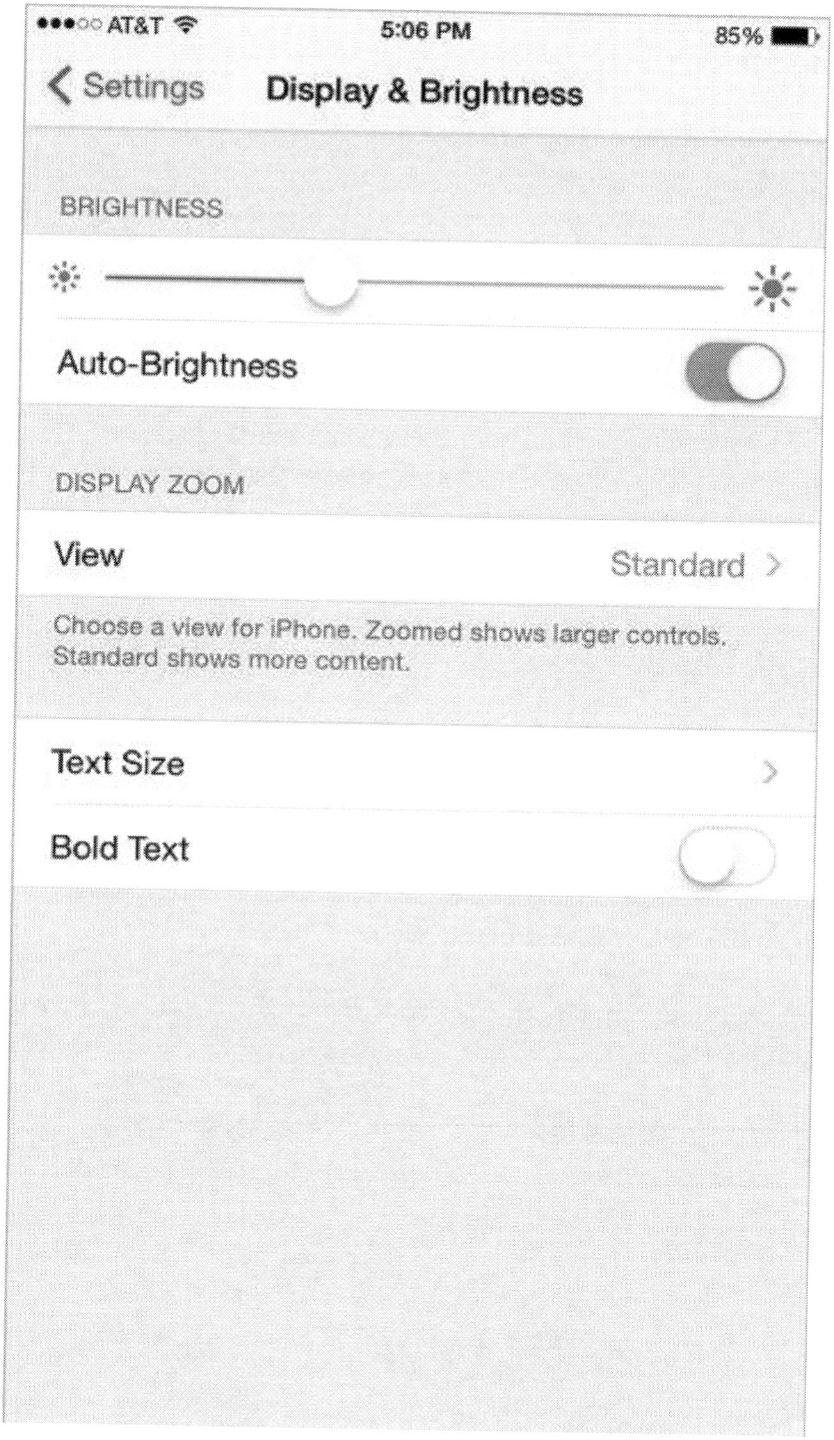

Figure 4: Display & Brightness Settings Screen

3. Assigning a Passcode Lock or Fingerprint Lock

The phone can prompt for a four-digit or alphanumeric password, or your fingerprint before unlocking.
To set up a password lock:

1. Touch the ⊚ icon. The Settings screen appears.
2. Touch **Touch ID & Passcode**. The Touch ID & Passcode screen appears, as shown in **Figure 5**.
3. Touch **Turn Passcode On**. The Set Passcode screen appears, as shown in **Figure 6**, if the Simple Passcode feature is turned on. The Set Password screen appears, as shown in **Figure 7**, if the Simple Passcode feature is turned off.
4. Enter a passcode. A confirmation screen appears.
5. Enter the passcode again. The new passcode is set.
6. Touch one of the following options on the Passcode Lock screen to change the corresponding setting:

   - **Require Passcode** - Set the time the phone waits before asking the user for the passcode. It is recommended to choose the default, **Immediately**, since an unauthorized user will not have access to your phone for any period of time if this option is chosen. Choosing one of the other options causes the phone to wait a set amount of time after being locked before requiring a passcode.
   - **Simple Passcode** - Allows you to enter a four-digit passcode. When turned off, you must enter an alphanumeric password when setting the passcode.
   - **Erase Data** - Erases all data after a user enters the passcode incorrectly ten times in a row.

Warning: You will not be able to recover your data if this feature is on when an incorrect passcode is entered ten times consecutively.

Set Fingerprint Lock

To set up a fingerprint lock:

1. Set up a password lock. Refer to the instructions **above** to learn how.
2. Touch **Add a fingerprint**. The Fingerprint Setup screen appears.
3. Lift and rest your finger on the Home button repeatedly. Keep doing this until the Fingerprint Confirmation screen appears, as shown in **Figure 8** . Your fingerprint can now be used to unlock the phone. To unlock the phone, activate the screen by pressing the Home or Sleep/Wake button, and scan your fingerprint.

Note: You must use the same thumb that you scanned in step 3 to unlock your phone every time.

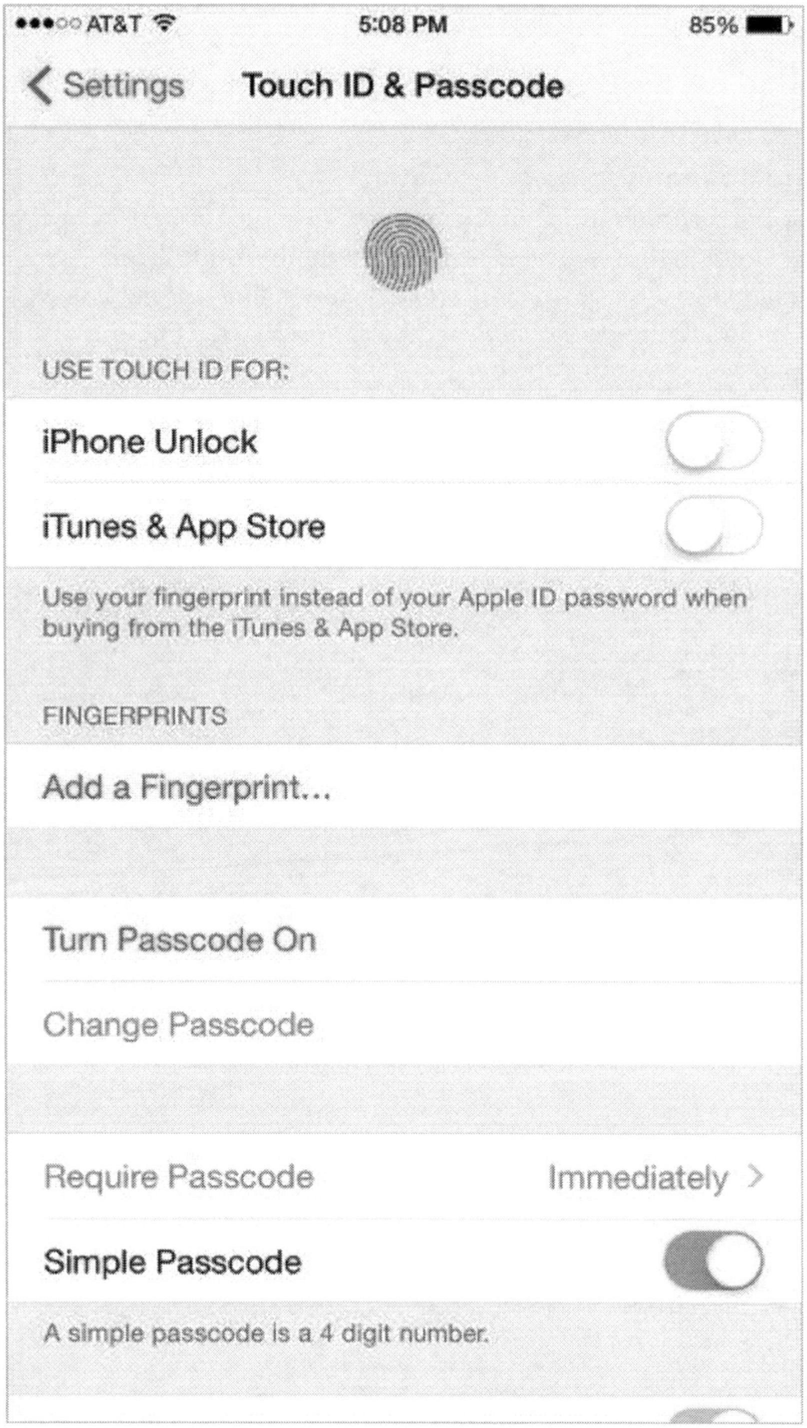

Figure 5: Touch ID & Passcode Screen

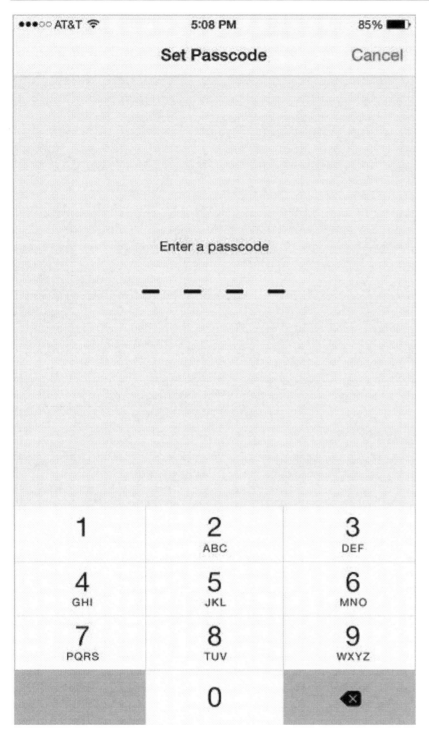

Figure 6: Set Passcode Screen

Figure 7: Set Password Screen

Figure 8: Fingerprint Confirmation Screen

4. Turning 24-Hour Mode On or Off

The phone can display the time in regular 12-hour mode or in 24-hour mode, commonly referred to as military time. To turn 24-hour mode on or off:

1. Touch the ⦿ icon. The Settings screen appears.
2. Touch **General**. The General Settings screen appears.
3. Scroll down and touch **Date & Time**. The Date & Time screen appears, as shown in **Figure 9**.

4. Touch the ⬭ switch next to '24-Hour Time'. The ⬤ switch appears 24-Hour mode is turned on.

5. Touch the ⬤ switch next to '24-Hour Time'. The ⬭ switch appears and 24-Hour mode is turned off.

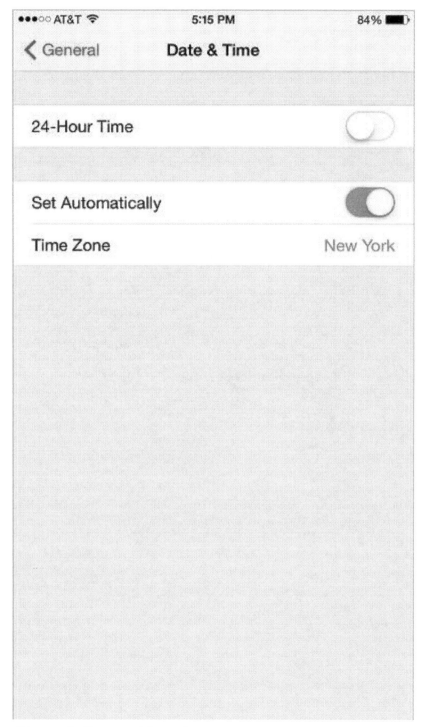

Figure 9: Date & Time Screen

5. Resetting the Home Screen Layout

You can reset the Home screen on your phone to look like it did when you first purchased it. To reset the Home Screen Layout:

Note: Resetting the Home screen layout does not delete any applications, but simply rearranges them on the Home screen.

1. Touch the icon. The Settings screen appears.
2. Touch **General**. The General Settings screen appears.
3. Scroll down and touch **Reset**. The Reset screen appears, as shown in **Figure 10**.
4. Touch **Reset Home Screen Layout**. A confirmation dialog appears at the bottom of the screen.
5. Touch **Reset Home Screen**. The Home Screen Layout is reset.

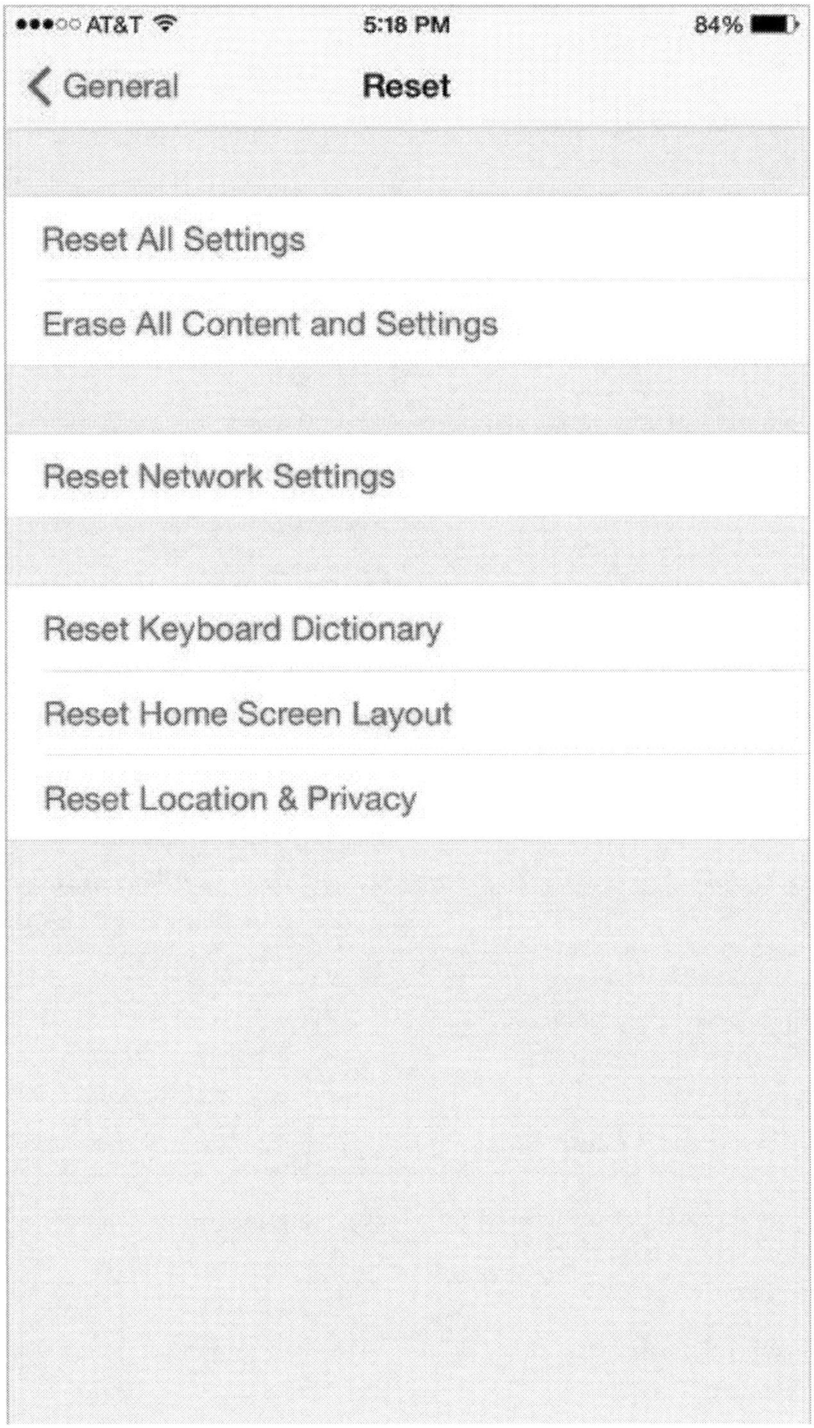

●●●○○ AT&T 🛜   5:18 PM   84% 🔋

❮ General   **Reset**

Reset All Settings

Erase All Content and Settings

Reset Network Settings

Reset Keyboard Dictionary

Reset Home Screen Layout

Reset Location & Privacy

Figure 10: Reset Screen

6. Resetting All Settings

You can reset all of the settings on your phone to the state they were in when you first purchased it. To reset all settings:

Note: Resetting the settings will NOT delete any data from your phone.

1. Touch the ⊚ icon. The Settings screen appears.
2. Touch **General**. The General Settings screen appears.
3. Scroll down and touch **Reset**. The Reset screen appears.
4. Touch **Reset All Settings**. A confirmation dialog appears at the bottom of the screen. You will also need to enter your passcode, if you have one.
5. Touch **Reset All Settings**. All settings are reset to defaults.

7. Erasing and Restoring the Phone

You can delete all of the data and reset all settings to completely restore the phone to its original condition. To erase and restore the phone to its original condition:

Warning: Any erased data is not recoverable. Make sure that you back up all of the data that you wish to keep.

1. Touch the ⊚ icon. The Settings screen appears.
2. Touch **General**. The General Settings screen appears.
3. Touch **Reset**. The Reset screen appears.
4. Touch **Erase All Content and Settings**. A confirmation appears at the bottom of the screen.
5. Touch **Erase iPhone**. The phone is erased and restored to its original condition.

8. Managing Notification Settings

You may customize the types of notifications that appear in the Notifications Center. To manage notification settings:

1. Touch the ⊙ icon. The Settings screen appears.
2. Touch **Notifications**. The Notifications Settings appear, as shown in **Figure 11**.
3. Touch one of the notification types, such as Phone or Messages, to turn the notifications on or off, or to customize the number of notifications that appear. The Notification Customization screen, as shown in **Figure 12** (Phone Notification Customization).
4. Touch the ⬤ switch next to 'Allow Notifications'. The ◯ switch appears and notifications will no longer appear for the selected type.
5. Touch one of the following options to customize the notifications:

Note: The following options will vary based on the notification type:

- **Show in Notification Center** - Select the number of recent items that should appear in the Notifications Center for the selected type.
- **Notification Sound** - Select the sound that plays when a new notification of the selected type arrives.
- **Badge App Icon** - Turn the notification type icon that appears next to a notification on or off.
- **Show on Lock Screen** - Allow notifications of the selected type to appear on the Lock screen.
- **Alert Style When Unlocked** - Touch **None**, **Banners**, or **Alerts** to select the way in which notifications appear for the selected type.

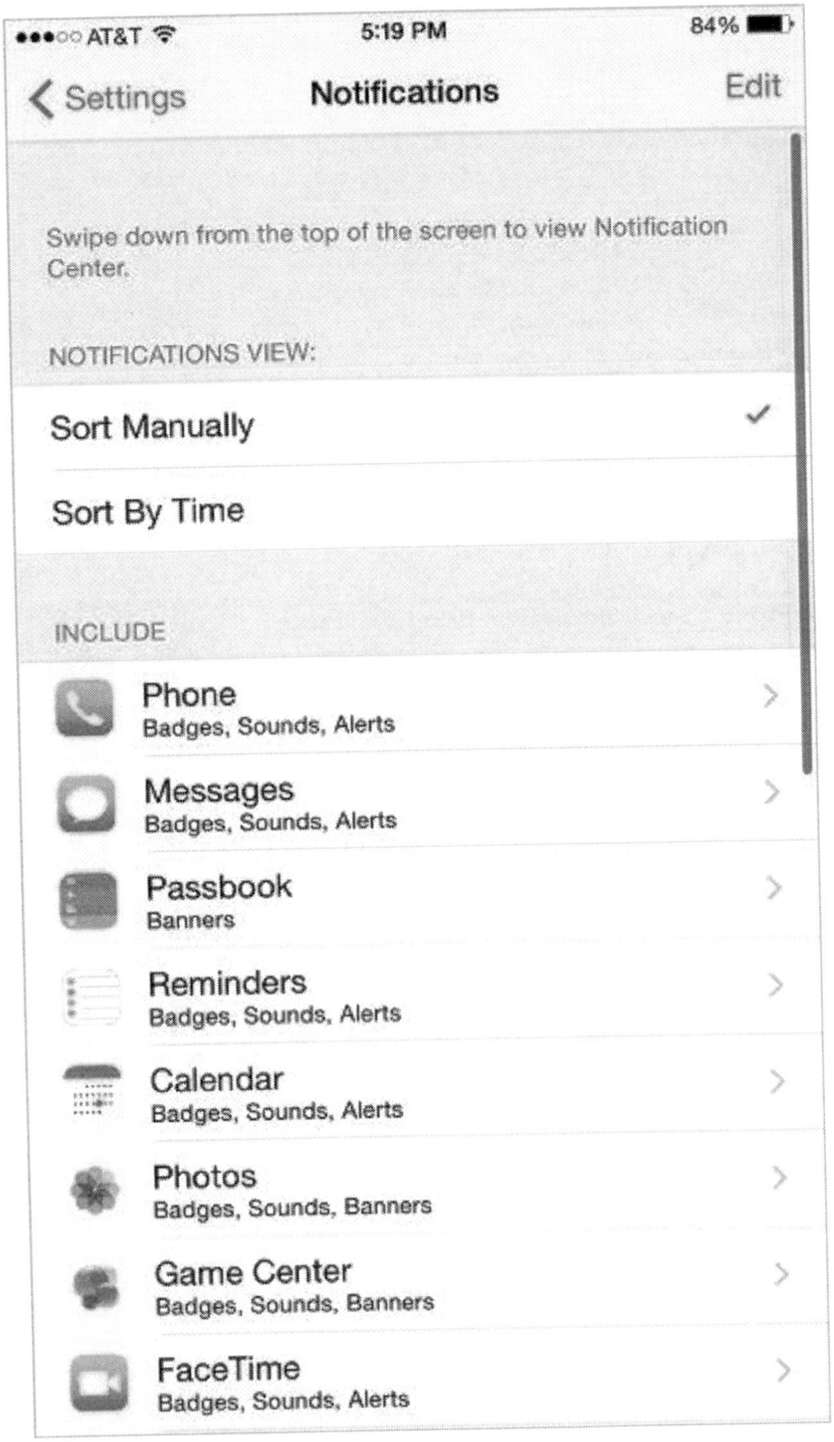

Figure 11: Notifications Settings

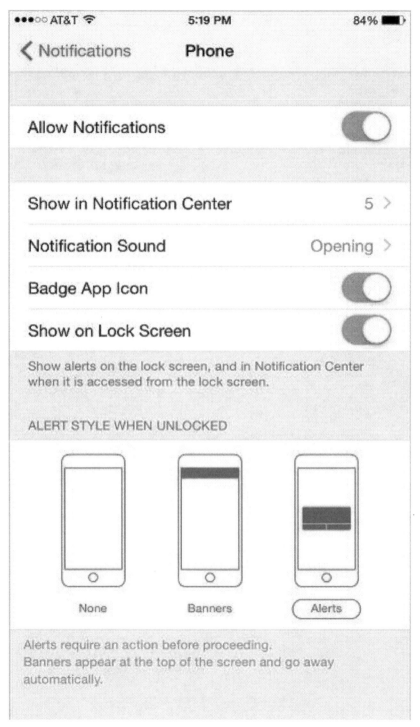

Figure 12: Notification Customization Screen

9. Changing the Wallpaper

The wallpaper is the image that appears on the Lock screen, and on the Home screen behind the application icons. To change the wallpaper:

1. Touch the ⚙ icon. The Settings screen appears.
2. Scroll down and touch **Wallpaper**. The Wallpaper Settings appear, as shown in **Figure 13**.
3. Touch **Choose a New Wallpaper**. The Wallpaper Selection screen appears, as shown in **Figure 14**.
4. Touch the image above 'Dynamic' or 'Stills', or touch one of the photo albums under 'Photos'. The corresponding image thumbnails appear.
5. Touch an image thumbnail. The image appears in full-screen, as shown in **Figure 15**.
6. Touch **Set**. The screen selection menu appears, as shown in **Figure 16**. Alternatively, touch **Cancel** to select another image.
7. Touch **Set Lock Screen**, **Set Home Screen**, or **Set Both** to set the corresponding wallpaper. The new wallpaper is set.

Figure 13: Wallpaper Settings

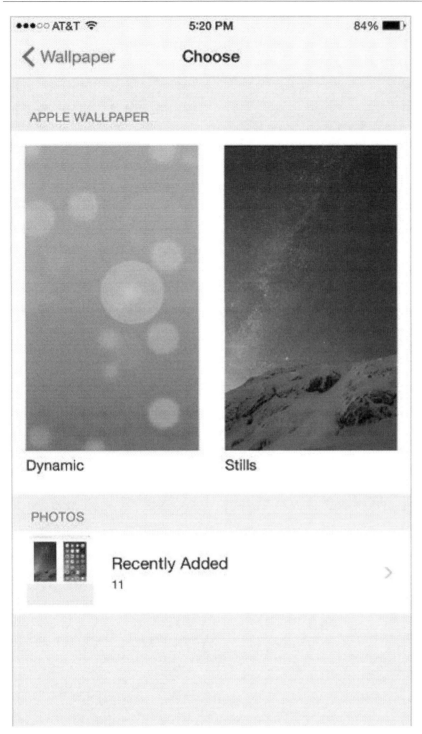

Figure 14: Wallpaper Selection

Figure 15: Wallpaper Image in Full-Screen

Figure 16: Screen Selection Menu

10. Restricting Access to Private Information

Some applications may request to use your some of the information stored on your phone, or even to access your camera. If you touch **Allow**, the application will have access to the requested information until you take away the access. To restrict access to private information:

1. Touch the icon. The Settings screen appears.
2. Touch **Privacy**. The Privacy Settings screen appears, as shown in **Figure 17**.
3. Touch one of the information types, such as 'Contacts' or 'Calendars'. The list of applications appear that have requested access to the selected type of information, as shown in **Figure 18** (Contacts).

4. Touch the switch next to the name of the requesting application. The switch appears, and the selected application will no longer have access to the type of information selected in step 3.

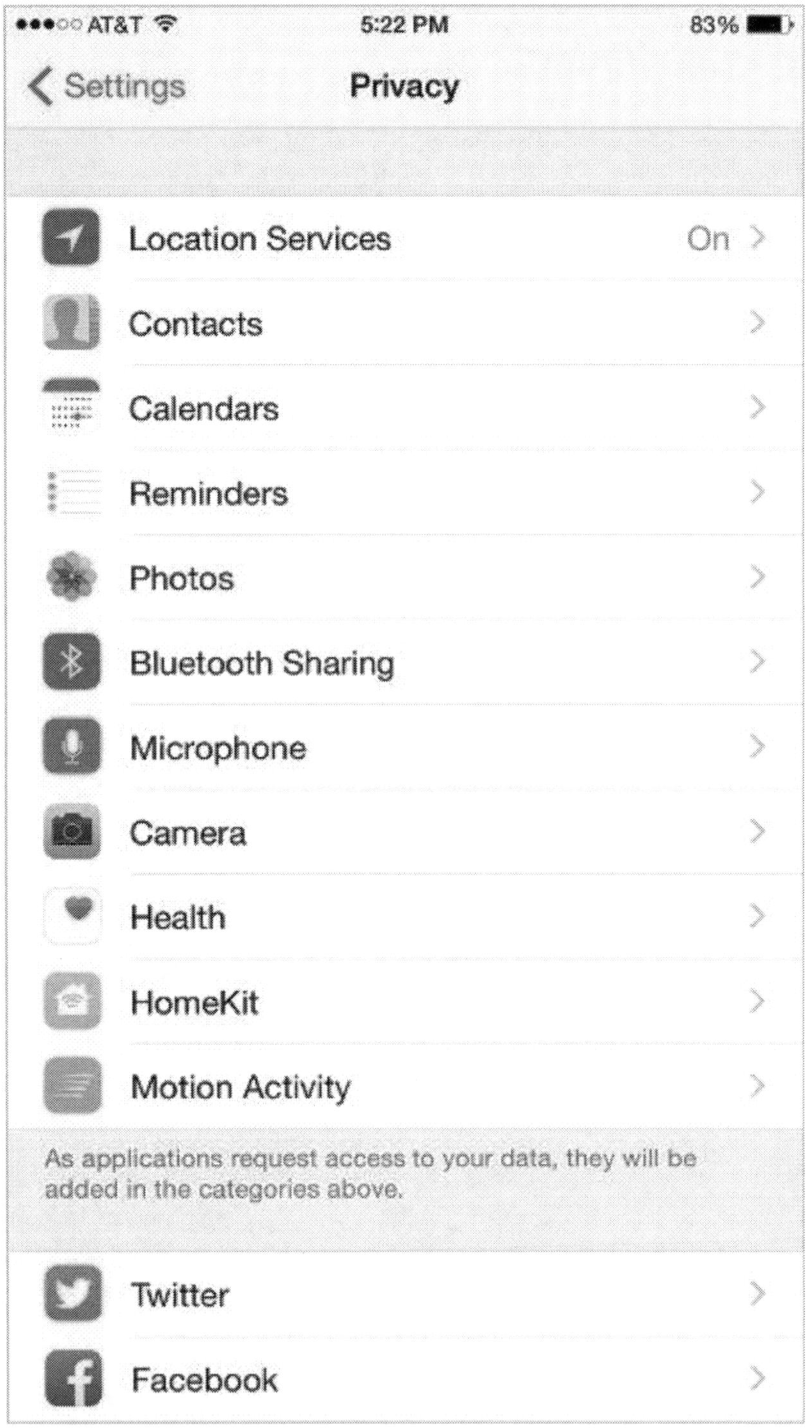

●●●○○ AT&T 📶   5:22 PM   83% ▆▆▆▷

< Settings   **Privacy**

◢ Location Services   On >

👥 Contacts   >

📅 Calendars   >

☰ Reminders   >

✿ Photos   >

* Bluetooth Sharing   >

🎤 Microphone   >

📷 Camera   >

♥ Health   >

🏠 HomeKit   >

📄 Motion Activity   >

As applications request access to your data, they will be added in the categories above.

🐦 Twitter   >

f Facebook   >

Figure 17: Privacy Settings Screen

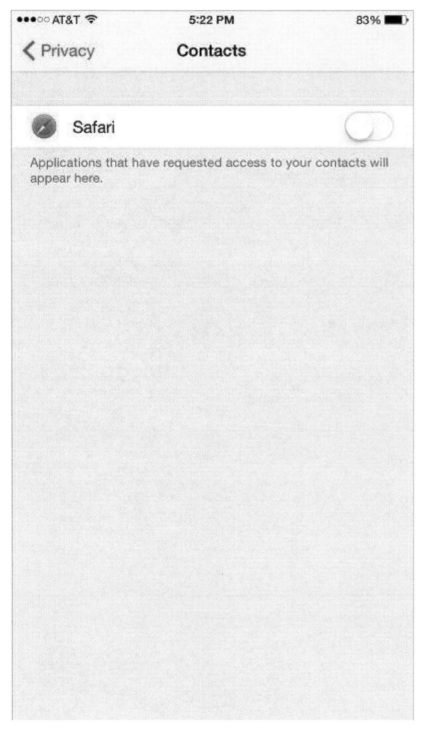

Figure 18: List of Applications that Have Requested Access

11. Setting the Display Zoom

The iPhone 6 and 6 Plus allow you to customize the size of icons and text on the display to your preference. There are two display zoom modes available: Standard and Zoomed. You will also have the ability to view the Messages screen, Mail Inbox, and extended keyboard when using the Standard view. To set the display zoom:

1. Touch the ⊚ icon. The Settings screen appears.
2. Touch **Display & Brightness**. The Display & Brightness Settings screen appears.
3. Touch **View** under 'Display Zoom'. The Display Zoom Settings screen appears, as shown in **Figure 19**.
4. Touch **Standard** or **Zoomed**. The corresponding display zoom mode is selected.
5. Touch **Set** in the upper right-hand corner of the screen. A confirmation dialog appears at the bottom of the screen.
6. Touch **Use Zoomed** or **Use Standard**, depending on your selection in step 4. The corresponding Display Zoom mode is enabled.

Note: You also have the chance to select the Display Zoom when setting up the phone for the first time. Refer to "Setting Up the Phone for the First Time" *on page 17 to learn more.*

Figure 19: Display Zoom Settings Screen

Adjusting Accessibility Settings

Table of Contents

1. Managing Vision Accessibility Features

Vision accessibility features allow people with visual disabilities to use the phone with greater ease. To manage vision accessibility features:

*   Touch the ![icon] icon. The Settings screen appears, as shown in **Figure 1**.
*   Touch **General**. The General Settings screen appears, as shown in **Figure 2**.
*   Touch **Accessibility**. The Accessibility Settings screen appears, as shown in **Figure 3**.
*   Touch one of the following options to turn vision accessibility features on or off:
*   **VoiceOver** - This feature speaks an item on the screen when you touch it once, activates it when you touch it twice, and scrolls through a list or page of text when you touch the screen with three fingers.
*   **Zoom** - This features zooms in on an item when you touch the screen twice using three fingers, moves around when you drag three fingers on the screen, and changes the level of zoom when you touch the screen with three fingers twice and drag.
*   **Invert Colors** - This feature inverts all of the colors on the screen. For instance, black text on a white screen becomes white text on a black screen.
*   **Grayscale** - This feature changes all color on the phone's screen to black and white.
*   **Speak Selection (touch Speech to access)** - This feature allows all text on the screen to be spoken aloud when you select it and touch **Speak**.
*   **Speak Screen (touch Speech to access)** - This feature allows all the contents of the screen to be described when you touch the top of the screen with two fingers and slide down.
*   **Speak Auto-text (touch Speech to access)** - This feature speaks every auto-correction or auto-capitalization as you enter text in any text field, including text messages and emails.

*   **Larger Text** - This feature increases the default size of the font. Use the font slider to adjust the default font size.

- **Bold Text** - This feature makes all text on the phone bold in order to make it easier to read. Enabling or disabling this feature requires you to restart the phone.
- **Button Shapes** - This feature allows all buttons, such as the back button in the upper left-hand corner of each menu screen, to have outlines.
- **Increase Contrast** - This feature improves the contrast on certain backgrounds in order to make it easier to read certain text.
- **Reduce Motion** - This feature turns off all screen animations, such as when you close an application to return to the Home screen.

- **On/Off Labels** - This feature turns and switches into and switches, respectively.

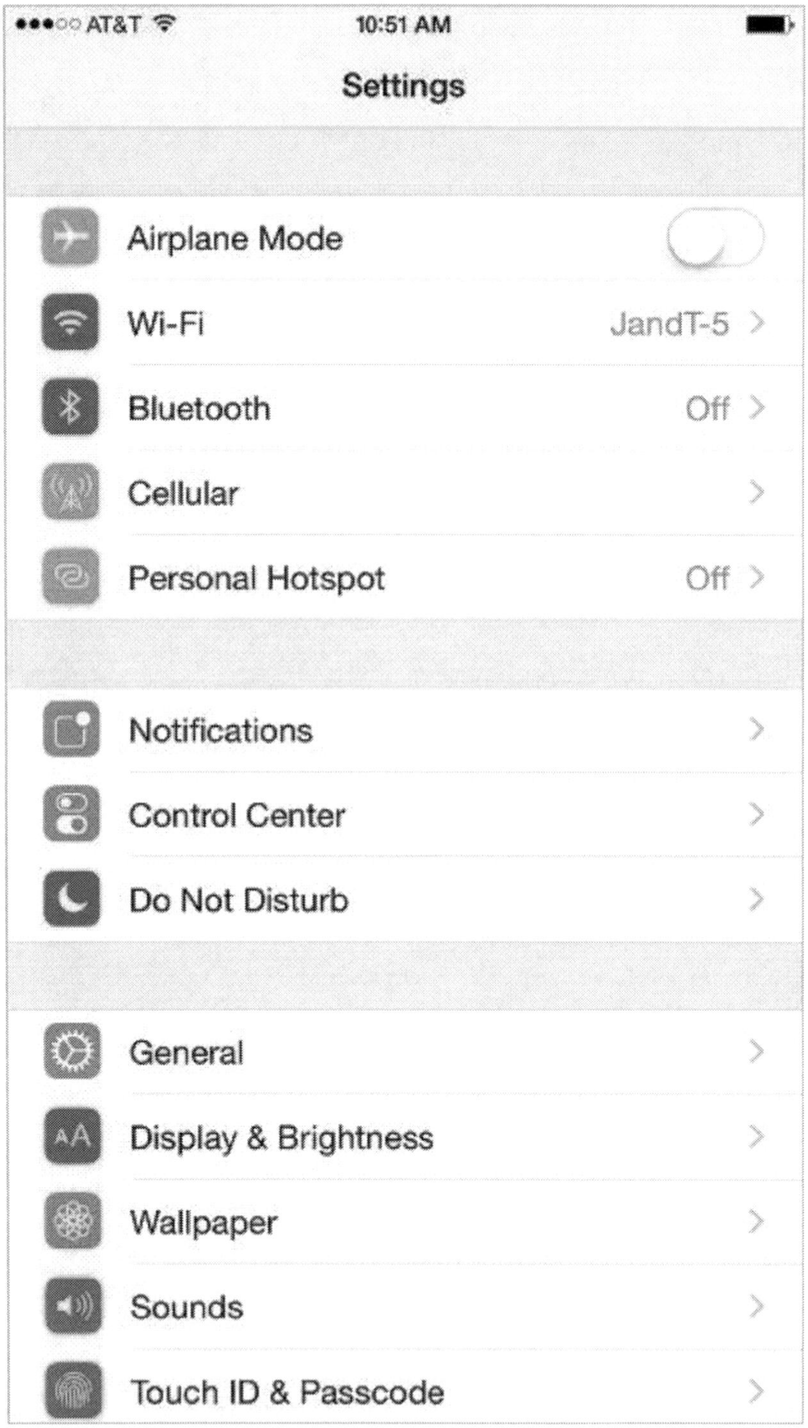

Figure 1: Settings Screen

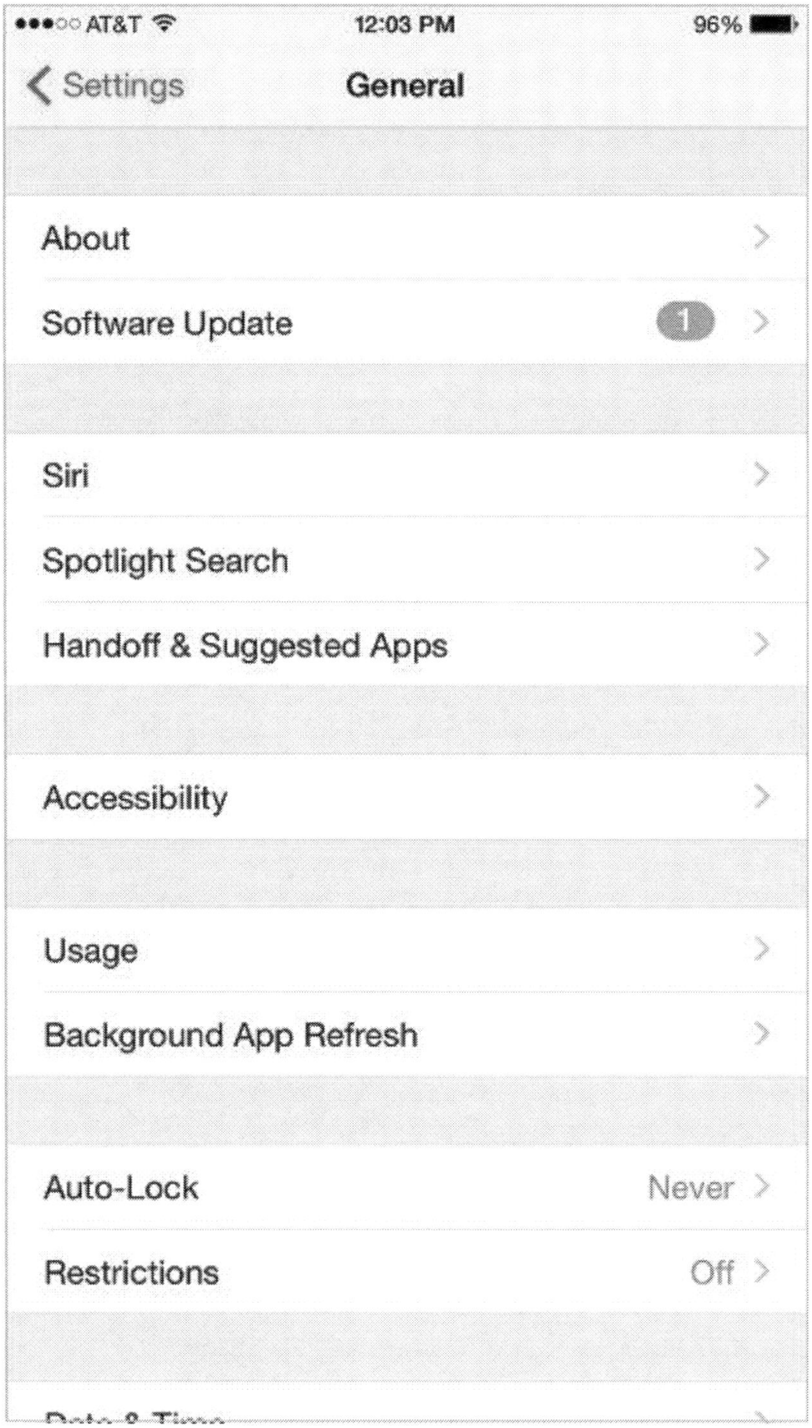

●●●○○ AT&T 📶   12:03 PM   96% 🔋

‹ Settings   **General**

About	›
Software Update	**1** ›
Siri	›
Spotlight Search	›
Handoff & Suggested Apps	›
Accessibility	›
Usage	›
Background App Refresh	›
Auto-Lock	Never ›
Restrictions	Off ›

Figure 2: General Settings Screen

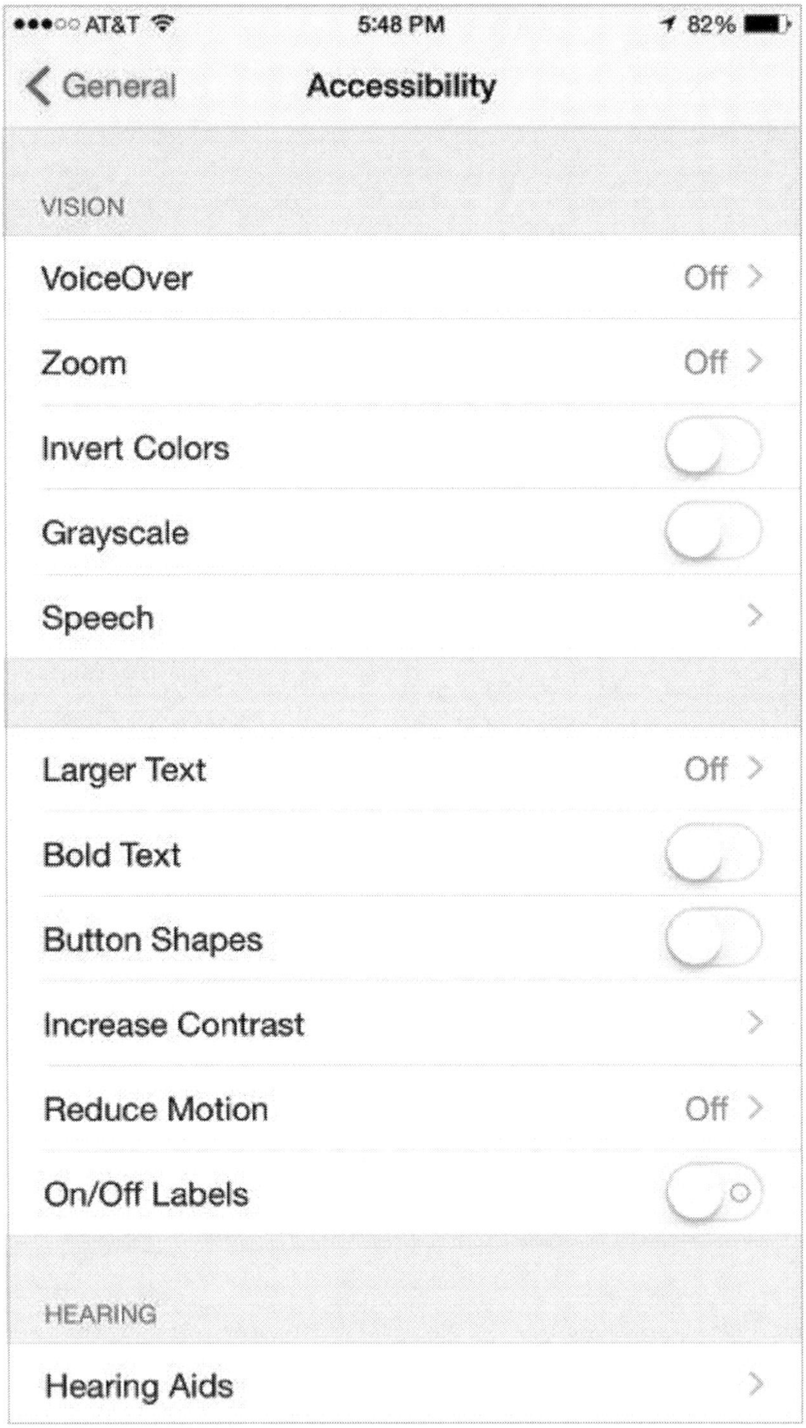

Figure 3: Accessibility Settings Screen

2. Managing Hearing Accessibility Features

Hearing accessibility features allow people with hearing disabilities to use the phone with greater ease. To manage hearing accessibility features:

1. Touch the ![icon] icon. The Settings screen appears.
2. Touch **General**. The General Settings screen appears.
3. Touch **Accessibility**. The Accessibility Settings screen appears.
4. Touch one of the following options to turn hearing accessibility features on or off:

   - **Hearing Aids** - This feature automatically manages the antenna in the phone to avoid interference with standard hearing aids and improve overall performance. However, cellular reception may be reduced when using this feature.
   - **Subtitles & Captioning** - This feature allows subtitles and closed captioning to be enabled for videos, where available.
   - **LED Flash for Alerts** - This feature allows the camera flash to be used to provide notification alerts, such as incoming calls or text messages.
   - **Mono Audio** - This feature turns off stereo audio, leaving only one speaker working.

3. Turning Guided Access On or Off

Guided Access is a feature that is made for people with learning disabilities, allowing the user to stay in a single application and control the features that are available. To turn Guided Access on or off:

1. Touch the ![icon] icon. The Settings screen appears.
2. Touch **General**. The General Settings screen appears.
3. Touch **Accessibility**. The Accessibility Settings screen appears.
4. Scroll down and touch **Guided Access**. The Guided Access Settings screen appears, as shown in **Figure 4**.
5. Touch the ![switch] switch next to 'Guided Access'. Guided Access is turned on.
6. Touch **Set Passcode** to set up a passcode that will allow you to exit the application when you are done using it.

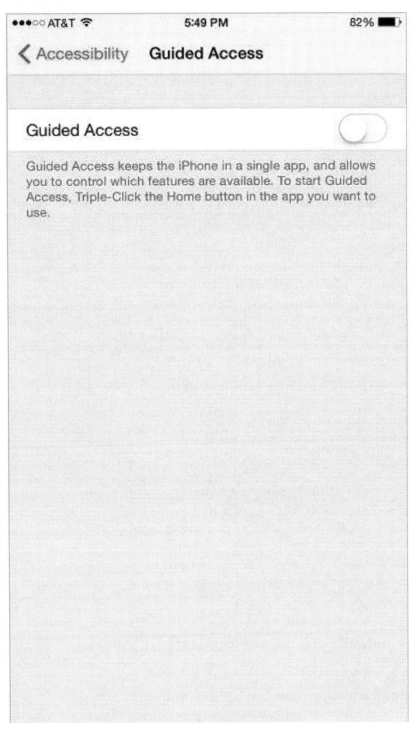

Figure 4: Guided Access Settings Screen

4. Managing Physical & Motor Accessibility Features

Physical and Motor accessibility features allow people with motor disabilities to use the phone with greater ease. To manage physical & motor accessibility features:

1. Touch the icon. The Settings screen appears.
2. Touch **General**. The General Settings screen appears.
3. Touch **Accessibility**. The Accessibility Settings screen appears.
4. Touch one of the following options to turn physical and motor accessibility features on or off:

   - **Switch Control** - This feature allows an adaptive accessory to be used to highlight items on the screen to control the functions of the phone. The Switch Control screen allows various settings, such as timing, switch stabilization, point scanning, audio, and visual settings, to be adjusted.
   - **Assistive Touch** - This feature allows you to create custom gestures in order to access various services on the phone.
   - **Home-click Speed** - This feature allows you to slow down the speed at which you need to press the Home button to access certain features.
   - **Call Audio Routing** - This feature allows you to answer calls directly on your headset or speakerphone by default.
   - **Accessibility Shortcut** - This feature allows you to select an accessibility feature that will be turned on when you press the Home button three times quickly at any time. If you choose more than one feature, a menu will appear allowing you to select the Accessibility feature that you wish to enable.

Adjusting Phone Settings

Table of Contents

1. Turning Call Forwarding On or Off

The phone can be set to forward all calls to a specified number. To turn Call Forwarding on or off:

1. Touch the ⊚ icon. The Settings screen appears, as shown in **Figure 1**.
2. Scroll down and touch **Phone**. The Phone Settings screen appears, as shown in **Figure 2**.
3. Touch **Call Forwarding**. The Call Forwarding screen appears.
4. Touch the ⬭ switch next to 'Call Forwarding'. The 'Forward to' field appears, as shown in **Figure 3**.
5. Use the keypad to enter the phone number to which the phone should forward. When finished, touch **Call Forwarding** at the top of the screen. Call Forwarding is set up, and the Call Forwarding screen appears.

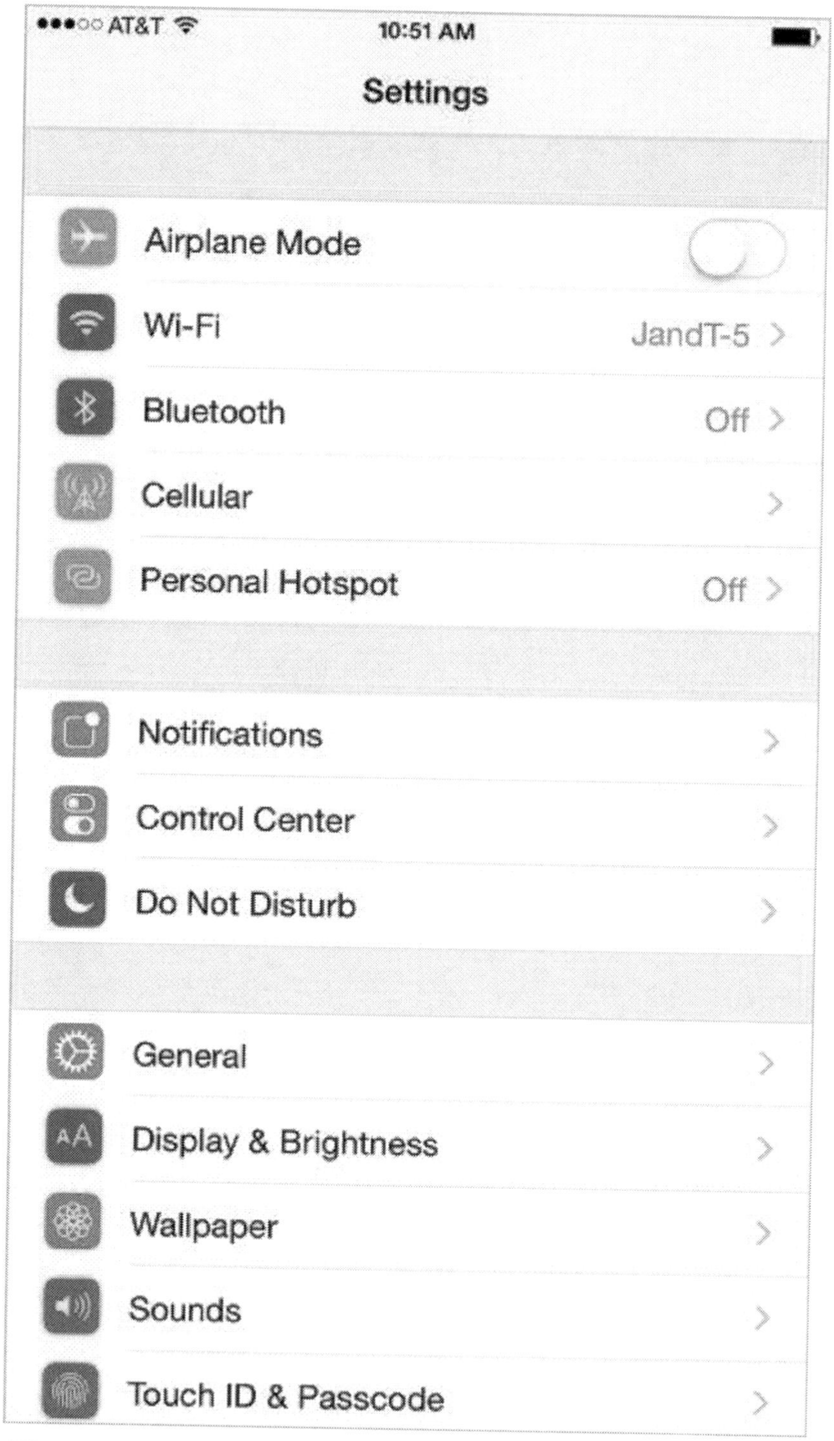

Figure 1: Settings Screen

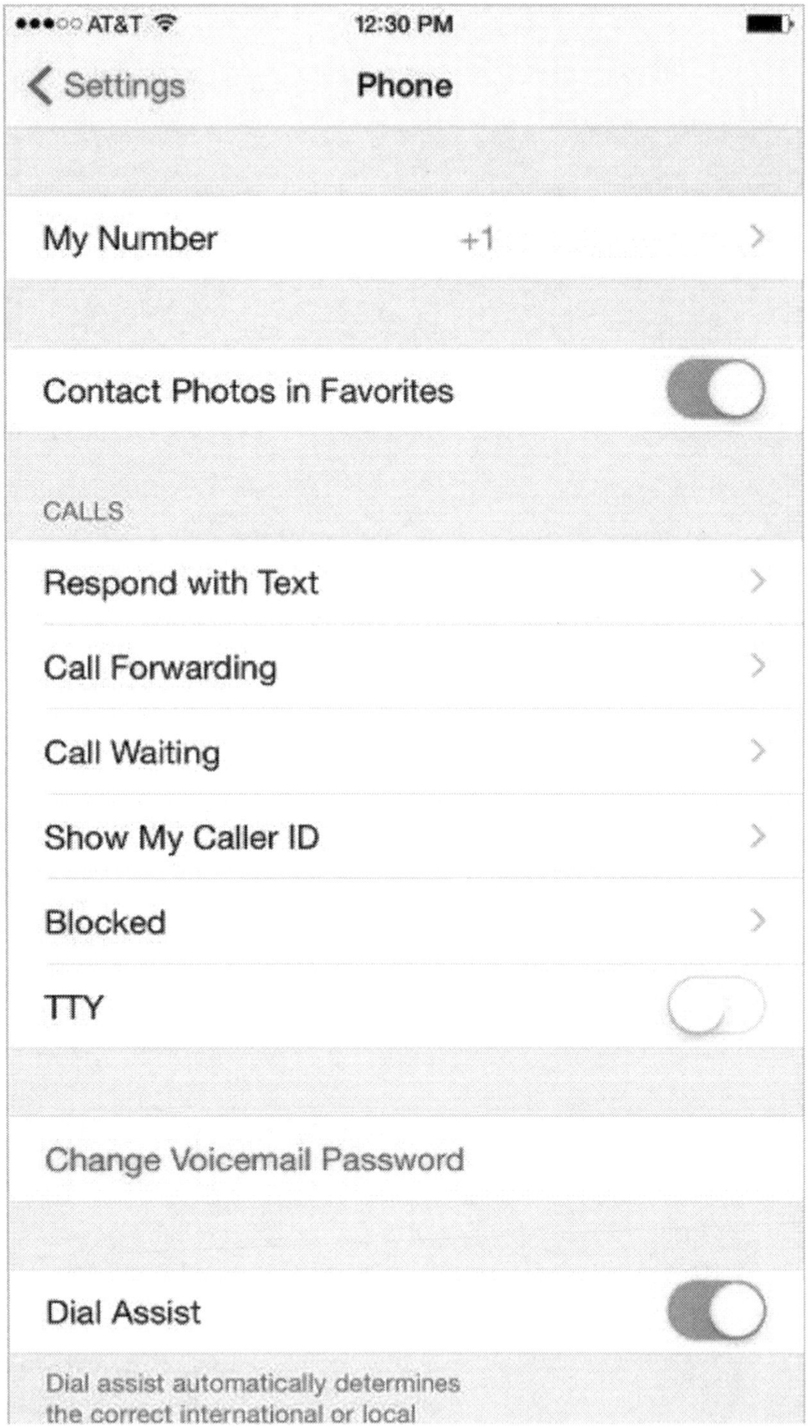

●●●○○ AT&T 📶   12:30 PM   ▬▶

‹ Settings   **Phone**

My Number   +1   ›

Contact Photos in Favorites   ⬤

CALLS

Respond with Text   ›

Call Forwarding   ›

Call Waiting   ›

Show My Caller ID   ›

Blocked   ›

TTY   ◯

Change Voicemail Password

Dial Assist   ⬤

Dial assist automatically determines
the correct international or local

Figure 2: Phone Settings Screen

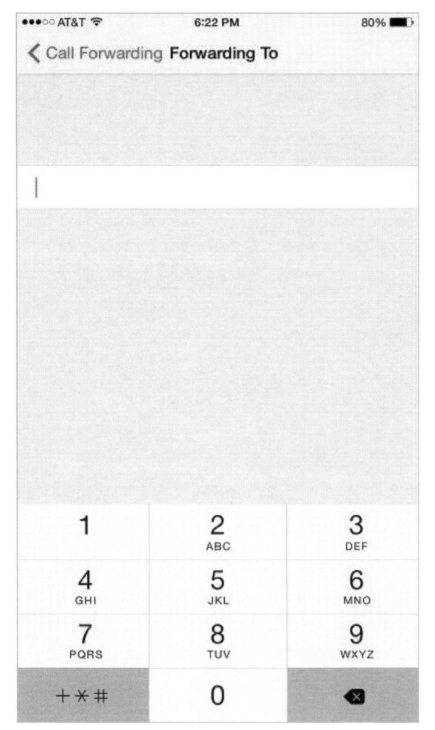

Figure 3: Forwarding To Screen

2. Turning Call Waiting On or Off

While you are on the line with someone, the Call Waiting feature allows the phone to alert you when there is a second incoming call. To turn Call Waiting on or off:

1. Touch the ⊚ icon. The Settings screen appears.
2. Scroll down and touch **Phone**. The Phone Settings screen appears.
3. Touch **Call Waiting**. The Call Waiting screen appears, as shown in **Figure 4**.

4. Touch the ⬤ switch next to 'Call Waiting'. The ◯ switch appears and Call Waiting is turned off.

5. Touch the ◯ switch next to 'Call Waiting'. The ⬤ switch appears and Call Waiting is turned on.

Figure 4: Call Waiting Screen

3. Turning Caller ID On or Off

The Caller ID feature shows your phone number or name (if your number is stored in the recipient's Phonebook) on the called party's phone. In order to preserve privacy and make your phone number appear as "Private Number", turn the Caller ID feature off. To turn Caller ID on or off:

1. Touch the ⚙ icon. The Settings screen appears.
2. Scroll down and touch **Phone**. The Phone Settings screen appears.
3. Touch **Show My Caller ID**. The Show My Caller ID screen appears, as shown in **Figure 5**.

4. Touch the ⬤ switch next to 'Show My Caller ID'. The ◯ switch appears and Caller ID is turned off.

5. Touch the ◯ switch next to 'Show My Caller ID'. The ⬤ switch appears and Caller ID is turned on.

Note: When Caller ID is turned off, even those who have your phone number stored in their Phonebook will not be able to view your number when receiving a call from you.

Figure 5: Show My Caller ID Screen

4. Turning TTY Mode On or Off

TTY stands for 'text telephone' or 'teletypewriter'. Using a special TTY machine when this mode is enabled allows speech and hearing impaired users to read incoming speech as text, and to type responses. The typed text is converted to speech on the other side of the conversation.
Search **Google for TTY machine** to purchase one. You will also need an Apple TTY Adapter, which can be purchased online at the Apple Store, in order to plug in a TTY machine to the phone. To turn TTY Mode on or off:

1. Touch the ⚙ icon. The Settings screen appears.
2. Scroll down and touch **Phone**. The Phone Settings screen appears.
3. Touch the ⬯ switch next to 'TTY'. The ⬮ switch appears and TTY mode is turned on.
4. Touch the ⬮ switch next to 'TTY'. The ⬯ switch appears and TTY mode is turned off.

5. Turning the International Assist On or Off

The International Assist feature is useful while traveling abroad. This feature will automatically add the correct international prefix to every phone number you dial when calling a U.S. phone number. To turn International Assist on or off:

1. Touch the ⚙ icon. The Settings screen appears.
2. Scroll down and touch **Phone**. The Phone Settings screen appears.
3. Touch the ⬯ switch next to 'Dial Assist'. The ⬮ switch appears and International Assist is turned on.
4. Touch the ⬮ switch next to 'Dial Assist'. The ⬯ switch appears and International Assist is turned off.

Note: The International Assist feature does not work in all areas.

6. Blocking Specific Numbers

The phone can block contacts with specified numbers from calling or texting you. In order to block a number, you must first add it to your Phonebook. Refer to *"Adding a New Contact"* on page 58 to learn how. To specify numbers to block:

1. Touch the icon. The Settings screen appears.
2. Scroll down and touch **Phone**. The Phone Settings screen appears.
3. Touch **Blocked**. The Blocked Numbers screen appears, as shown in **Figure 6**.
4. Touch **Add New**. Your Phonebook appears.
5. Touch a contact. The contact's number is added to the Blocked list.

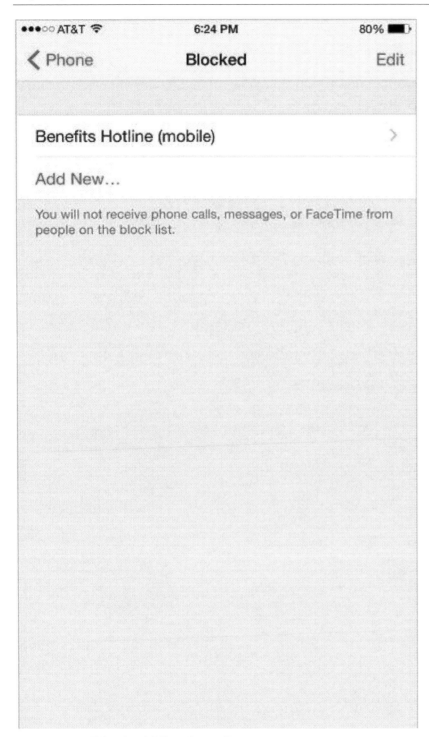

Figure 6: Blocked Numbers Screen

7. Editing Preset Text Message Responses

The phone allows you to respond with a preset text if you are unable to answer a call. To edit the preset text message responses:

1. Touch the ![icon] icon. The Settings screen appears.
2. Scroll down and touch **Phone**. The Phone Settings screen appears.
3. Touch **Respond with Text**. The Respond with Text screen appears, as shown in **Figure 7**.
4. Touch one of the messages under 'Respond With' to edit it.
5. Touch **Phone** at the top of the screen. The new preset text messages are saved.

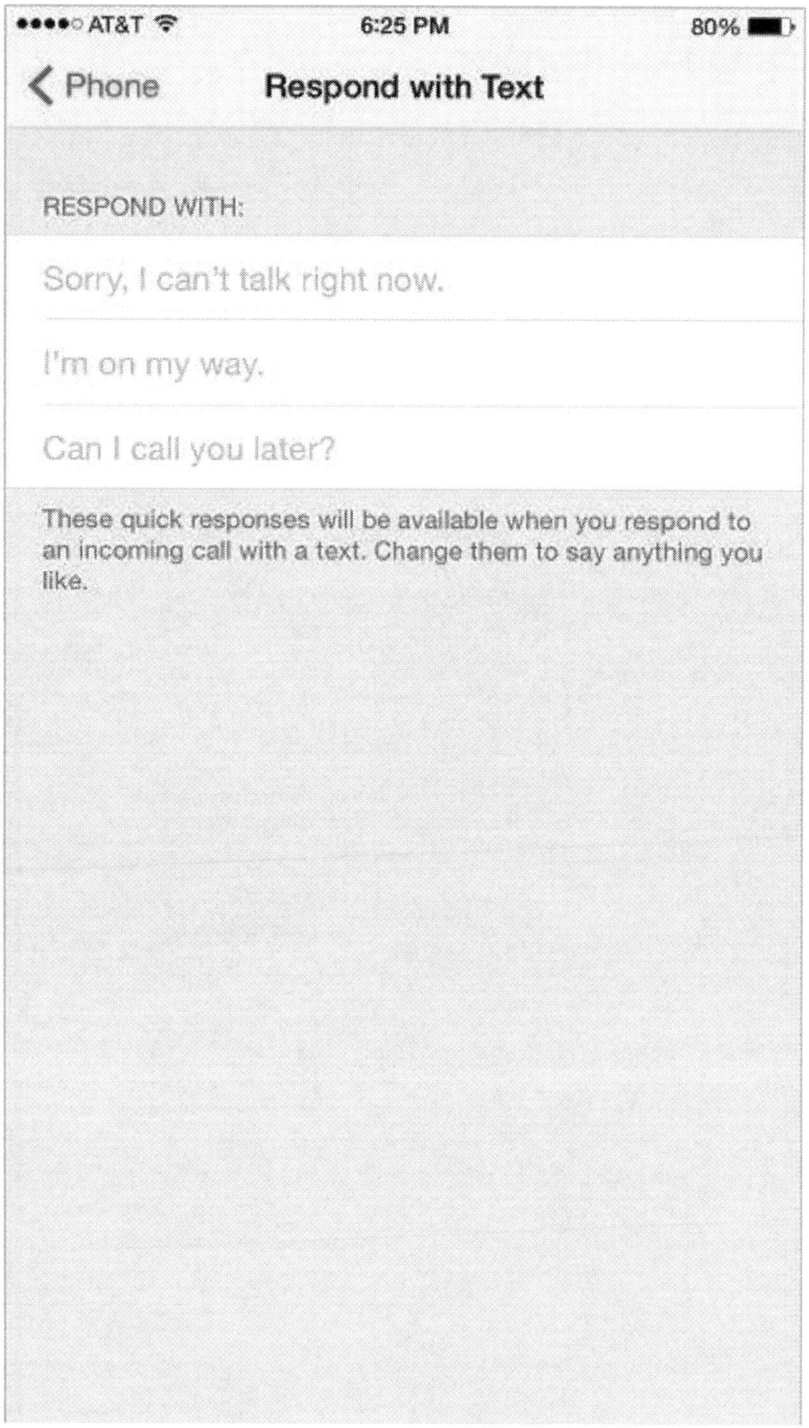

●●●●○ AT&T 📶 　　　　　6:25 PM　　　　　80% 🔋▷

< Phone　　**Respond with Text**

RESPOND WITH:

Sorry, I can't talk right now.

I'm on my way.

Can I call you later?

These quick responses will be available when you respond to an incoming call with a text. Change them to say anything you like.

Figure 7: Respond with Text Screen

Adjusting Text Message Settings

Table of Contents

1. Turning iMessage On or Off

The iMessage feature allows you to send free text messages to iPhone, iPad, or iPod Touch. Turn on iMessage to send a message to another iPhone, or to an iPad or iPod touch, using the email address assigned to the recipient's iMessage account. By default, iMessage is turned on. When iMessage is turned off and you send a text message to another Apple device, standard text messaging rates apply as set forth by your network provider. To turn iMessage on or off:

1. Touch the ⚙ icon. The Settings screen appears, as shown in **Figure 1**.
2. Scroll down and touch **Messages**. The Message Settings screen appears, as shown in **Figure 2**.

3. Touch the ⬜ switch next to 'iMessage'. The 🔘 switch appears and iMessage is turned on.

4. Touch the 🔘 switch next to 'iMessage'. The ⬜ switch appears and iMessage is turned off.

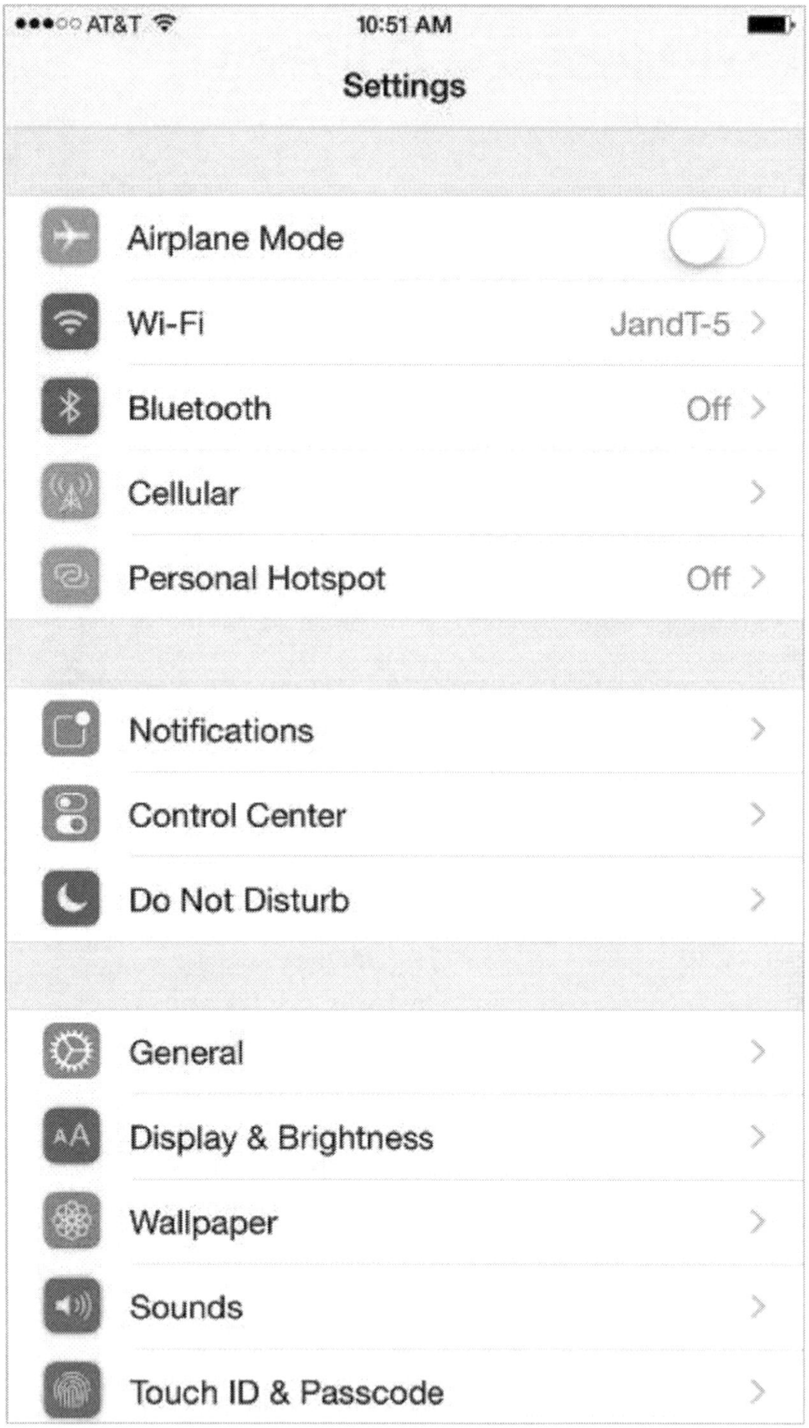

Figure 1: Settings Screen

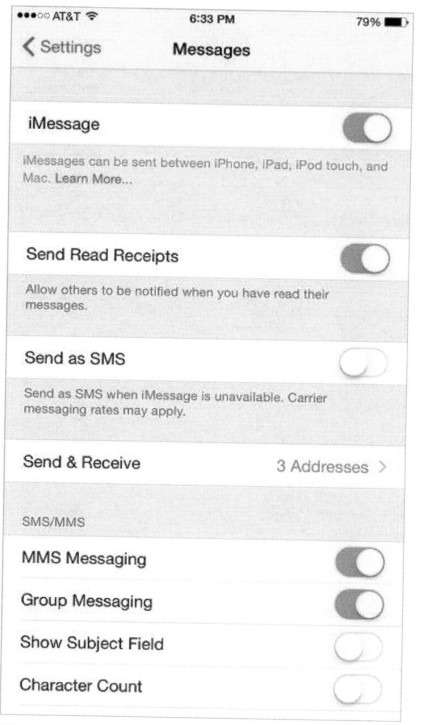

Figure 2: Message Settings Screen

2. Turning Read Receipts On or Off in iMessage

After receiving and opening a message from an iPhone, iPad, or iPod Touch, your phone can notify the sender that you have opened and read the message. These notifications are called Read Receipts, and appear under the original message on the sender's screen as "Read", followed by a time. Read Receipts are only compatible with iPhones, iPads, and iPod Touch devices. To turn Read Receipts on or off:

1. Touch the 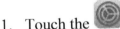 icon. The Settings screen appears.
2. Scroll down and touch **Messages**. The Message Settings screen appears.
3. Touch the ⬜ switch next to 'Send Read Receipts'. The 🔵 switch appears and Read Receipts are turned on.
4. Touch the 🔘 switch next to 'Send Read Receipts'. The ⚪ switch appears and Read Receipts are turned off.

3. Turning 'Send as SMS' On or Off

When a message cannot be sent via iMessage, your phone can attempt to send it as a regular text message, also known as an SMS. To turn Send as SMS on or off:

1. Touch the 🔘 icon. The Settings screen appears.
2. Scroll down and touch **Messages**. The Message Settings screen appears.
3. Touch the ⬜ switch next to 'Send as SMS'. The 🔵 switch appears and 'Send as SMS' is turned on.
4. Touch the 🔘 switch next to 'Send as SMS'. The ⚪ switch appears and 'Send as SMS' is turned off.

Note: When 'Send as SMS' is turned off, you will only be able to send a message to an iPhone, iPad, or iPod Touch, which has iMessage enabled.

4. Turning MMS Messaging On or Off

When you are running low on data, it can be useful to disable MMS messaging, also known as media messaging, to avoid receiving unwanted picture messages that will use up the data too quickly. To turn MMS messaging on or off:

1. Touch the [icon] icon. The Settings screen appears.
2. Scroll down and touch **Messages**. The Message Settings screen appears.
3. Touch the [switch] switch next to 'MMS Messaging'. The [switch] switch appears and MMS Messaging is turned off.
4. Touch the [switch] switch next to 'MMS Messaging'. The [switch] switch appears and MMS Messaging is turned on.

5. Turning the Subject Field On or Off

The phone can attach a subject to each text message it sends when the subject field is enabled. On most phones, the subject will appear in parentheses preceding the message content. To turn the subject field on or off:

1. Touch the [icon] icon. The Settings screen appears.
2. Scroll down and touch **Messages**. The Message Settings screen appears.
3. Touch the [switch] switch next to 'Show Subject Field'. The [switch] switch appears and the Subject field is turned on.
4. Touch the [switch] switch next to 'Show Subject Field'. The [switch] switch appears and the Subject field is turned off.

6. Turning the Character Count On or Off

The Messaging application can show you the number of characters that you have typed when entering a message. To turn the character count on or off:

1. Touch the icon. The Settings screen appears.
2. Scroll down and touch **Messages**. The Message Settings screen appears.
3. Touch the ⬭ switch next to 'Character Count'. The ⬤ switch appears and the Character Count is turned on.
4. Touch the ⬤ switch next to 'Character Count'. The ⬭ switch appears and the Character Count is turned off.

7. Turning Group Messaging On or Off

When sending a text message, you can include multiple recipients at the same time. This feature is known as Group Messaging. To turn Group Messaging on or off:

1. Touch the ⬤ icon. The Settings screen appears.
2. Scroll down and touch **Messages**. The Message Settings screen appears.
3. Touch the ⬭ switch next to 'Group Messaging'. The ⬤ switch appears and the Group Messaging is turned on.
4. Touch the ⬤ switch next to 'Group Messaging'. The ⬭ switch appears and the Group Messaging is turned off.

8. Setting the Amount of Time to Keep Messages

When using iMessage, text messages can be automatically deleted after a certain period of time. To set the amount of time to keep messages:

1. Touch the ⬤ icon. The Settings screen appears.
2. Scroll down and touch **Messages**. The Message Settings screen appears.
3. Touch **Keep Messages**. The Keep Messages screen appears, as shown in **Figure 3**.
4. Touch **30 Days** or **1 Year** to select the amount of time, or touch **Forever** to prevent the phone from erasing any messages.

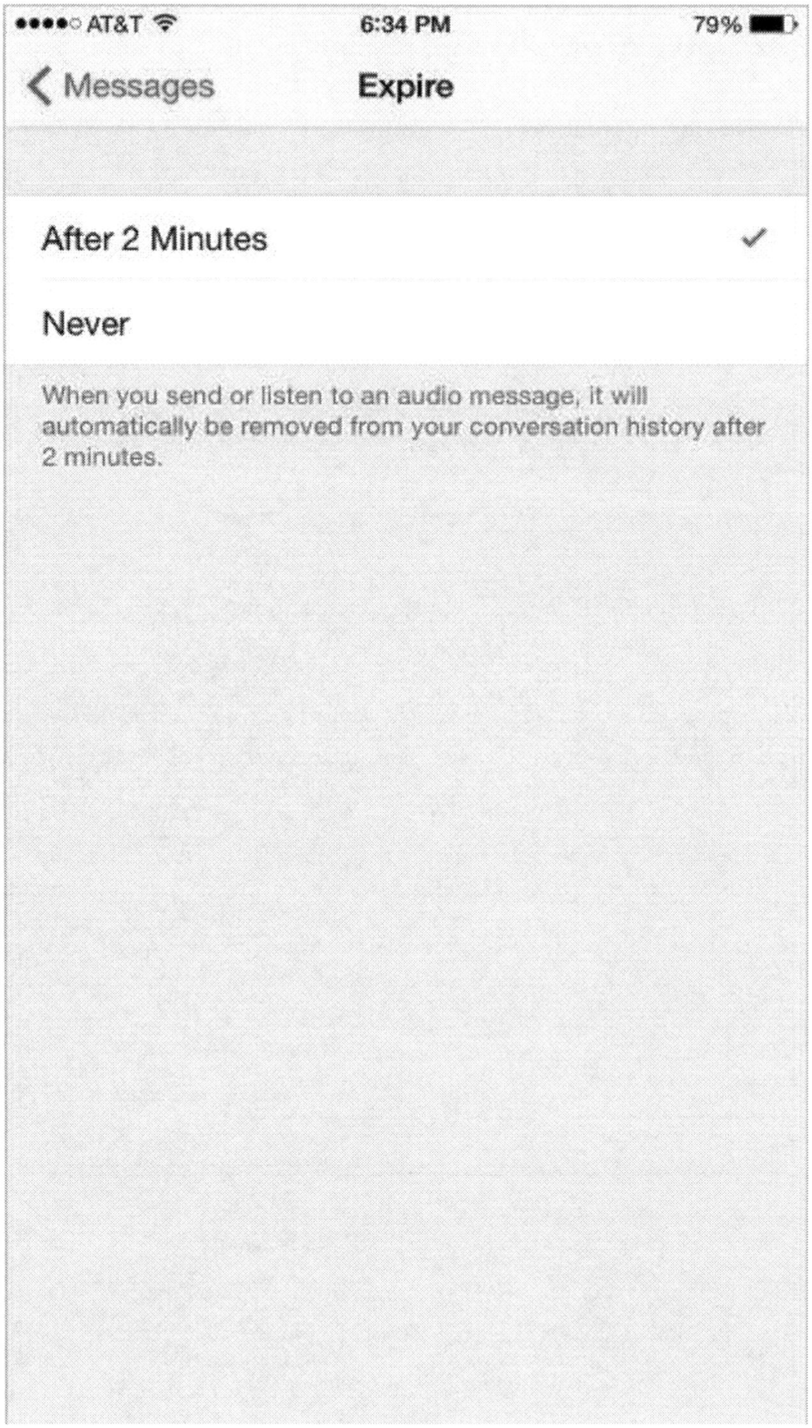

••••○ AT&T 🛜   6:34 PM   79% ▬▬◻

‹ Messages   **Expire**

After 2 Minutes   ✓

Never

When you send or listen to an audio message, it will automatically be removed from your conversation history after 2 minutes.

Figure 3: Keep Messages Screen

9. Setting the Expiration Time for Audio Messages

When an audio message is sent using iMessage, it can be set to expire after two minutes, at which point it is removed from your phone. Refer to *"Adding a Voice Message to a Conversation (iMessage Only)"* on page 103 to learn how to attach audio messages in iMessage. To set the expiration time for audio messages:

1. Touch the ⊚ icon. The Settings screen appears.
2. Scroll down and touch **Messages**. The Message Settings screen appears.
3. Touch **Expire** under 'Audio Messages'. The Audio Message Expiration screen appears, as shown in **Figure 4**.
4. Touch **After 2 Minutes**, or touch **Never** to keep audio messages.

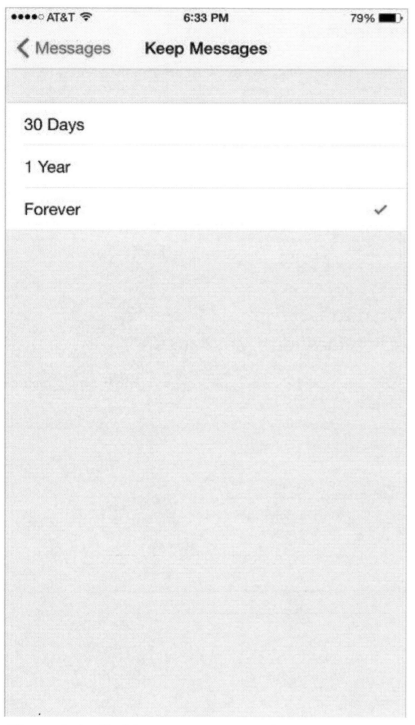

Figure 4: Audio Message Expiration Screen

10. Turning Raise to Listen On or Off

The Raise to Listen feature allows you to raise the phone to your ear to listen to audio messages. To turn Raise to Listen on or off:

1. Touch the icon. The Settings screen appears.
2. Scroll down and touch **Messages**. The Message Settings screen appears.
3. Touch the ⬭ switch next to 'Raise to Listen'. The ⬤ switch appears and the Raise to Listen is turned on.
4. Touch the ⬤ switch next to 'Raise to Listen'. The ⬭ switch appears and the Raise to Listen is turned off.

11. Setting the Expiration Time for Video Messages

When a video message is sent using iMessage, it can be set to expire after two minutes, at which point it is removed from your phone. Refer to *"Quickly Adding a Video or Photo to a Conversation (iMessage Only)"* on page 105 to learn how to attach video messages in iMessage. To set the expiration time for video messages:

1. Touch the icon. The Settings screen appears.
2. Scroll down and touch **Messages**. The Message Settings screen appears.
3. Touch **Expire** under 'Video Messages'. The Video Message Expiration screen appears.
4. Touch **After 2 Minutes**, or touch **Never** to keep video messages.

Adjusting Music Application Settings

Table of Contents

1. Turning 'Shake to Shuffle' On or Off

When the 'Shake to Shuffle' feature is enabled, the phone can shuffle the songs it is currently playing when you shake the phone. To turn 'Shake to Shuffle' on or off:

1. Touch the ⊙ icon. The Settings screen appears, as shown in **Figure 1**.
2. Scroll down and touch **Music**. The Music Settings screen appears, as shown in **Figure 2**.
3. Touch the ⬤ switch next to 'Shake to Shuffle'. The ◯ switch appears and 'Shake to Shuffle' is turned off.
4. Touch the ◯ switch next to 'Shake to Shuffle' under the 'Ringer and Alerts' section.

    The ⬤ switch appears and 'Shake to Shuffle' is turned on.

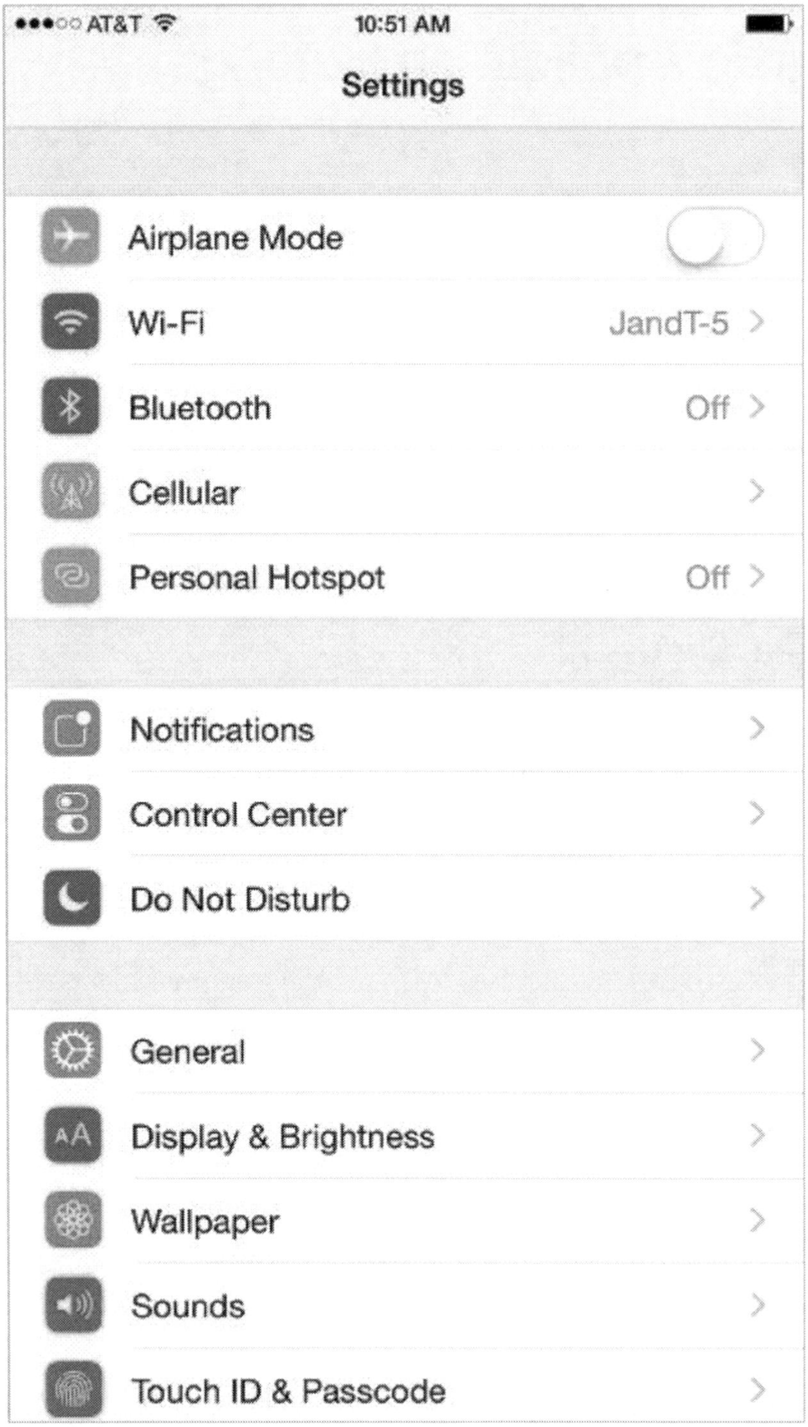

Figure 1: Settings Screen

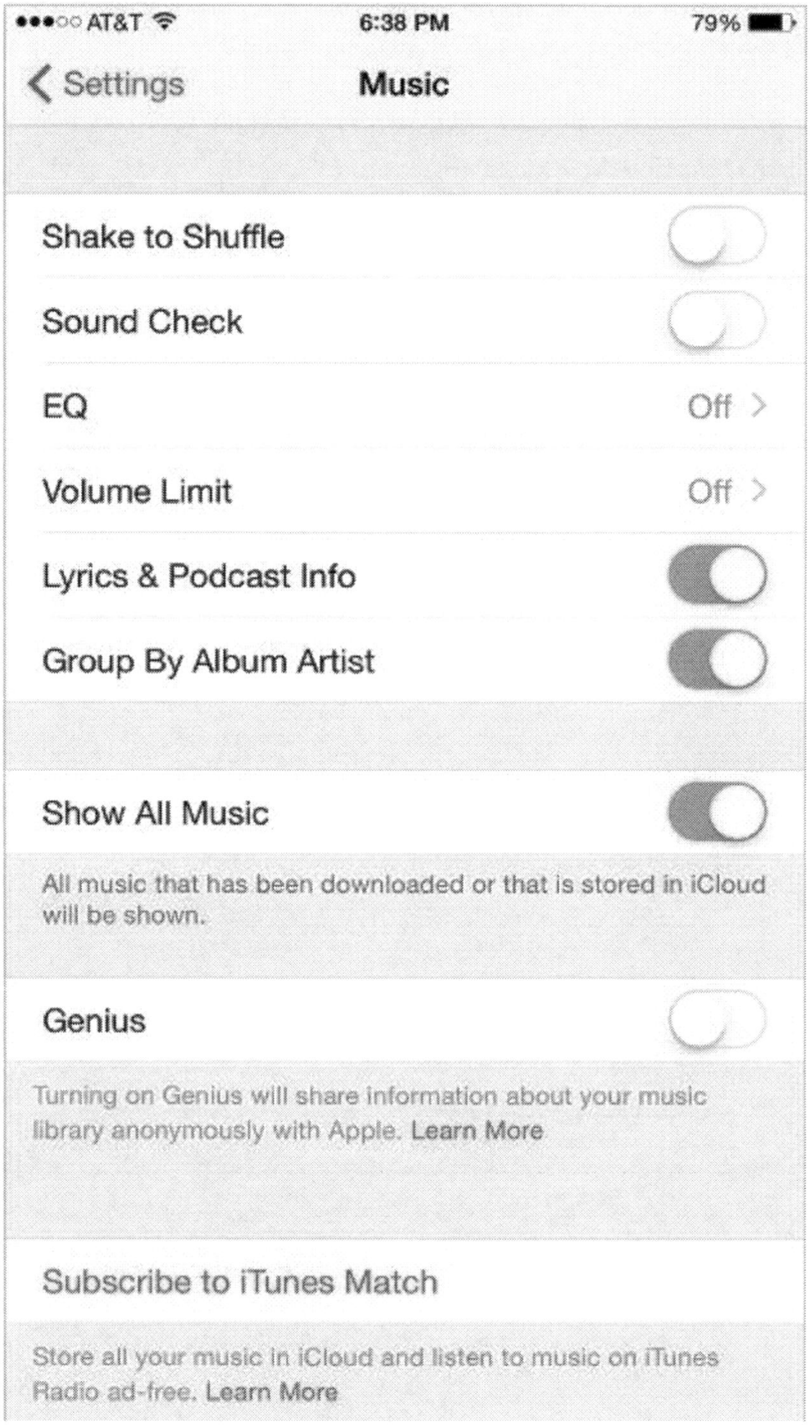

●●●○○ AT&T 🛜   6:38 PM   79% 🔋▸

‹ Settings   **Music**

Shake to Shuffle

Sound Check

EQ   Off >

Volume Limit   Off >

Lyrics & Podcast Info

Group By Album Artist

Show All Music

All music that has been downloaded or that is stored in iCloud will be shown.

Genius

Turning on Genius will share information about your music library anonymously with Apple. **Learn More**

Subscribe to iTunes Match

Store all your music in iCloud and listen to music on iTunes Radio ad-free. **Learn More**

Figure 2: Music Settings Screen

2. Selecting a Pre-Loaded Equalization Setting

The phone has several custom, pre-loaded Equalization settings that can be applied in order to improve the sound of your music. To select an Equalization setting:

Note: In order to quickly select the optimal EQ setting for you, turn on some music before performing the steps below. Refer to "Using the Music Application" *on page 165 to learn how.*

1. Touch the icon. The Settings screen appears.
2. Scroll down and touch **Music**. The Music Settings screen appears.
3. Touch **EQ**. A list of EQ settings appears, as shown in **Figure 3**.
4. Touch an EQ setting. The EQ setting is applied to all music that plays via the Music application.
5. Touch **Music** in the upper left-hand corner of the screen. The EQ setting is saved.

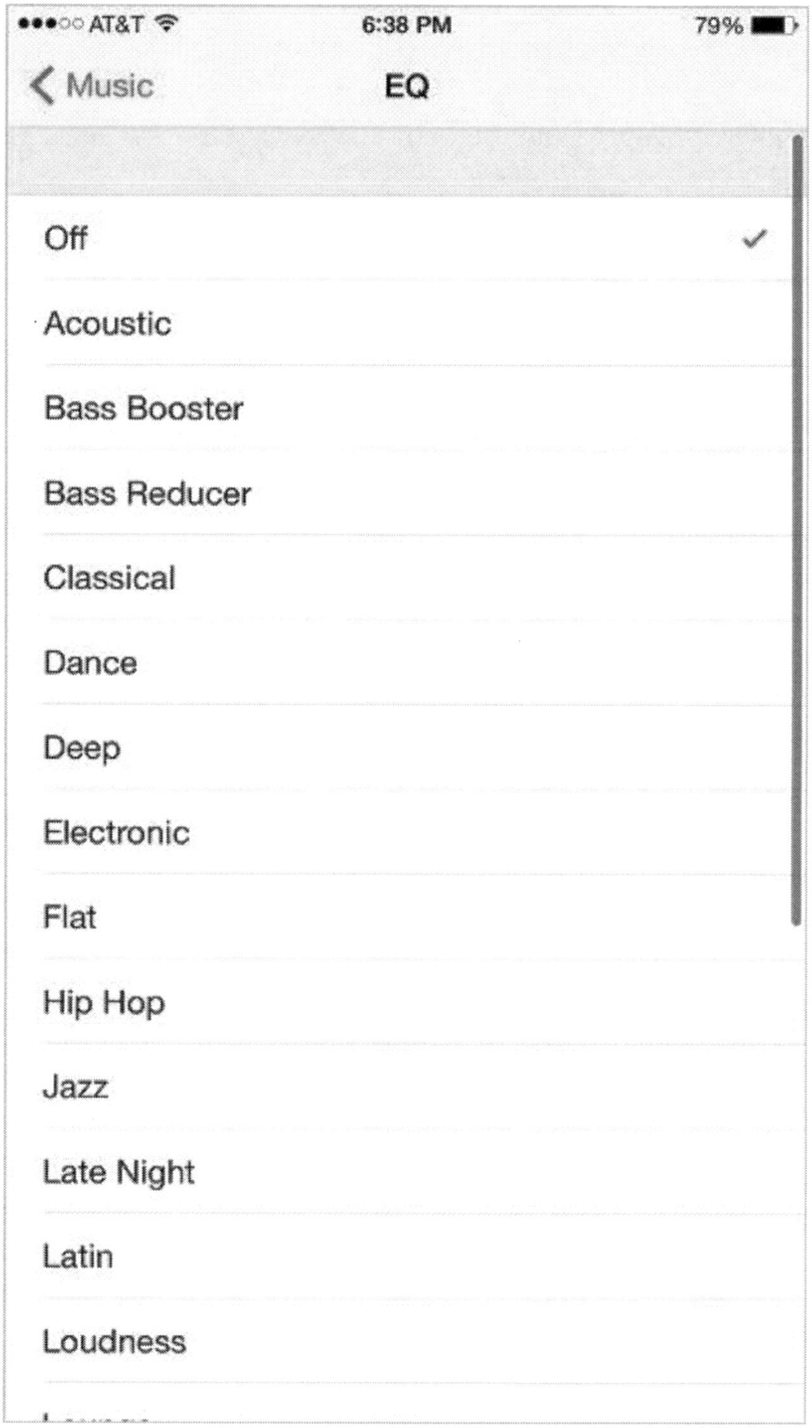

●●●○○ AT&T 📶 6:38 PM 79% 🔋

< Music **EQ**

Off ✓

Acoustic

Bass Booster

Bass Reducer

Classical

Dance

Deep

Electronic

Flat

Hip Hop

Jazz

Late Night

Latin

Loudness

Figure 3: List of EQ Settings

3. Setting a Volume Limit

In order to prevent increasing the volume in the Music application by accidentally pressing the volume buttons, try setting a Volume Limit. To set a Volume Limit:

1. Touch the ⚙ icon. The Settings screen appears.
2. Scroll down and touch **Music**. The Music Settings screen appears.
3. Touch **Volume Limit**. The Volume Limit screen appears, as shown in **Figure 4**.
4. Touch the ⬤ on the ━━━━━━━━⚪ bar and drag it to the desired location. The new volume limit is selected.
5. Touch **Music** in the upper left-hand corner of the screen. The Volume Limit is saved.

Figure 4: Volume Limit Screen

4. Turning Lyrics and Podcast Info On or Off

The phone can automatically display the lyrics of a song or the details of a podcast while one of these is playing in the Music application. To turn 'Lyrics and Podcast Info' on or off:

1. Touch the ⚙ icon. The Settings screen appears.
2. Scroll down and touch **Music**. The Music Settings screen appears.
3. Touch the ⬜ switch next to 'Lyrics & Podcast Info'. The 🔵 switch appears and Lyrics and Podcast Info is turned on.
4. Touch the 🔵 switch next to 'Lyrics & Podcast Info'. The ⬜ switch appears and Lyrics and Podcast Info is turned off.

5. Choosing which Music Appears in the Music Application

The Music application can either display all of your music, both in the Cloud and on your phone, or just the music on your phone. To choose which music appears in the music application:

1. Touch the ⚙ icon. The Settings screen appears.
2. Scroll down and touch **Music**. The Music Settings screen appears.
3. Touch the ⬜ switch next to 'Show All Music'. The 🔵 switch appears and both music on your phone and in the Cloud will be shown in the Music application.
4. Touch the 🔵 switch next to 'Show All Music'. The ⬜ switch appears and only the music on your phone will be shown in the Music application.

6. Turning iTunes Match On or Off

iTunes Match is a service that Apple offers at $24.99 per year, which allows you to play songs from Apple's Cloud at the highest quality, as long as the song already exists in your library. iTunes Match songs can be played on any one of your registered Apple devices. To use iTunes Match, you must first subscribe (at this website: **https://www.apple.com/itunes/itunes-match/**), and then enable it through iTunes on your computer. Click **Store** and then click **Turn On iTunes Match** in iTunes on your computer. You will need to enter your Apple credentials. To turn iTunes Match on or off on the phone:

1. Touch the ⚙ icon. The Settings screen appears.
2. Scroll down and touch **Music**. The Music Settings screen appears.
3. Touch the ⬜ switch next to 'iTunes Match'. The Password prompt appears.
4. Enter your Apple credentials and touch **OK**. The 🔵 switch appears and iTunes Match is turned on.
5. Touch the 🔵 switch next to 'iTunes Match'. The ⬜ switch appears and iTunes Match is turned off.

Adjusting Photo and Video Settings

Table of Contents

1. Turning Photo Stream On or Off

Photo Stream allows you to instantly load photos you have taken on your phone to your other registered Apple devices. It accomplishes this by automatically uploading them to the iCloud and then downloading them to the necessary devices. To turn Photo Stream on or off:

1. Touch the ⊙ icon. The Settings screen appears, as shown in **Figure 1**.
2. Scroll down and touch **Photos and Camera**. The Photo Settings screen appears, as shown in **Figure 2**.

3. Touch the ⬭ switch next to 'My Photo Stream'. The ⬤ switch appears and Photo Stream is turned on.

4. Touch the ⬤ switch next to 'My Photo Stream'. The ⬭ switch appears and Photo Stream is turned off.

Note: You can also touch the ⬭ switch next to iCloud Photo Library to upload your photos and videos to iCloud for safekeeping.

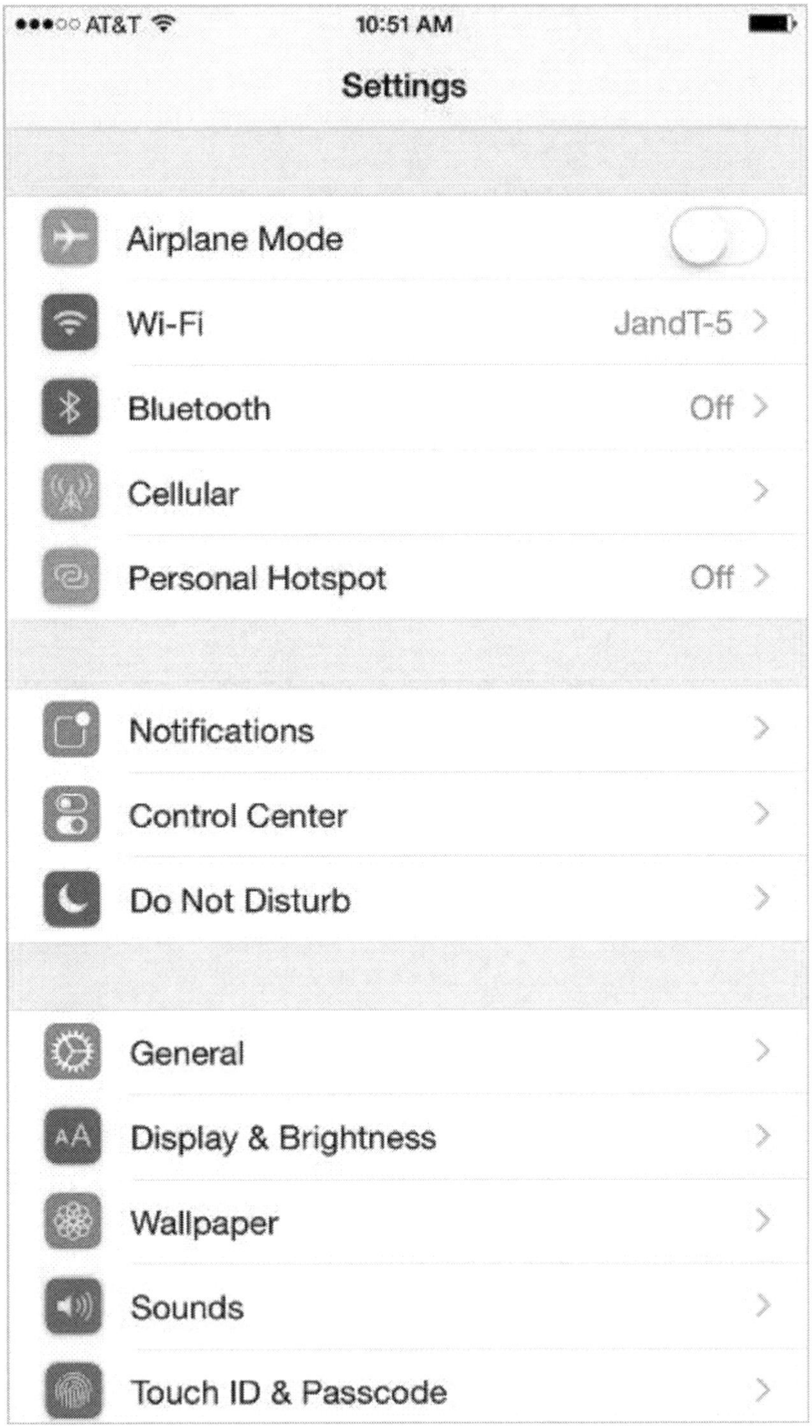

Figure 1: Settings Screen

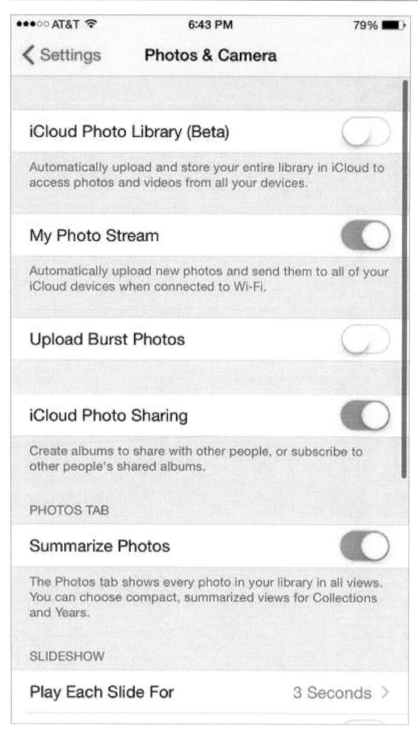

Figure 2: Photo Settings Screen

2. Customizing Slideshow Settings

You can customize the slideshow settings on your phone. Refer to *"Starting a Slideshow"* on page 147 to learn how to turn on a slideshow. To customize Slideshow settings:

- Touch the ⚙ icon. The Settings screen appears.
- Scroll down and touch **Photos and Camera**. The Photo Settings screen appears.
- Touch one of the following options under the 'Slideshow' section to change the corresponding setting:

  - **Play Each Slide For** - Sets the amount of time that each photo remains on the screen during a slideshow.
  - **Repeat** - Sets the slideshow to start again from the beginning of the current album after reaching the end.
  - **Shuffle** - Sets the photos to appear in random order during a slideshow.

Note: Turning both 'Repeat' and 'Shuffle' on at the same time plays your photos continuously and in random order.

3. Customizing High Dynamic Range (HDR) Camera Settings

When taking photos with the phone, you can enable HDR, which will improve picture quality by taking several photos in order to represent actual lighting much more accurately than in a photo taken by a non-HDR camera. To turn on HDR, touch **HDR Off** at the top of the screen while the camera is running. When HDR is turned on, a non-HDR copy of each photo is stored by default. To customize HDR settings:

1. Touch the ⚙ icon. The Settings screen appears.
2. Scroll down and touch **Photos and Camera**. The Photo Settings screen appears.

3. Touch the ⬤ switch next to 'Keep Normal Photo'. The ◯ switch appears and the phone will now delete non-HDR photos while keeping the HDR copy.

4. Touch the ◯ switch next to 'Keep Normal Photo'. The ⬤ switch appears and the phone will keep the non-HDR photo in addition to the HDR copy when taking photos.

Note: An HDR photo takes up more memory on your phone than a non-HDR one.

4. Customizing Video Playback Settings

After a video is stopped (not paused), the phone can resume playing it from the beginning or from where you last left off. To customize Video Playback settings:

1. Touch the ⊚ icon. The Settings screen appears.
2. Scroll down and touch **Videos**. The Video Settings screen appears, as shown in **Figure 3**.
3. Touch **Start Playing**. The Start Playing screen appears, as shown in **Figure 4**.
4. Touch **From Beginning**. Videos will now resume from the beginning.
5. Touch **Where Left Off**. Videos will now resume where they last left off.
6. Touch **Videos** in the upper left-hand corner of the screen. Your video playback selection is saved.

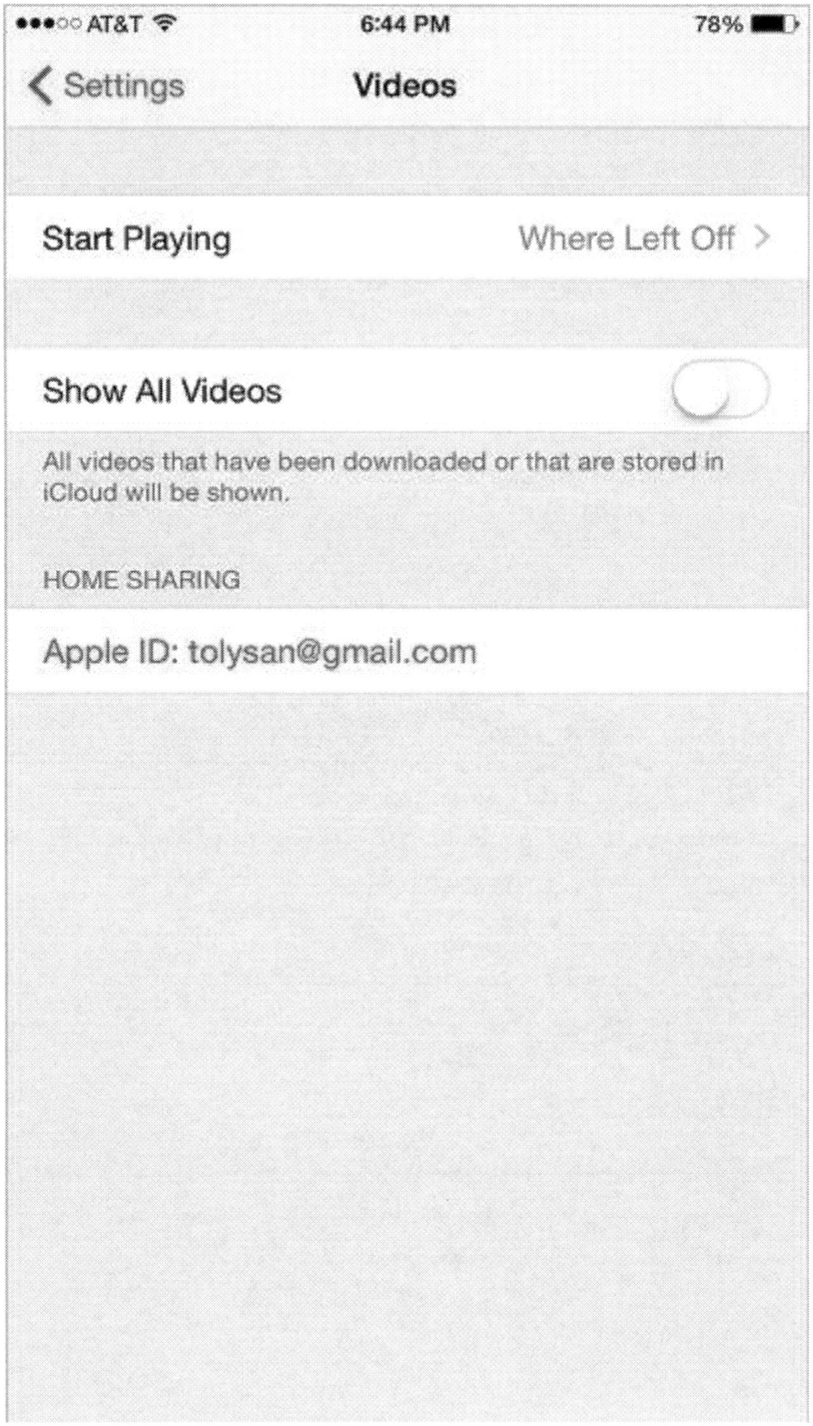

Figure 3: Video Settings Screen

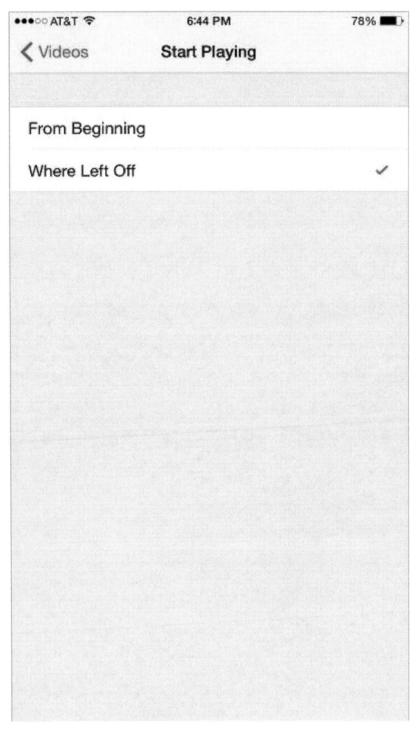

Figure 4: Start Playing Screen

5. Choosing which Videos Appear in the Videos Application

The Music application can either display all of your videos, both in iCloud and on your phone, or just the videos on your phone. To choose which music appears in the music application:

1. Touch the ⊚ icon. The Settings screen appears.
2. Scroll down and touch **Videos**. The Video Settings screen appears.

3. Touch the ⬜ switch next to 'Show All Videos'. The ⬤ switch appears and all videos, both on your phone and in the Cloud will appear in the Videos application.

4. Touch the ⬤ switch next to 'Show All Videos'. The ⬜ switch appears and only videos on your phone will appear in the Videos application.

Tips and Tricks

Table of Contents

1. Maximizing Battery Life

There are several things you can do to increase the battery life of the iPhone 6.

- Lock the iPhone 6 whenever you are not using it. To lock the iPhone 6, press the **Sleep/Wake** button at the top of the phone. Refer to *"Button Layout"* on page 10 for the location of the Sleep/Wake button.
- Keep the Auto-lock feature on and set it to a small amount of time. Refer to *"Changing Auto-Lock Settings"* on page 280 to learn how to change Auto-lock settings.
- Turn down the brightness and turn off Auto-Brightness. Refer to *"Adjusting the Brightness"* on page 284 to learn how.
- Turn on Airplane mode in areas where there is little or no signal, as the iPhone 6 will continually try to search for service. Refer to *"Turning Airplane Mode On or Off"* on page 237 to learn how to turn on Airplane Mode. This tip is for iPhone and iPad 4G only.
- Make sure to let the battery drain completely and then charge it fully at least once a month. This will help both short-term and long-term battery life.
- Turn off Wi-Fi when it is not in use. Refer to *"Using Wi-Fi"* on page 29 to learn how.
- Turn off Location Services when it is not in use. Refer to *"Turning Location Services On or Off"* on page 239 to learn how.
- Turn on the Grayscale accessibility feature. This will prevent you from seeing any colors, but is a great feature to use when your battery is running low. Refer to *"Managing Vision Accessibility Features"* on page 310 to learn how.

Refer to the tips below to learn more. In addition, you can view a list of applications that are using up most of your battery. To view battery usage:

1. Touch the icon. The Settings screen appears.
2. Touch **General**. The General Settings screen appears.
3. Touch **Usage**. The Usage screen appears.
4. Touch **Battery Usage**. The Battery Usage screen appears, showing all of the applications that are draining your battery, and the percentage of the battery that each has drained. Refer to *"Closing an Application Running in the Background"* on page 224 to learn how to cut down on the amount of battery used by applications.

2. Taking a Screenshot

To capture what is on the screen and save it as a photo, press and hold the **Home** button, and then press the **Sleep/Wake** Button. Release the buttons and the screen will momentarily flash white. The screenshot is saved to the 'Recently Added' album.

3. Scrolling to the Top of a Screen

Touch anywhere in the notification bar at the very top of the screen to quickly scroll to the top of a list, website, etc. The notification bar is where the clock and battery meter are located.

4. Saving an Image While Browsing the Internet

To save an image from Safari to the iPhone 6, touch and hold the picture until the Image menu appears. Touch **Save Image**. The image is saved to the 'Recently Added' album.

5. Inserting a Period

When typing a sentence, touch the space bar twice quickly to insert a period and a space.

6. Adding an Extension to a Contact's Number

When entering a number for a stored contact, you can add an extension that will be dialed following a short pause after the call is connected. While entering a number, touch the $+ * \#$ button in the lower left-hand corner of the screen, and then touch **Pause**. A comma appears, and you can now enter an extension. Each comma represents one second that the phone will wait after dialing the number.

7. Navigating the Home Screens

Typically, you navigate to another Home screen by touching the screen and sliding your finger to the left or right. Alternatively, touch one of the gray dots at the bottom of a Home screen to go to the corresponding screen.

8. Typing Alternate Characters

When typing a sentence, insert other characters, such as Á or Ñ, by touching and holding the base letter. A menu of characters appears above the letter. Slide your finger to a character to insert it.

9. Quickly Deleting Recently Typed Text

This feature is quite a secret. If you have just typed several lines of text and do not want any of it, just give the phone a good shake. A menu appears asking whether to undo the typing.
Touch **Undo**. The typed text is erased. Give the phone another shake to redo the typing. This works in any application, or while text messaging.

10. Resetting the Phone

If the iPhone 6 or an application freezes up or is acting strangely, you may wish to reset the iPhone 6. This will NOT wipe any data, but simply restart the operating system. To reset the iPhone 6, hold the **Home** button and **Sleep/Wake** button together until the phone completely shuts off.

Continue to hold the buttons until the logo appears. The phone resets and starts up.

11. Calling a Phone Number on a Website

You can call a phone number on a website directly. The number will be blue and underlined, much like a link. Touch the number. The iPhone 6 calls it. If the number is on a website, the iPhone 6 will ask whether to call the number. Touch **Call**. This may not work with all websites.

12. Taking Notes

A convenient way to take notes is by using the built-in Notes application and emailing the notes to yourself. To take notes, touch the [ ] icon on the Home screen. Touch **New** at the top of the screen to add a note. Touch the [ ] icon at the bottom of the screen and then touch **Mail** to email the note.

13. Recovering Signal After Being in an Area with No Service

Sometimes the iPhone 6 has trouble finding signal after returning from an area where your network was not available. This issue can sometimes be fixed by turning Airplane Mode on and then back off. Refer to *"Turning Airplane Mode On or Off"* on page 237 to learn how.

14. Changing the Number of Rings Before the iPhone 6 Goes to Voicemail

There is a hidden way to change the number of times the iPhone 6 rings before going to Voicemail. The maximum number of seconds the phone can ring is 30. Have a pen and paper ready, as you will need to enter a long number. To change the number of times the iPhone 6 rings before going to Voicemail:

1. Turn off Call Forwarding. Refer to *"Turning Call Forwarding On or Off"* on page 318 to learn how.
2. Touch the [ ] icon and then touch the [ ] icon. The Keypad appears.
3. Dial ***#61#** exactly as it appears here and touch **CALL**. When the call is completed, the Voicemail Configuration screen appears.
4. Write down the number that follows "Forwards to." Skip the '+' since you will be typing it in later anyway.
5. Touch **Dismiss**. The call is ended.

6. Dial ***61*+1XXXXXXXXXX*11*tt#** exactly as it appears here, where the X's represent the number you just wrote down and "tt" is the number of seconds you want for the iPhone 6 to ring before going to Voicemail. For example, if the number you wrote down is 1234567890 and the number of seconds you prefer is 30, you would dial *61*+11234567890*11*30#. To make the plus sign appear when dialing a phone number, touch and hold**0**.

7. Touch **CALL.** The number of seconds the iPhone 6 rings is changed and a confirmation appears.

8. Touch **Dismiss**. The call is ended.

Note: To change the ring time back, just repeat these steps. The number you wrote down in step three does not change, so you can proceed to step four if you know it. The default ring time for the iPhone 6 is 20 seconds.

15. Changing the Navigation Icons in the iPod Application

You can change the arrangement of the Navigation icons in the iPod application. While using the iPod Application, touch the icon. The More screen appears. Touch **Edit** at the of the screen, and then touch any icon on the page and drag it to the bottom of the screen. Release it over another icon. The icons are swapped. You can also rearrange the icons at the bottom of the screen in the same way.

16. Deleting a Song in the Music Application

To delete a song from your iPhone 6, touch the song and swipe your finger to the left. **DELETE** appears. Touch **DELETE**. The song is deleted.

17. Taking a Picture from the Lock Screen

To take a picture without unlocking the phone, touch the icon and slide your finger up. The camera turns on. Press the **Volume Up** button. The camera takes a picture.

18. Assigning a Custom Ringtone to a Contact

You can assign a custom ringtone to any contact in the Phonebook. To assign a ringtone to a contact:

1. Touch the ![icon] icon. The Phonebook appears.
2. Find and touch the contact to whom you wish to assign a custom ringtone. The Contact Info screen appears. Refer to *"Finding a Contact"* on page 60 to learn how.
3. Touch **Edit** in the upper right-hand corner of the screen. The Contact Editing screen appears.
4. Touch **Ringtone**. A list of available ringtones appears.
5. Touch a ringtone. The ringtone plays.
6. Touch **Done** at the top of the screen. The ringtone is selected and the Contact Editing screen appears.
7. Touch **Done** at the top of the screen. The ringtone is assigned to the contact.

Note: Refer to "Buying Music and Ringtones in iTunes" *on page 156 to learn how to purchase additional ringtones.*

19. Opening the Photos Application without Closing the Camera

To open the Photos application while the camera is turned on, touch the photo thumbnail in the bottom left-hand corner of the screen.

20. Inserting Emoticons

The Emoji keyboard contains over 460 new emoticons that can be used when entering text. To learn how to add the Emoji keyboard, refer to *"Adding an International Keyboard"* on page 265, and touch **Emoji** in step 6. After adding the Emoji keyboard, touch the ![emoji key] key, if the Emoji keyboard is the only one that you have added, or touch the ![globe key] key if there are other keyboards in addition to English and Emoji. The Emoji keyboard appears. If you touched the ![globe key] key, you may need to touch it again to cycle through the keyboards until the Emoji keyboard turns on.

21. Hiding the Keyboard in the Messages Application

While reading a text message, you can hide the keyboard to view more of the conversation at once. Touch the last visible message in the conversation and slide your finger down to the keyboard. The keyboard is hidden.

22. Controlling Web Surfing Using Gestures

Instead of touching the ⟨ and ⟩ buttons to go back and forward, respectively, you can touch the screen and slide your finger the left or right, respectively.

23. Navigating the Menus Using Gestures

Instead of touching the text in the upper left-hand corner of the screen to return to the previous menu, just touch the left-hand side of the screen and slide your finger to the right. This works in most applications as well, such as the Music application.

24. Pausing or Cancelling an Application Download

If you are downloading more than one application at a time, you may wish to pause one of the downloads so that one of the other applications downloads first. To pause an application download, touch the application icon of the application that you wish to pause. Touch the icon again to resume the download. You may also cancel the download by deleting the application. Refer to *"Deleting an Application"* on page 225 to learn how.

Note: If you cancel a download by deleting the application, you will still be charged if the application was not free. You may still download the application later. Refer to "Buying an Application" *on page 220 to learn how.*

25. Making a Quick Note for a Contact

You may take a quick note for a contact without having to edit the entire contents of the contact. To make a quick note for a contact, touch **Notes** on the contact's information screen. Touch **All Contacts** at the top of the screen to save the note.

26. Using a Search Engine that Does Not Track Your Searches

Safari now allows you to use a new search engine, called DuckDuckGo. This search engine comes from a start-up company, and allows you to search the Web without tracking your searches like Google. Refer to *"Changing the Search Engine"* on page 124 to learn how to change your search engine to DuckDuckGo.

27. Preventing Applications from Refreshing in the Background

Certain applications, such as Podcasts and Weather will refresh their content even when the application is closed. This can drain your battery more quickly. To prevent applications from refreshing in the background:

1. Touch the ⊚ icon. The Settings screen appears.
2. Touch **General**. The General Settings screen appears.
3. Touch **Background App Refresh**. The Background App Refresh screen appears.
4. Touch the ⬤ switch next to 'Background App Refresh'. The ⬭ switch appears and the feature is turned off.

28. Leaving Your Home Screen Free of Icons

If you are a wallpaper connoisseur, you may wish to leave your main Home screen empty. In iOS 7 and earlier, if you tried to move all of your icons to other screens, the second Home screen took the place of the first. Starting in iOS 8, you may now move all of your icons to other screens, and leave your main Home screen empty. This way, you can look at your wallpaper all day long without the intrusion of those pesky icons.

29. Call Waiting in FaceTime

FaceTime now allows you to accept another call while you are already on a call. To accept a call and end the current one, touch **End & Accept**. To reject an incoming call, touch **Decline**.

30. Adding an Event Mentioned in a Text Message to the Calendar

You may add a planned event from a text message directly to your calendar. Touch the blue underlined text, such as "dinner tonight", and then touch Create Event or Show in Calendar, if the event already exists and you need to change some of the details.

Troubleshooting

Table of Contents

1. Phone does not turn on

If the phone does not power on, try one or more of the following tips:

- **Recharge the phone** - Use the included wall charger to charge the battery. If the battery power is extremely low, the screen will not turn on for several minutes. Do NOT use the USB port on your computer to charge the phone.
- **Replace the battery** - If you purchased the phone a long time ago, you may need to replace the battery. Contact Apple to learn how.
- **Reset the phone** - This method will not erase any data. Hold down the **Home** button and **Sleep/Wake** button at the same time for 10 seconds. Keep holding the two buttons until the logo appears and the phone restarts.

2. Phone is not responding

If the phone is frozen or is not responding, try one or more of the following. These steps solve most problems on the phone.

- **Exit the application** - If the phone freezes while running an application, hold the **Home** Button for six seconds. The application quits and the phone returns to the Home screen.
- **Turn the phone off and then back on** - If the phone is still frozen, try pressing the **Sleep/Wake** button to turn the phone off. Keep holding the **Sleep/Wake** Button until "Slide to Power Off" appears. Slide your finger from left to right over the text. The phone turns off. After the screen is completely black, press the **Sleep/Wake** button again to turn the phone back on.
- **Restart the phone** - Hold the **Home** button and **Sleep/Wake** button at the same time for 10 seconds or until the ⌂ logo appears.
- **Remove Media** - Some downloaded applications or music may freeze up the phone. Try deleting some of the media that may be problematic after restarting the phone. Refer to *"Deleting an Application"* on page 225 to learn how to delete an application. You may also erase all data at once by doing the following:

Warning: Once erased, data cannot be recovered. Make sure you back up any files you wish to keep.

1. Touch the ⚙ icon. The Settings screen appears.
2. Touch **General**. The General Settings screen appears.
3. Touch **Reset**. The Reset screen appears.
4. Touch **Erase All Content and Settings**. A confirmation dialog appears.

3. Can't make a call

If the phone cannot make outgoing calls, try one of the following:

- If "No Service" is shown at the top of the screen, the network does not cover you in your location. Try moving to a different location, or even to a different part of a building.
- Try walking around to find more signal.
- Turn off Airplane Mode if you have it turned on. If that does not work, try turning Airplane Mode on for 15 seconds and then turning it off. Refer to *"Turning Airplane Mode On or Off"* on page 237 to learn how.
  - Make sure you dialed 1 and an area code with the phone number.
  - Turn the phone off and back on.

4. Can't surf the web

If you have no internet access, there may be little or no service in your area. Try moving to a different location or turning Wi-Fi, if available. Refer to *"Using Wi-Fi"* on page 29 to learn how to turn on Wi-Fi. If you still cannot access the Web, refer to *"Phone is not responding"* on page 368 for further assistance.

5. Screen or keyboard does not rotate

If the screen does not rotate, or the full, horizontal keyboard does not appear when you rotate the phone, it may be one of these issues:

- The application does not support the horizontal view.
- The phone is lying flat. Hold the phone upright to change the view in applications that support it.

- The rotation lock is on. The rotation is locked if the 🔒 icon appears next to the battery life at the top of the screen. Touch the bottom of the screen and slide your finger up to access the Control Center. In the control center, touch the 🔒 icon to unlock the rotation.

On an iPad, if you do not see the 🔒 icon in the Control Center, then the rotation can be controlled using the Side switch above the Volume Controls.

6. iTunes does not detect phone when connected to a computer

If iTunes does not detect the phone when connecting it to your computer, try using a different USB port. If that does not work, turn the phone off and on again while it is plugged in to the computer. If the phone indicates that it is connected, the problem might be with your computer. Try restarting your computer or reinstalling iTunes. Otherwise, refer to *"Phone is not responding"* on page 368 for assistance.

7. Phone does not ring or play music, can't hear while talking, can't listen to voicemails

Make sure the volume is turned up. Refer to *"Button Layout"* on page 10 to find the Volume Controls. Check whether you can still hear sound through headphones. The headphone jack is located on the top of the phone. If you can hear sound through headphones, try inserting the headphones and taking them out several times. Sometimes the sensor in the headphone jack malfunctions.

8. Low microphone volume, caller can't hear you

If you are talking to someone who can't hear you, try the following:

- Take off any cases or other accessories as these may cover up the microphone.
- When you first take the phone out of the box, it comes with a piece of plastic covering the microphone. Make sure to take this plastic off before using the phone.
- If the caller cannot hear you at all, you may have accidentally muted the conversation. Refer to *"Using the Mute Function During a Voice Call"* on page 52 to learn how turn Mute on or off.

9. Camera does not work

If the phone camera is not functioning correctly, try one of the following:

- Clean the camera lens with a polishing cloth.
- Take off any cases or accessories that may interfere with the camera lens on the back of the phone.
- Hold the phone steady when taking a picture. A shaky hand often results in a blurry picture. Try leaning against a stationary object to stabilize your hand.
- If you cannot find the icon on your Home screen, try the following:

1. Touch the icon. The Settings screen appears.
2. Touch **General**. The General Settings screen appears.
3. Touch **Restrictions**. The Restrictions screen appears.
4. Touch **Disable Restrictions**. The Restrictions Passcode screen appears.

5. Enter the passcode that you set up when you enabled the restrictions. All restrictions are disabled.

10. Phone shows the White Screen of Death

If the phone screen has gone completely white, try restarting or restoring the phone. Refer to *"Phone is not responding"* on page 368 to learn how.

11. "Phone needs to cool down" message appears

If you leave the phone in your car on a hot day, or expose it to direct sunlight for too long, one of the following may happen:

- Phone stops charging
- Weak signal
- Screen dims
- Phone breaks completely
- "Phone needs to cool down" message appears.

Before using the phone, allow it to cool. The phone works best in temperatures between 32°F and 95°F (0°C to 35°C). While it is turned off, store the phone at temperatures between -4°F and 113°F (-20°C to 45°C).

12. Display does not adjust brightness automatically

If the phone does not brighten in bright conditions, or does not become dimmer in dark conditions, try taking any cases or accessories off. A case may block the light sensor, located at the top of the phone near the earpiece. Also, check to make sure that Auto-Brightness is turned on. Refer to *"Adjusting the Brightness"* on page 284 to learn how to turn on Auto-Brightness.

Index

22491761R00212

Made in the USA
San Bernardino, CA
08 July 2015